Modern Irish Poetry

Tradition and Continuity
from Yeats to Heaney

ROBERT F. GARRATT

Modern Irish Poetry

Tradition and Continuity from Yeats to Heaney

UNIVERSITY OF CALIFORNIA PRESS

Berkeley   Los Angeles   London

University of California Press
Berkeley and Los Angeles, California

University of California Press, Ltd.
London, England

Copyright © 1986 by The Regents of the University of California

Library of Congress Cataloging-in-Publication Data

Garratt, Robert F.
  Modern Irish poetry.

  Includes index.
    1. English poetry—Irish authors—History and
criticism.   2. English poetry—20th century—History
and criticism.   3. Ireland in literature.   I. Title.
PR8771.G37   1986   821'.91'099415   85–28838
ISBN 0–520–05567–5 (alk. paper)

Printed in the United States of America

1 2 3 4 5 6 7 8 9

To Barbara

Contents

Preface

In presenting a view of Irish literary history, this book argues that the nature of poetics in Ireland changed about the year 1940. The deaths of Yeats in 1939 and Joyce in 1941 forced the question of the future of Irish writing. Poetry in Ireland during the first forty years of this century was characterized essentially by romanticism and Yeatsian abstraction, both of which combined to conjure up an Ireland of the mind. After 1940, in an effort to cultivate their individuality, post-Yeatsian poets rooted their art in a Joycean realism, the bedrock of everyday experience. That Yeats and Joyce should figure in the great shift in twentieth-century Irish poetry is both appropriate and inevitable. The history of modern literature would be very different without them and the Irish contribution to twentieth-century English literature would be severely diminished. Moreover, the literary values that have been connected with their works—the romantic and inherently conservative vision of Yeats's poetry and the realistic and aggressively modernist mode of Joyce's fiction—influence the tendencies in modern Irish poetry.

Post-Yeatsian poetry, though blessed with astonishing performances by talented writers, has had to struggle with the mantle of tradition shaped by Yeats and many of the poets of the Revival. Revivalism itself—the sentimental and romantic treatment of rural Ireland—had worn thin even for the first post-Yeatsians, Austin Clarke and Patrick Kavanagh, but the sense of tradition was still very strong for these poets. Both Clarke and Kavanagh, in opposite ways, were obsessed with the idea of an Irish poetic tradition and wrote with that idea in mind. Clarke's and Kavanagh's wrestling with the concept of tradition cleared the ground for those poets who followed. Thomas Kinsella and John Montague, both of whom began writing in the 1950s, could move to a more complicated problem in their poetry, that of continuity or the connection with tradition. Kinsella describes this shift in poetic consciousness as an awareness of isolation and the realization that the promise of the Revival to restore and reclaim ancient Irish culture can never be fulfilled because of the death of the Irish language. It is first the recognition and then the acceptance of a broken literary tradition which inform the work of Kinsella, Montague, Seamus Heaney, and Derek Mahon, major voices of post-Yeatsian poetry. Each poet in his way accepts discontinuity as a dominant feature of his cultural past and responds in his poetry accordingly. Kinsella's psychological quest, Montague's historiography, Heaney's examination of the given life, and Mahon's modernism—all take root in a shift from tradition to continuity.

I have described this shift by concentrating first on the perpetuation of tradition in Yeats and in the followers of the Revival. The reaction to tradition comes as a Joycean countertruth, described in a chapter on Joyce's reaction to the Revival and the triumph of modernism in his fiction. The remainder of the book traces the tension between tradition and continuity in the poetry of Clarke, Kavanagh, Kinsella, Montague, Heaney, and Mahon. I devote a chapter to each of these poets.

Two writers whom I only mention in the final chapter, Louis MacNeice and Richard Murphy, would merit greater treatment in a less thematic study of post-Yeatsian poetry. I restrict my discussion of each of these poets because I felt I would reduce their poetic achievement too much to fit my thesis. MacNeice's work, while Irish in part, seems to range well beyond the Irish poetic tradition. Murphy's new book, *The Price of Stone*, appeared too late for me to include in my discussion.

As I move toward the contemporary period I am especially aware of interesting work by poets whose reputations while established are still growing with recent publications. I would like to have included a detailed discussion of contemporary Ulster poetry that is attracting a growing recognition among critics and readers of modern poetry. I can only touch on the work of Derek Mahon and make the briefest mention of one or two other contemporary poets in my concluding chapter. The scope of my argument demands limits, and I have arbitrarily drawn a line through some very good work produced by contemporary poets. I do so for organization reasons and for a concern over the length of my essay, not out of disregard for the poetic achievement. It is also true, however, that many of the most recent generation, like Paul Muldoon and Tom Paulin, are promising young talents whose poetics, still evolving, are not ripe for judgment. Even in the work they have produced, however, I sense the concern over the problem of continuity.

I owe a great deal of thanks to a number of people for support and assistance during the writing of this book: to Frank Peterson and the Enrichment Committee of the University of Puget Sound for two grants that allowed me to travel to Ireland, and for a typing award that enabled me to prepare the typescript; for the National Endowment for the Humanities for a year long research fellowship and a summer seminar grant; to the University of Puget Sound for a unit of released time in my teaching load at a crucial time during my writing; to Seamus Deane and Anthony Bradley who read an early version of this study; and to Robert Ryf, Audrey Eyler, Floyd Skloot, and Kingsley Weatherhead, who read individual chapters—these colleagues have offered valuable criticism that has reduced the infelicities and the mistakes I make here. I also wish to thank colleagues in my department at Puget Sound who challenged my thinking on Yeats; to Frank and Denise Coyne and Margaret Wagner for their kindness, hospitality and generosity during my visits to Ireland; to the library staffs at Trinity College, Dublin, National Library of Ireland, and University College, Dublin; to Kathleen Wells, Doris Johnson, June Lang, Diane Harris, and Shelley Bott for their patience and their excellent preparation of copy; to Bonnie Newton and Michael Mays for editorial assistance; to James Kubeck for helpful advice; and especially to my wife Barbara, whose support and encouragement were important to me at every stage of my work.

R. F. G.

Introduction

The following essay offers a reading of Irish poetry since Yeats and attempts to explain a main current, or preoccupation, in the writing of certain poets from the 1930s to the 1970s. As a reading it is selective both in its choice of poets and in its critical vantage point. I have chosen these particular poets because I believe that they represent the major voices in Irish poetry after Yeats. In most cases I do not anticipate any arguments; enough critical attention already has been paid to these writers to justify their inclusion in any book about twentieth-century Irish poetry. When dealing with very recent or contemporary poets, my choices were made somewhat difficult because of the continual publication of new work as I was writing this book. As a result, I chose to discuss the most recent generation, those writers whose reputations are still evolving, by emphasizing the works of Seamus Heaney and Derek Mahon, the most established and best known among them. Any gathering of writers which purports to reveal a direction in literature can be criticized for its omissions; I respond in advance that the poets whom I discuss here represent the personal selection necessary to develop my argument.

My critical vantage point has also limited and controlled my remarks. To paraphrase Roy Harvey Pearce, what follows is not a comprehensive literary history that surveys the making of poetry in Ireland since 1930 but rather a particular history that certain poems have made.[1] The pattern of that history reveals a conscious awareness of a poetic tradition involving a sense of the past and of its importance to the present.[2] As I attend in my arguments to the various expressions of a poetic tradition—its acceptance, rejection, even revision—I necessarily understate, but never deny, the diversity of subject matter and the artistic vitality of each poet represented here.

The purpose of any critical perspective is to interpret the poems themselves, especially those which deserve most to be read and discussed because they tell us emphatically and poignantly about human experience. In twentieth-century Ireland, that experience has been inextricably tied to the forging of a new nation within the context of older cultures and customs, a process that has demanded energetic reflection from intellectuals, artists, and writers. It is not surprising, then, that the identities of both the individual and the nation have emerged as dominant themes in the poetry of the period. Since the faint stirrings of nationalism in the early nineteenth century, literature, especially poetry, has played an important role in forming political and cultural attitudes. This role grew with the establishment in the 1920s of the Irish Free State. In essays, in newspaper articles, in plays, stories, and poems, writers consistently calibrated and criticized the national identity in the hopes of shaping and assuring its evolution.

With politics and literature so closely linked in Ireland, the question of identity took on poetic dimensions, demanding a particularly Irish solution. Thus began a highly self-conscious preoccupation with what might be called the problem of native voice, from its discovery and development under Yeats and the founders of the Literary Revival in the 1890s to its reconsideration and revision among contemporary Ulster poets. The latter include John Montague, Seamus Heaney, and Derek Mahon, who are acutely aware of the Janus-faced (British and Gaelic) nature of their cultural heritage.[3] The articulation of both the social and personal sides of Irish identity reveals a subtle but nonetheless clear tension in twentieth-century Irish poetry. Post-Yeatsian poets have exhibited that sense of tension by eschewing a version of the literary tradition which, a generation earlier, provided new metaphors to make Ireland's heart begin to beat. Less idealistic than their elders about the promise of Irish culture, these poets have sought out continuity, a sense of the past which insists upon its own reality, grounded in life as it is actually experienced and reflected in a hardened, nonromantic aesthetic.

Framework

Since the Literary Revival possessed extraordinary staying power—its themes and subject matter appeared well into the 1930s—it is easy to forget that the notion of a tradition in Irish literature is a very recent thing, confined essentially to this century. The enormous success and influence of this notion were due primarily to the efforts in the 1890s of the young William Butler Yeats, whose indefatigable promotion of an Irish voice in literature encouraged the industry of others. Most of those who immediately followed Yeats, however, were writers whose imaginations were more imitative than inventive, and while they featured Irish material in their works, they tended to repeat rather than to expand the early success of the Revival. Poets such as Joseph Campbell, Padraic Colum, and others who were featured in AE's (George Russell's) anthology *New Songs* (1904) believed that poetic success depended upon patriotism and the sentimental treatment of rural life and landscape; they gathered their material not by holding a mirror up to nature but by reading other poets, especially the early Yeats, and borrowing conventional imagery such as purple twilight and misty glens. These poets' continual use of the same themes and subjects rendered the practice of the Revival obsolete by the mid-1920s. Thus the generation of writers coming into their own in the 1930s faced the unusual discovery that a newly established poetic tradition had quickly become stifling and cliché-ridden.

Part of the explanation lay with the direction the Revival had taken in the 1910s and 1920s, when it was dominated by writers whose main concern seemed to be apologetics rather than the cultivation of the imagination. Romantic treatment of

Irish materials by writers like Campbell, Seamus O'Sullivan, and even the young Austin Clarke and F. R. Higgins eventually bred an attitude that criticized Irish writers for ignoring national subject matter. At its best, this critical perspective merely reiterated the early idealism of the Revival; at its worst, it produced a rigid and defensive view of literature that denied any realistic handling of Irish subject matter on the grounds that reality might be too blunt and too harsh for an evolving and fragile Irish identity. This inward-looking romanticism eventually led to the jingoistic literary theory of Daniel Corkery, whose criticism of writers focused on their respective degrees of Irishness.[4] The later work of Yeats himself was undervalued by revivalist critics such as Corkery because it moved away from Irish materials to more universal themes.[5]

This literary chauvinism came about because of the great paradox of the modern Irish poetic tradition: although it was created or invented out of a need to connect and identify with ancient Celtic Ireland, its manifestation depended upon its use of English, which qualified (if indeed it did not call into question) the Celtic-Gaelic origins. Yeats, who knew no Irish, could speak of "Gaelic memories and Gaelic habits of our mind"[6] and of "an unexhausted and inexhaustible Irish mythology which would provide symbols and characters for poems."[7] A generation later, Austin Clarke, whose knowledge of Irish allowed him to read these myths in the original, would criticize Yeats and the founders of the Revival for their lack of real understanding of "the drama of racial conscience."[8]

Clarke's charge was less a comment on Yeats's early use of Celtic materials, which Clarke favored on poetic if not scholarly grounds, than a response to Yeats's later work, which launched another version of an Irish poetic tradition, one that emphasized the great writers of the Protestant, Anglo-Irish Ascendancy, especially Swift, Burke, and Berkeley. Yeats's shift, embodied in the powerfully rhetorical poetry of *The Tower* (1928) and *The Winding Stair* (1933), was made primarily for aesthetic purposes, but also sprang from a psychological need to assert his own values and character amid what he saw as the growing tyranny of an alien majority culture. The conjuring of the spirit of Anglo-Irish Ascendancy provided Yeats with a tradition that served him poetically and personally; it also directed the course of new generations of poets. The success of Yeats's mythmaking in his later poems undoubtedly inspired Clarke, Thomas Kinsella, and other Catholic poets to explore their own idioms, pushing them deeper into yet another layer of history: that of Catholic, Gaelic Ireland and the culture of a conquered and dispossessed people who trace their lineage back beyond the Protestant Ascendancy. Clarke's and Kinsella's responses, every bit as personal as Yeats's, focus upon dissociation in modern Irish culture and connect the loss of the Irish language with a death of part of their imagination. For them, as for Yeats, the richness of the past implied a poverty of the present. The crucial difference is, however, that they arrived at their conclusions by a separate route.

Critical Perspective

The central argument of this essay assumes a change among a younger generation of writers in their attitudes toward tradition. The need to create and establish a tradition in literature no longer appears foremost in their thoughts nor has it produced the definitions and the apologetics that demanded so much from the young Yeats and the early revivalists. Indeed, by the 1920s the notion of a literary tradition within the context of the Irish Revival had been fully accepted by writers and scholars alike. Clarke, F. R. Higgins, and Liam O'Flaherty, all born in 1896, during the decade of the misty and shadowy Celtic Twilight, began their literary careers seeking inspiration and subject matter from the myths and folklore popularized by the revivalists. Clarke and O'Flaherty eventually outgrew this youthful enthusiasm, but as young nationalists their poetry and fiction, as well as their aggressive journalism and criticism, defended what Higgins ambiguously called "Gaelic consciousness," and their keen endorsement of romantic Ireland confirmed the lasting power of the Revival long after Yeats, its principal designer, had pronounced it dead and gone. This validation of the Revival by younger writers has prompted the view, held by Maurice Harmon and accepted by many literary historians, that by 1925 an Irish poetic tradition was fact and not fabrication.

> There was one great advantage for the Irish writer who began his literary career after the Literary Revival had reached its peak: he could then aspire to a tradition that had been widely recognized and accepted. By the mid-twenties the idea of a separate and distinct Irish tradition in English literature could not be denied.[9]

This may have appeared undeniable to a growing number of younger writers, but it eventually proved untenable. By mid-century many poets, including an older and wiser Austin Clarke and a young Thomas Kinsella, had granted the presence of tradition, recognizing it as a by-product of the Revival, but they sought to expand the concept, stressing the idea of continuity, the possibility of reclaiming or even identifying with their Gaelic past. Tradition as it was understood and practiced by the revivalists created false historical assumptions predicated on the reclamation of Gaelic culture. For the post-Revival poets, this romantic view of history restricted rather than expanded the poetic imagination. Armed with a knowledge of the Irish language which their elders never had, this new generation of poets saw the limitations and even the duplicity in any attempts to reclaim Gaelic culture; moreover, these poets detected a major fissure in the Irish literary tradition which suggested not a connection but an unalterable break with the past. There is a great irony connected with this attitude. These younger writers had genuine facility with the Irish language and could therefore make real contact with the ancient culture. Yet it was precisely this contact that convinced post-Yeatsian poets of the impossibility of reconstructing the past. Indeed, familiarity with the ancient heritage verified its opposite: the disappearance of traditional cultural values from twentieth-century life.

Language and Identity

The death of language and the accompanying cultural loss are such persistent themes in modern Irish poetry that it is worth reflecting briefly upon the function of the Irish language in modern literature. While the number of Irish speakers continues to shrink in the twentieth century, causing scholars to predict the language's imminent death, Irish nonetheless has made a living contribution to both spoken and written English. P. W. Joyce, in a famous study of the Irish dialect of English, notes the "give and take" where the Irish and English languages have mixed, producing a special vitality and colorful phrasing.[10] The well-known lilt and turn of phrase in the English spoken by Irish men and women owe much to the infiltration of the Irish language into English speech. Hugh Kenner has explained that this distinct richness of expression results from the tenacity of the older Gaelic syntax and idioms in retaining their shape when "pushed" by the younger English language.

> So an English comes to be spoken that has nothing grammatically wrong with it but with still something strange about it, a strangeness frequently obtained by the Irish habit of concentrating on states but supplementing the feeble English verb "to be" with verbs like "put," "leave," "have," which are used to indicate how a state of things has been effected: "She has him crying" (she has made him cry); "I put the fear of God on him" (I frightened him severely); "Have it off him" (take it from him).[11]

While the results of this strange bilingualism have been used to great advantage by writers such as Synge, O'Casey, and Flann O'Brien, colorful speech and rich expression seem scant recompense to those haunted by the death of the Irish language.[12] Many Irish writers in the twentieth century—even the greatest wordsmith of them all, James Joyce—have acknowledged their linguistic identity crisis. In chapter 5 of *A Portrait of the Artist as a Young Man* (1916), as Stephen mulls over his conversation with his English Jesuit master, he expresses the essential tension over language felt by the modern Irish writer:

—The language in which we are speaking is his before mine. How different are the words "home," "Christ," "ale," "master," on his lips and on mine! I cannot speak or write these words without unrest or spirit. His language, so familiar and so foreign, will always be for me an acquired speech. I have not made or accepted its words. My voice holds them at bay. My soul frets in the shadow of his language.[13]

The significance of language to poetry and poetic identity has been expressed clearly by T. S. Eliot, whose interest in tradition is well known. According to Eliot, the direct duty of the poet is to his language,

. . . to preserve, and second to extend and improve. In expressing what other people feel he is also changing the feeling by making it more conscious; he is making people more aware of what they feel already, and therefore teaching them something about them-selves . . . it will be equally true that the quality of our poetry is dependent upon the way in which the people use their language: for a poet must take as his material his own as it is actually spoken around him. If it is improving, he will profit; if it is deteriorating, he must make the best of it.[14]

And if it is disappearing or has disappeared, Eliot might have said if he were referring to modern Irish poetry, the poet surely will feel dislocated.

This rings hard and true for the modern Irish writer who writes in English about his Gaelic past and whose awareness of language leads to an inevitable discovery of loss. Facing up to that loss and attempting to reduce it constitute the prevailing problem of continuity in the poetry after Yeats; any attempt at reclaiming the lost culture merely repeats the central irony of the Revival: that the reclamation is done in English, thus con-firming the Irish poet's separation from a part of himself. This dilemma becomes especially crucial in poetry, as Roy Harvey Pearce has argued, because the poet's real concern is the articula-tion of cultural identity: "Poetry is thus a means whereby, through the imaginative use of language, we may be made aware of the values of a culture as they have (and have not) made possible the communal life of the individuals of whom it is composed."[15] In Ireland the case is further complicated by a confusion about community which itself is tied to a confusion about language. Seamus Deane, one of contemporary Ireland's most astute literary critics, believes that the linguistic problems of Irish literature reveal a divided and disturbed literary consciousness.

> In Ireland, the problem of language as used by Irish writers is not in the end separable from the problem of the Irish language. A place deprived of its speech is rendered deaf to its traditions. Yet, having experienced this, Ireland, in the course of two centuries, has attempted to master, not only a new language, but also the new traditions that go with it while still feeling, sometimes profoundly, sometimes with irritation, the necessity to keep some sort of formative contact with the "Hidden Ireland" and its old language.[16]

Thus the modern Irish writer views his role as artist paradoxically, as both preserver and destroyer of his cultural heritage.

This curious circumstance has directed recent Irish critical thinking to challenge the assumption that the Irish Literary Revival provided continuity for modern writers. Kinsella has asserted that the modern Irish tradition is "gapped," and his understanding of a Gaelic heritage merely points up discontinuity. He is aware that he stands "on one side of a great rift," with the Irish language and Irish culture on the far side.[17] John Montague, echoing Kinsella, has explained that Irish poetry in English faces the uneasy prospect that the larger part of its past lies in another language.[18] Seamus Deane, denying a single revivalist tradition, has identified a number of Irish literary factions including Yeats's Anglo-Irish, Protestant Ascendancy, Padraic Pearse's heroic revolutionary idealism, and Joyce's practice of repudiation. Deane has argued that the continuity of any one strain of tradition in Ireland necessary involves some sort of betrayal of another, due to the presence of colonial and native strains in Irish culture.[19] Insistence upon the unquestionably rich and great Protestant Ascendancy of Swift, Grattan, Burke, and Berkeley unavoidably alienates the Irish Catholic community, whose recollection of the Ascendancy's greatness are unfortunately tinged with memories of discrimination, the penal days, and their own servitude. The equally rich Celtic heritage of literature and language is inaccessible to the Irish Protestant community and even to a growing number of Catholics.

The sense of separation from the past tilts the poetic struggle subtly away from tradition and toward continuity, pushing Irish poetry toward the modernist and post-modernist concern with poetic and psychological identity. The struggle will always have an Irish context, because of the bipartite nature of Irish culture and the self-consciousness of its literary tradition, but its obsession with the poetic consciousness mirrors the direction of modern American, English, and European poetry. Much of post-Yeatsian Irish poetry takes as its subject the grave difficulties of writing poems within a culture becoming increasingly blind to its own past. Irish poets since Yeats have eschewed the romantic treatment of Irish history which characterized the practice of the early decades of the century and have turned instead to a consideration of both the place of poetry in the modern world and the role of the poet as the voice of his culture. The Irish version of the modern poet's search for identity demands a recognition of a severed tradition and an awareness of bipolarity. We sense the shift toward this cultural understanding in recent remarks by the contemporary poet Eavan Boland:

> Let us be rid at last of any longing for cultural unity, in a country whose most precious contribution may be precisely its insight into the anguish of disunity; let us be rid of any longing for imaginative collective dignity in a land whose final and only dignity is individuality.
>
> For there is, and at last I recognize it, no unity whatsoever in this culture of ours.[20]

In the face of this kind of critique from writers and scholars, the insistence upon one aspect of Irish culture as the authentic Irish experience, the most eloquent and powerful being Yeats's Ascendancy myth, is itself restrictive and discontinuous.

This is not to suggest that the notion of discontinuity or incoherence in an Irish literary tradition is only a very recent discovery. The two modern writers most responsible for the resurgence of Irish literature recognized in different, characteristic ways the difficulties of connecting with the past. James Joyce not only identified incoherence in modern Irish culture but accepted it as the culture's intrinsic feature. His early criticism and journalism attacked the tenets of the Revival which posited a reunification with the past. He shaped the political and cultural tensions in *A Portrait* by depicting the gulf between Victorian Ireland and her Gaelic past; in *Ulysses* (1922) he builds an aesthetic upon the problem of discontinuity, describing Irish art, especially the literature of the Revival, as "the cracked lookingglass of a servant." Joyce's apt image implies two fundamental problems in Irish literature: the distortion of any reality caught in a cracked mirror and the servitude inherent in a literature written for export to entertain foreign readers with Irish wit and humor.[21]

Yeats, too, recognized the fissure in Irish thought but sought to overcome it by sheer strength of poetic personality. As a young writer he attempted to express the consciousness of two cultures in his own work, hoping to translate the values of ancient Ireland for the modern world. This high romanticism was self-serving, of course, since the young Yeats needed Ireland every bit as much as he insisted that Ireland needed him. But it also indicates the clear fragility of Yeats's design and the essentially remedial direction of the Revival, predicated as it was on the hope, as Denis Donoghue has pointed out, "that the broken tradition of Ireland might still be mended."[22] Yeats, after his long running battle with middle-class opinion, eventually gave up his aim; his later poetry concentrates on isolation from the mainstream and celebrates the distance between the old Irish aristocracy and the new Ireland of the Catholic bourgeoisie. While he continued to look to the past for values, he cast a cold eye on modern Ireland, insisting upon her imperviousness to the civility and customs of history. His eulogy of the Ascendency at once grants tragic, heroic stature to the declining Anglo-Irish gentry and denies the possibility of greatness to rising modern Ireland.

Literary Values

It is precisely this concern with tradition and continuity which has engaged and, as this essay argues, haunted Irish poetry since Yeats. Post-Yeatsian poets have admitted the idea of tradition but have rejected the particular version advanced by the literature of the Revival. Understandably, this version of tradition proved too romantic for the simple tastes of younger poets, less idealistic than their elders. Clarke's and Kinsella's generation denied the Revival's central fiction that ancient Ireland offered modern Ireland its cultural identity; indeed they have insisted upon the opposite: although Gaelic Ireland can be recalled, it can never be recovered, much less re-created.

In the face of this realization, the poetic task has become not a retelling of Ireland's heroic agenda as the Revival urged but a reflection from Joyce's cracked looking glass showing the fractured character of Irish identity. Accordingly, the direction of Irish poetry in the twentieth century has shifted gradually from the casting of eyes on other days to a scrutiny of the here and now. Not only does the recent poetry criticize contemporary Irish society, it also reflects upon the difficulties of the poetic act, which must simultaneously draw upon a bifurcated history and shape the consciousness of the present. The Joycean tenor of post-Yeatsian poetry corrects the tendency of the Revival to idealize Irish life by converting a poetry of feeling into a poetry of thought.[23]

Turning to Joyce provided a different and much-needed direction for poets writing after the heyday of the Revival and during the early years of the Free State; it did not, however, completely solve the imposing problem of Yeats, whose stature and achievement demanded special attention from those who followed him. The responses toward Yeats from younger poets has varied from direct confrontation with his ideas to attempts to isolate him from the mainstream of contemporary literature. But while the responses vary, the acute anxiety in every case remains constant: how to distance oneself from Yeats, how to find a new poetic direction that leads away from Yeatsian practice. Often this has resulted in a contemplative, inward-looking poem that takes as its subject the responsibility of the artist or the role of poetry in modern society. The poem becomes a meditation upon society, poetic process, the poet, or the poem itself. The scrutiny and the criticism of romance and sentimentality may have rendered obsolete the high heroics of Irish myth for the modern age; they have also created a void that demands a new heroism, as John Montague notes in "Speech for an Ideal Election":

> Now the extraordinary hour of calm
> And day of limitation.
> The soft grasses stir
> Where unfinished dreams
> Are buried with the Fianna
> In that remote rock cave.
>
> Who today asks for more
> —Smoke of battle blown aside—
> Than the struggle with casual
> Graceless unheroic things,
> The greater task of swimming
> Against a slackening tide?[24]

This self-questioning seems a logical development in a poetic tradition that has been so thoroughly absorbed with its own identity. The new task—to make poems out of "graceless unheroic things"—demands poetic strategy antithetical to the Revival and antithetical also, as Montague subtly suggests, to those who wrote in defiance of the Revival. For poetry at mid-century could no longer battle against revivalism; that conflict was over. Rather, the poet had to swim against a slackening tide, a greater task because he met no resistance and therefore had to determine his poetic direction from within, not in response to some external condition. The most recent generation of poets, therefore, has recognized the achievement of the past, but also has proclaimed the pastness of the past. They know that Yeats and, in other ways, the minor poets of the Revival made a return to the old, high way of poetry impossible. As a result, they believe that they have inherited a brave new world. These poets not only have shouldered the usual accumulating burden of the past, as every new generation must, but they have also faced the self-conscious nationalism that has dominated twentieth-century Irish literature. In their attempts to discover their own voices and individual expressions, they have revised and extended their literary inheritance and taken their places within an ongoing poetic tradition; by making poetic identity an important subject for poetic treatment, the poets of mid-century passed on to yet a new generation an expanded sense of tradition, one that accommodated the problem of continuity.

Direction and Perimeters

In discussing the significance of tradition in Irish poetry since Yeats, I will concentrate on six poets whose work reflects a particular literary history. The fact that I also consider these poets to be the major figures of the period from 1930 to 1980 adds, I feel, to the cogency of my argument, although any ranking of poets is incidental to my design and purpose. By "major" I mean important and central, in this case, writers who have over a span of time produced a significant body of material which has received attention from reviewers, critics, scholars, and other poets. Occasionally, some poets—such as Thomas McGreevy, Brian Coffey, Denis Devlin, and Samuel Beckett who have been identified with a movement or a group and who flirted with European modernism in the 1930s—are treated here as part of a larger discussion. But on the whole I do not survey schools or movements. I have not, for example, linked poets with specific periodicals in order to explain strategies and directions in post-World-War-II poetry.[25] My coverage, then, is restricted by my selection of poets, deliberately limited in order that I might give more detailed attention to, and analysis of, a few rather than briefly survey many.

The treatment of individual poets is itself also limited to the discussion of my theme. While I am sensitive to the variety and expression of poetic achievement in each case, I am chiefly interested in the way in which artistic identity and the struggle with tradition are themselves subjects of the poetry. The compulsion of Irish poets, particularly since Yeats, to reconsider and redefine the Irishness of poetic expression is dominant. To consider this subject thoroughly, I stress certain aspects of the poetry, sometimes understating, though not overlooking, other topics or themes. What I attempt here, then, is neither the construction of a pantheon of twentieth-century Irish poetry nor a survey accounting for all the poets who have written since the death of Yeats. Rather, I am interested in illuminating a specific literary problem, which, I hope to show, has profoundly affected the work of a number of important modern poets.

A word about documentation. In my citations of primary sources, I have used the most recent or the most easily available publications. Almost all references to the works of the principal poets considered in this study are included in the text, with the edition indicated in an early note. Works cited infrequently, such as autobiographies, letters, essays, and novels, are cited in notes. All secondary material is documented in the usual manner in notes and is used conventionally to expand or illuminate portions of my argument.

Writing soon after the death of Yeats and Joyce, Frank O'Connor, himself a benefactor as well as a critic of the Literary Revival, reflected upon the past and the present and speculated on the future of Irish literature.

> Irish literature, as I understand it, began with Yeats and Synge and Lady Gregory; it has continued with variations of subject and talent through a second generation. Is there to be a third, or will that sort of writing be re-absorbed into the mainstream of English letters?[26]

The following essay offers an interpretive answer to O'Connor's question.

1

Tradition and Isolation: W. B. Yeats

It is tempting in a study of recent Irish poetry to ignore completely the work of W. B. Yeats, to adopt a tight-lipped policy in which one dares not speak his name, the mere mention of which might spoil the party. Yet so essential was the role Yeats played in determining the direction of modern Irish poetry that those poets who followed him, try as they would, could neither ignore him nor escape his influence. For them, particularly for the generation of Austin Clarke, Padraic Fallon, F. R. Higgins, and Patrick Kavanagh, Yeats was the omnipresent specter whose achievement in poetry, when coupled with his domination in the affairs of Irish letters, exerted an unavoidable pressure upon their work. They admired his productivity and admitted his genius, but quite naturally, as Clarke has explained, wanted their own place in the sun: "Yeats was rather like an enormous oak-tree, which, of course, kept us in the shade and of course we always hoped that in the end we would reach the sun, but the shadow of that great oak-tree is still there."[1] "Great upas tree" would have been more apt, for the difficulties in facing up to Yeats cost the poets of Clarke's generation dearly. Of those who immediately followed Yeats, only Clarke and Kavanagh managed to develop individual voices, and the individuality of both emerged only after great artistic struggle.

Yeats's Achievement and Reputation

With Yeats's death in 1939, the Irish poetic landscape seemed to offer little that was undiscovered or uncharted. For those young poets exploring it, the territory had very few places that did not show signs of other travelers. The poets' plight was aggravating; in Seamus Heaney's words, "Every layer they strip/ Seems camped on before." As the younger poets looked for new directions or fresh material, they invariably uncovered some reminder of the great Yeats, whose long and prolific literary career changed modern literature and made Ireland a land of imagination for readers all over the world.

From the very beginning of his career, Yeats showed a remarkable facility with language which allowed him to excel in every poetic mode he attempted. The exquisite beauty of early lyrics results from simple repetition of words, control of rhythm and rhyme, and the development of imagery.

> I went out to the hazel wood
> Because a fire was in my head,
> And cut and peeled a hazel wand
> And hooked a berry to a thread
> And when white moths were on the wing,
> And moth-like stars were flickering out,
> I dropped the berry in a stream
> And caught a little silver trout.[2]

The lyric success culminated in *The Wind Among the Reeds* (1899) and pushed Yeats toward the development of a public voice in such political poems as "September 1913" and "Easter 1916." The public poetry continued in the great poems of the 1920s, "Prayer for My Daughter" and "The Tower," and in the elegiac and majestic celebration of the Protestant Ascendancy in poems such A "Blood and the Moon" and the famous lines from "Coole Park and Ballylee, 1931":

> We were the last romantics—chose for theme
> Traditional sanctity and loveliness;
> Whatever's written in what poet's name

The book of the people; whatever most can bless
The mind of man or elevate a rhyme;
But all is changed that high horse riderless,
Though mounted in that saddle Homer rode,
Where the swan drifts upon a darkening flood.

(*YP.*, 245)

The depth of feeling in these lines, the conviction and authority grown from a personal view of history, all join with the mastery of language to present a powerful poetic sensibility and personality. During this later period Yeats also mastered both the meditative and the philosophic poem, giving us some of the greatest monuments of our language, "Among School Children," "Lapis Lazuli," and "Circus Animals' Desertion." The range is as extraordinary as it is revealing; when Yeats had succeeded in one form, he moved on to another—until he mastered that—and on again—"I, through the terrible novelty of light, stalk on, stalk on." At the end he had achieved greatness in many poetic modes.

The excellence of Yeats's achievement made it impossible for poets on either side of the Irish Sea to ignore his work. Ezra Pound and T. S. Eliot, both in London, learned much from him; W. H. Auden, C. Day Lewis, and Stephen Spender borrowed regularly from Yeats in their early poems. But English poets could borrow from Yeats without being stifled by him, since, according to Eliot, his real impact came not in poetic practice but rather in posture and attitude: "His idiom was too different for there to be any danger of imitation . . . the influence of which I speak is due to the figure of the poet himself, to the integrity of his passion for his act and craft which provided such an impulse for his extraordinary development."[3]

The matter of influence proved more serious, however, for the Irish poet whose idiom was similar to Yeats's. Moreover, in addition to sharing an idiom, younger Irish poets had to contend with the poetic personality, since Yeats saw himself throughout his life as the impresario of Irish letters. From the very beginning of his career, he assumed the chair of modern Irish literature, speaking *ex cathedra* on all aspects of Irish culture, organizing literary societies, directing a national theater, founding a national academy, editing, writing, debating, constantly agitating for his idea of a distinct voice in Irish literature. Over the course of time Yeats shifted his emphasis in regard to the definition of a national culture, but his purposeful commitment to the stewardship of Irish letters remained steadfast. Near the end of his life, in a series of radio broadcasts, he reminded audiences of his part in recent literary history, that he had "founded Irish literary societies, an Irish theatre, . . . had become associated with the projects of others."[4] Not content simply to reminisce in old age, he remained an active apologist until the very end, as he explains in a letter to Dorothy Wellesley dated 13 August 1937:

> I am well enough to face the public banquet and make the necessary senatorial speech. "Our movement is essential to the nation—only by songs, plays, stories can we hold our thirty millions together, keep them one people from New Zealand to California. I have always worked with this purpose in my mind."[5]

Even in the ordering of his *Collected Poems* (1956), the celebrated advice to future poets appears as a final legacy in a grand design.[6]

It was in this context of literary history that younger Irish poets like Clarke, Kavanagh, and Kinsella preferred their Yeats. They ignored his modernism, his visionary schema, and his philosophy, considering him first and foremost a nationalist writer, one who placed Ireland at the heart of his work in order to give it imaginative shape. More important, they saw him as the primary force behind the Revival, the apologist, if not the inventor, of the notion of an Irish poetic tradition. In testing their own poetic wings, they felt the necessity to limit the boundaries of Yeats's poetics, the better to respond to it. They did this by reading his work as a quest for continuity which eventually failed, taking refuge in a heroic individualism that denied any communal sense of Ireland. The final stages of this quest for continuity, the celebration of the Protestant Ascendancy, suggest a deliberate isolation from the mainstream of twentieth-century Irish life.

Although limited only to certain aspects of Yeats's poetry, this view held by the younger generation has its own validity, particularly as an explanation of the importance of tradition throughout Yeats's work. He had decided early in his career to follow the advice of John O'Leary and emphasize nationality in his writing. This, reasoned Yeats, would give him and other young writers in Ireland two advantages. It would set their poetry apart from the already crowded literary world dominated by the likes of Browning, Tennyson, Rossetti, Swinburne, and Morris. Moreover, as Yeats often reminded his contemporaries, historical themes and a newly discovered mythology would lend an authenticity to their work in the form of an established literary tradition that emphasized and defined Irishness.

Although Yeats utilized Irish material often in his work, nationality never commands his poetry as it does that of so many of his early contemporaries; indeed, Irish subject matter disappears in some phases of Yeats's career, and at other times the Irish voice is only faintly audible. Yet in two important stages in the poetry—the early Revival work and the later poems celebrating the Protestant Ascendancy—Yeats not only treated but emphasized Irish material, attempting in the process to define and shape versions of an Irish poetic tradition. In doing so, he invited those who followed him to read him as a nationalist poet.

The story of Yeats's influence on the direction of the Irish Literary Revival is certainly well known, having been told by Yeats himself, by other luminaries who took part in its unfolding, and by a number of literary historians.[7] Despite the many and varied accounts, despite even George Moore's gossipy and witty version which attempts to poke fun at the participants, one fact remains consistent throughout: above all others, Yeats was the guiding force and the dominant personality behind the movement. In an astonishing flurry, from 1889 to 1899, the crucial years during which the Irish Literary Revival was launched, he published four books of poetry, two books of Irish stories and tales, three anthologies of Irish poetry or Irish stories, countless articles and letters to newspapers. He also began work on his plays and lectured often on Irish literature to societies in Dublin and London. As if his example was not enough, he personally encouraged other writers through letters and conversation to seize the advantages of authenticity and originality offered by an Irish literary movement.

The enthusiasm and vigor that Yeats applied to the promotion of the Revival was motivated in part by idealistic national feelings and the hope for cultural identity in Ireland. He alludes to this hope in his *The Trembling of the Veil* (1922):

> Might I not, with health and good luck to aid me, create some new Prometheus Unbound; Patrick or Columbkil, Oisin or Fion, in Prometheus' stead; and instead of Causausus, Cro-Padric or Ben Bulben. . . . We had in Ireland imaginative stories, which the uneducated classes knew and even sang, and might we not make those stories current among the educated classes, rediscovering for the work's sake what I have called "the applied arts of literature," the association of literature, that is, with music, speech, and dance; and at last, it might be, so deepen the political passion of the nation that all, artist and poet, craftsman and day-laborer would accept a common design.[8]

The promotion of cultural unity in Victorian Ireland was politically so unrealistic, however, that it cannot serve as the most important reason that Yeats was committed to the Revival. Even the dreamy and idealistic young poet understood the deep political division in Irish society. Moreover, Yeats's own aesthetic and critical sensibility opposed poetry that announced or advocated political nationalism. Even though he claimed Davis, Mangan, and Ferguson as his poetic ancestors, Yeats generally felt that the sentimental patriotism of most nineteenth-century poetry weakened its literary achievement. Poetry, according to Yeats, should never serve nationalism; indeed, precisely the reverse should occur.

Nationalism was far too valuable a commodity to market solely to raise social and political consciousness. Yeats's real interest in Irish nationalism lay in its application to aesthetic theory and practice. The crucial early stage of his poetic development, between 1889 and 1899, demanded a particular focus, a narrowing of the field for the young writer whose interests at this time, Richard Ellmann has told us, went everywhere.[9] Thus commitment to the Revival allowed Yeats to channel his energies and, at the same time, gave him a framework for his art. Poetic rather than political reasons made an Irish literary movement appealing to him. To put it another way, the young Yeats's interest in stimulating the momentum of an Irish literature was self-serving more than it was nation-serving.

It is a credit to Yeats that he understood and developed the use of poetic tradition at such an early stage in his career. From the outset of his involvement as spokesman for the Revival, he recognized the advantages a national literary movement would provide to younger writers eager to break in upon the scene. In a letter written in January 1889, Yeats encourages a hopeful poet to use Irish legends as the basis of her work by saying "It helps originality and makes one's verses sincere, and gives one less numerous competitors. Besides one should love best what is nearest and most interwoven with one's life."[10]

Originality, sincerity, less competitiveness: these precepts appeared frequently during this period in Yeats's letters, essays, and poems. His advice to the young poet, like many of his remarks about the promise of the Irish mode, had meaning for Yeats himself, confirming the choice of his own poetic direction. He was understandably worried about his own development and his opportunities in the presence of competitors, especially the Victorian poets then in vogue, Rossetti and Swinburne. By avoiding the established mode of the Pre-Raphaelites and the decorous verse of London's aesthetes, Yeats sought originality. By insisting upon the cultivation of national themes and subject matter by younger Irish writers, he developed the context for fresh metaphors and new symbols. In 1887 he wrote to Katherine Tynan, "by being Irish as you can, you will be more original and true to yourself and in the long run more interesting, even to English readers" and again, in 1891, "a book such as you are doing should be Irish before all else . . . every poem that shows English influence in a marked way should be rejected."[11]

To be non-English was to avoid the dominant literary tradition, the first step toward originality for Irish writers. But since the Irish tradition lacked a definitive shape and an established continuity, where could these writers look to give their art a framework, a sense of reference, and a connection with the past? Yeats solved this dilemma by emphasizing the evolving nature of the tradition and its open-endedness. Irish writers could not only turn to a native tradition for sources and inspiration but in their use of Irish materials, they could also help create the tradition. In an essay on contemporary Irish poetry, Yeats identifies the work of AE, Katherine Tynan, and others, including but not mentioning himself, as

> . . . examples of the long and continued and resolute purpose of the Irish writers to bring their literary tradition to perfection, to discover fitting symbols for their emotions, or to accentuate what is at once Celtic and excellent in their nature, that they may be at last tongues of fire uttering the evangel of the Celtic people.[12]

Participation in the tradition, then, involved not merely drawing from it but also extending it.

An evolving literary tradition demanded a strong apologist, and Yeats willingly accepted the task. Throughout the 1890s he campaigned for an Irish poetic tradition, with two important results. He not only pumped life into a national movement by encouraging the participation of other writers but he also strengthened the conviction of his own poetics. Most of his efforts were aimed at establishing continuity, stressing not only ties with familiar nineteenth-century writers, especially the Young Ireland movement, but also with the Celtic myths and legends that had become available to English readers through the work of translators and philologists during the mid-nineteenth century. The Celtic materials appealed to Yeats because of their rich symbolic potential for modern literature: "the Welsh legends are held by almost as many masters as the Greek legends, while the Irish legends move among known woods and seas, and have so much of a new beauty that they may well give the opening century its most memorable symbols."[13]

While Yeats could easily accommodate the ancient Celtic materials into a poetic tradition, he had more difficulty with the popular ballads of nineteenth-century poets. In the well-known lines from "To Ireland in the Coming Time," he hints at his identification with certain of these writers:

> Know, that I would accounted be
> True brother of a company
> That sang, to sweeten Ireland's wrong.
> Ballad and story, rann and song . . .
> Nor may I less be counted one
> With Davis, Mangan, Ferguson.
>
> (*YP.*, 50)

Outside the dramatic context of this poem, however, Yeats's identification appears more qualified. In essays and reviews on Irish writing, he opposed the tendency of Davis' Young Ireland movement to use poetry for political purposes; moreover, he criticizes the lack of technique in many of these poets' work. Yet in his concern for continuity, Yeats sought a link with folk tradition and the poetry of the people, both of which could be found in recent popular writers. Thus for the sake of defining a poetic tradition, he surrendered some of his own critical principles.

In a running debate with Edward Dowden, Professor of Literature at Trinity College and opponent of the Irish movement in literature, Yeats defended his loyalty to the Young Ireland movement on the grounds of poetic sympathy. When Dowden pointed to the nineteenth-century writers' propensity for rhetoric as one reason why the achievement of Irish literature had been insignificant, Yeats responded by reiterating his own standards and suggesting an evolving literature that would build upon the past and would therefore be tied to it:

> Our "movement" . . . has denounced rhetoric . . . has exposed sentimentality and flaccid technique, but, at the same time, it has added to that literature books of folklore, books of history, books of fiction, and books of verse, which, whatever be their faults, are yet the expression of the same dominant mood, the same creative, impulse which inspired Ferguson.[14]

The vigor which characterizes his response to Dowden's criticism demonstrates the importance that Yeats placed upon a defense of the Revival against those who disdained narrow, local, or provincial movements outside the mainstream of English literature. For Yeats, more than the integrity of the Irish Revival was at stake. His defense was also an explanation of his own poetic achievement to date and his rejection of the Victorians and the Pre-Raphaelite movement in poetry.

The fortunes of the Irish Revival and the acceptance of its tenets and principles were linked in Yeats's mind to his own early success as a poet. In his initial efforts to promote the Irish Revival, he sensed that the proper cultivation of literary sensibilities and the education of an audience determined to a large extent the favorable reception of Irish poetry, both his own and that of others. In an 1889 letter to Katherine Tynan, mildly complaining about the time he spent explaining Irish elements in literature, he makes the important connection between his role as apologist and the writing of poetry:

> . . . the journalism interests me more dimly, of course, being good work for many people, but no way, unless on Irish matters, good work for you or me. . . . At least I think this way about it, not with any poet's dignity, of course, but because so much in the way of writing is needed for Irish purposes. . . . Much may depend in the future on Ireland now developing writers who know how to formulate in clear expressions the vague feelings now abroad.[15]

These remarks show a clear recognition by a young enthusiast of the problems faced by writers who use unfamiliar materials and themes in their work. It is also revealing because it indicates Yeats's concern and desire that other writers join him in developing an Irish literature.

From a writer worried about competitors and rivals, this may seem inconsistent and paradoxical. Yet for the young Yeats, participation by other writers in the Irish movement offered more advantages than threats. For one thing, the competition would be healthy rather than severe, since all writers were beginners like himself, a situation much preferable to tussling with Browning, Tennyson, and Rossetti. Also, the movement, if it was to be called one at all, demanded a critical mass of writers working actively toward its development. Yeats recognized some important benefits in this. Encouraging wider participation proved less a drain on his own time than the demanding journalism—the explanation of the tradition, the outline of its progress, the discussion of its themes—in which he involved himself only out of a sense of duty. As more writers tapped Irish sources, the reading public's familiarity with the material became greater and the need for journalism to promote the Revival became smaller.

The young Yeats worked hard to encourage other Irish writers, not only minor ones such as Katherine Tynan and Lilly White but more important figures such as AE, Douglas Hyde, Lionel Johnson, Lady Gregory, and, later, John Millington Synge. All profited from Yeats's promotion of the Revival. Often, the encouragement came in reviews and articles praising their work, at other times in letters, either to the individual directly or to a third party, recommending that a particular writer's work be read.

Yeats was so insistent that Irish writers develop Irish subjects that he frequently let his enthusiasm outrun his critical judgment. Often in these early reviews and letters he praises a work for its subject matter alone, ignoring technique and language. His regard for Katherine Tynan's poetry, which from our present vantage point is surely higher than the poetry deserved, stemmed almost solely from her use of Irish themes. Occasionally, the process worked in reverse; a writer would be censured for neglecting Irish material.

> [William] Allingham had the making of a great writer in him, but lacked impulse and momentum, the very things national feeling could have supplied. Whenever an Irish writer has strayed away from Irish themes and Irish feelings, in almost all cases he has done no more than make alms for oblivion.[16]

The example of Allingham, a nineteenth-century writer who Yeats felt ignored his Irish background provided contemporary

Irish writers with a negative model; not to recognize the potential in native sources was to risk losing authenticity.

Not surprisingly, the effect of this promotional effort was not one-sided. These writers whom Yeats encouraged and promoted were in turn of great help to Yeats, increasing literary activity and thereby indirectly enhancing his own reputation. Hyde and AE, in particular, were great organizers in their own right and contributed to the Revival in unique ways. Hyde's interest in the Irish language led to the formation of the Gaelic League in 1893 and to the completion of a bilingual collection of folk lyrics, *Love Songs of Connacht* (1893), one of the important texts of the Revival and one that influenced future translators such as Frank O'Connor. AE wrote a book of poems, *Homeward: Songs By the Way* (1894), but his special contribution was as a founder and editor of literary journals and as a friend to young Irish writers, helping to get their work into print.

Once the Revival was launched, AE gradually assumed a more active role in discovering new writers until, by 1910, he, rather than Yeats, had become the *paterfamilias* of Irish literature. His personality seemed well suited to this role, and he genuinely enjoyed fostering the careers of others. Yeats, on the other hand, lost interest in encouraging younger writers. His new administrative responsibility with the Abbey Theater took much of his time and energy. Also, the success of the Revival had created its own momentum, attracting new writers to Irish materials, thereby reducing the need for the kind of proselytizing Yeats had begun in the early 1890's.

Chiefly, AE's assumption of leadership manifested a change in Yeats's and his respective poetic temperaments and artistic perspectives. AE's writing time became increasingly absorbed by editorial duties on various periodicals. Yeats, on the other hand, continued to grow as a writer. His promotion and explanation of the Revival and his encouragement of other writers stirred his own imagination and served as an important proving ground for his poetry. As he worked through these early stages, reaching certain levels of poetic achievement in the process, his need for the scaffolding of the Revival lessened, and his attitude toward it changed. Thus by 1910, he was able to be critical of young writers attempting merely to be Irish, thus reversing or at least revising his earlier sentiment and enthusiasm. In his diary he describes a visit to AE's weekly gathering of literary people, among them many fledgling poets.

> Went to Russell's Saturday night—everybody either too tall or too short, or crooked or lop-sided. . . . Ireland since the Young Irelanders has given itself up to apologetics. Every impression of life or impulse has been examined to see if it helped or hurt the glory of Ireland or the political claim of Ireland. Gradually sincere impressions of life became impossible; all was artificial apologetics.[17]

Nor was his criticism at this time always confined to the private pages of a diary. In a poem collected in *The Green Helmet and Other Poems* (1910), Yeats announces an end to his liberal praise of younger Irish poets and rebukes AE for encouraging imitators.

> You say, as I have often given tongue
> In praise of what another's said or sung,
> 'Twere politic to do the like by these;
> But was there ever dog that praised his fleas?
>
> (*YP.*, 95)

Culmination and Exhaustion

This interesting reversal in attitude toward the younger Irish poets came in part from Yeats's personal awareness of his own aesthetic development, which grew out of the 1899 book *The Wind Among the Reeds*. In a variety of ways the book not only culminates but also exhausts a certain kind of poetic expression. The Celtic Twilight materials from Yeats's earliest poems— especially the delicate, shadowy imagery, the combination of strange beauty and otherworldliness, and the interest in the dream state—become in this book the vehicle for a heightened emotionalism that has autobiographical significance.[18] *The Wind Among the Reeds* blends myth, folklore, and love poems, all of which are wrapped in a personal symbolism that reflects Yeats's unsettled emotional life during the 1890s. His unsuccessful love affairs and his growing awareness of the difficulties facing his hopes for cultural unity created a state of mind that fluctuated between desire and despair, and it was this state of mind that brought the poet to a painful dreaminess in the poetry.[19] The volume's opening poem, "The Hosting of the Sidhe," plunges the reader directly into Irish legend and, at the same time, introduces the personal theme of the book, the danger of the seductive dream state:

> The host is riding from Knochnarea
> And over the grave of Clooth-na-Bare;
> Coailte tossing his burning hair,
> And Niamh calling *Away, come away:*
> *Empty your heart of its mortal dream.*
> *The winds awaken, the leaves whirl round,*
> *Our cheeks are pale, our hair is unbound,*
> *Our breasts are heaving, our eyes are agleam,*
>
> *Our arms are waving, our lips are apart:*
> *And if any gaze on our rushing band,*
> *We come between him and the deed of his hand,*
> *We come between him and the hope of his heart.*
> The host is rushing 'twixt night and day,
> And where is there hope or deed as fair?
> Caoilte tossing his burning hair,
> And Niamh calling *Away, come away.*
>
> (*YP.*, 56)

The powerful attraction of the unseen world and the repetitious emphasis on escape create the distance between desire and fulfillment so prominent in these poems, the timeworn human world measured against the eternal, trouble-free dreamland of the fairies, where

> . . . time and the world are ever in flight;
> And love is less kind than the grey twilight,
> And hope is less dear than the dew of the morn.
>
> (*YP.*, 59)

The transition linking the dramatic love lyrics in *The Wind Among the Reeds* with poems treating Irish subject matter occurs in the pivotal poem "The Song of Wandering Aengus," which celebrates the figure who is associated with love in Irish myth and who in Yeats's poem searches for a mysterious woman. The story had considerable personal significance for the young Yeats, involved with Olivia Shakespear and in love with Maud Gonne, and is an early example of his tendency to give historical and literary materials an autobiographical shape and meaning. The love lyrics also underscore the mood of the entire volume through their delicate rhythms and fragile, dreamy quality. Consistently, almost hypnotically, the same phrases and images recur in the descriptions of love: "pale," "dim," "half-closed eyes," "pearl-pale hand," "pale breast," "dream-heavy, "cloud-pale eyelids."[20] The mysterious beauty of the otherworld of the Irish fairies and the seductive charm and power of the passion depicted in the love lyrics combine to establish a mood that is shown to be incapacitating to the human condition; the tension of the book exists, then, in the pull of the dream state upon the human heart.

This development of mood is clearly seen in "The Secret Rose," a poem that treats unrequited love and celebrates the powerful beauty of the beloved, here symbolized by the "far-off, most secret, and inviolate Rose."

> I, too, await
> the hour of thy great wind of love and hate,
> When shall the stars be blown about the sky
> Like the sparks blown out of a smithy, and die?
> Surely thine hour has come, thy great wind blows,
> Far-off, most secret, and inviolate Rose?
>
> (*YP.*, 70)

All the characters in the poem, Conchobar, Cuchullain, Caolte, and Fergus, meet their destinies while in search of some ideal or while completing some great action, and as a result they now "dwell beyond the stir/And tumult of defeated dreams," enfolded by the Rose. The speaker-poet also seeks his own destiny, and yet he senses the implications of finality, even death, and the fact that to have the Rose is also to be consumed by it.

The Wind Among the Reeds succeeds to a fault, as the final poems of the volume suggest. The poet-narrator in "The Secret Rose" calls for the Rose to enfold him, which would mean absorbing and consuming him personally and, by implication, poetically. Elsewhere, the sadness of the lover in "The Lover Speaks to the Hearers of his Songs in Coming Days," "The Poet Pleads With the Elemental Powers," and "He Wishes For the Cloths of Heaven" becomes so cultivated that it overwhelms the speaker-poet, taking on a life of its own beyond the poetic contexts.[21]

Yeats recognized the dangerous tendencies of his mood almost immediately. As early as 1905, while revising The Wind Among the Reeds, he saw that the direction of the book broke down caught between the world of action and the world of dream, and that the emotional excesses in the poetry had compromised the personal element. It may be, as has been suggested, that Yeats's profound sadness and sense of personal failure forced him to recognize that his poetic attempts to deal with life were really maneuvers to avoid it.[22] Or Yeats simply may have understood that as a poet he had moved as far as he could in one direction, that he had exhausted the life of his symbols, and that he needed to shift his poetic strategy. Whatever the cause, the poetry did begin to change after the turn of the century, gradually at first, but definitively, curbing excessive emotion with the emergence of a distinct sense of personality and a cultivation of the individual.

Yeats's conscious understanding that the achievement of The Wind Among the Reeds also meant a culmination and a turning point in his artistic development caused him to be wary of the Revival for the same reasons he promoted it—the desire for originality, the sense of poetic identity, and the fear of stultification by existing poetic modes. As his own poetic style began to shift and evolve out of self-criticism, he looked for that same sense of self-criticism in others. Yet what he found dissuaded him from the promise of the Revival. His younger contemporaries appeared unwilling to subject their work to the same intensive scrutiny and revision that he applied to his own poems. Moreover, he sensed stasis and even retrogression in a uninspired imitation and lack of imagination. The inventiveness Yeats always believed essential to the use of Irish materials was a quality he missed in AE's anthology *New Songs*. He wrote to AE in April 1904:

> Some of the poems I will probably underrate (though I am certain I would recognize a masterpiece come out of any temperament) because the dominant mood in many of them is one I have fought in myself and put down. In my *Land of Heart's Desire*, and in some of my lyric verse of that time, there is an exaggeration of sentiment and sentimental beauty which I have come to think unmanly.[23]

Although Yeats names only his early play *The Land of Heart's Desire*, produced in 1894, he is referring here to his Celtic Twilight period, to those works that evoke an excessively dreamy and sentimental mood. The crucial point here is Yeats's willingness, or need perhaps, to admit a change in his poetic temperament.[24] It is this view of his own work which allowed him to find fault with writers for tendencies he would have praised ten years earlier.

The Ascendancy Tradition

Yeats's shifting aesthetic sensibility and his developing poetic maturity explain in part his change in attitude toward revivalist writers and their use of Irish materials. But his coolness toward the younger generation also reflected intellectual changes, particularly in his feelings concerning the Revival's promise for a culturally united Ireland.[25] As Yeats dealt more and more with the Irish middle class, both in his capacity as a director of the Abbey Theater and as a champion of various artistic causes, he became discouraged by the public's narrow-minded morality and materialism. His embittered response was to turn his back upon middle-class Catholic Ireland and align himself with the aristocracy, a move which bred a critical attitude toward Catholic writers as well. In a letter to Florence Farr written in 1905, Yeats remarks:

> . . . the writers of this country who come from the mass of the people—or no, I should say, who come from Catholic Ireland, have more reason than fantasy. It is the other way with those who come from the leisured classes. They stand above their subject and play with it, and their writing is, as it were, a victory as well as a creation. The others, Colum and Edward Martyn, for instance, are dominated by their subject with the result that their work as a whole lacks beauty of shape, the organic quality.[26]

In 1905, during the early years of the Abbey Theater, Yeats remained idealistic enough about national culture to censure Catholicism only on literary grounds. A few years later, however, he had become sufficiently embittered socially to extend his views to Irish culture in general, claiming the superiority of the Protestant Ascendancy over Gaelic-Catholic Ireland: "The whole system of Irish Catholicism pulls down the able well-born if it pulls up the peasant, as I think it does. A long continuity of culture like that at Coole could not have arisen, and never has arisen, in a single Catholic family in Ireland since the Middle Ages."[27]

The critical stance Yeats assumed against the middle-class eventually found its way into his poetry, thus requiring a shift in aesthetic strategy. No longer could he see his work as leading toward a spiritually united Ireland, a community of the imagination based on an ancient Celtic heritage. In 1909, discouraged in his attempts to influence the public through poetry and drama, a disillusioned Yeats wrote in his journal, "the Irish people were not educated enough to accept as an image of Ireland anything more profound, more true of human nature as a whole, than the schoolboy thought of Young Ireland."[28] Against his failed communal ideal, then, Yeats set the notion of the heroic individual and began the search for a new perspective in his art.

He accomplished this during the 1920s by focusing upon the Protestant Anglo-Irish Ascendancy and, in effect, creating a new pantheon composed of the great public figures of Georgian Ireland: Swift, Grattan, Goldsmith, Burke, Berkeley, Tone, and Emmet. By doing this, Yeats expanded his conception of the Irish literary tradition so that it could accommodate the shift in his own poetics. His need for tradition at this stage of his career remained critical, but the Gaelic tradition no longer served as efficaciously since it came increasingly to connote Catholic Ireland. As Yeats grew continually more disdainful of the Catholic majority, which he characterized as being composed of merchants and clerks with timid breath, he dramatized and celebrated the heroic courage of the Anglo-Irish and mythologized their tradition, identifying himself and his ancestors with that heritage.

Yeats's most emphatic description of the importance of the Ascendancy tradition occurs in his famous attack in the Irish Senate on the Catholic position on divorce, which while an essentially legal argument had considerable relevance nonetheless for literary theory.

> I think it is tragic that within three years of this country gaining its independence we should be discussing a measure which a minority of this nation considers to be grossly oppressive. I am proud to consider myself a typical man of that minority. We against whom you have done this thing are no petty people. We are one of the great stocks of Europe. We are the people of Burke; we are the people of Grattan; we are the people of Swift, the people of Emmet, the people of Parnell. We have created the most of the modern literature of this country. We have created the best of its political intelligence.[29]

All the ingredients are here that would inform Yeats's later poetry: the historical sense, which looks back to those great Irish voices of the eighteenth century; the aristrocratic cultural conservatism; the declaration that Protestant Ireland was an essential and important aspect of the new Irish Free State; the continuity of the heroic Protestant tradition; and, finally, the criticism of the deficiency and shortsightedness of the Catholic middle-class majority.

Although the use of the Ascendancy tradition is prominent in the later poems, it appeared as early as the 1910 volume *The Green Helmet*, in a manner that would be characteristic of Yeats's public voice of the 1920s and 1930s. There is the explicit criticism of the new leveling tendency in Ireland:

> The weak lay hand on what the strong has done,
> Till that be tumbled that was lifted high
> And discord follow upon unison
> And all things at one common level lie.
>
> (*YP.*, 96)

There is also an accompanying mythologizing of the Anglo-Irish in "At Galway Races" with its portrait of "riders upon the galloping horses," even in this early poem an important emblem of courage, grace, action, and culture. Protestant Ireland offered the values that, like Lady Gregory's house and wood in "A Prayer for My Daughter," stood as a barrier to the roof-leveling wind that would crush all greatness, make all the same. Furthermore, we sense in this volume the same elegiac note that would resound throughout the later poems, signifying the finality of the Protestant achievement. The sun has fallen in these poems, the race is over, the great house "where passion and precision have been one" is threatened, and the vital horsemen are only a distant memory.

The gradual development of the importance of Ascendancy values grew from the few poems in *The Green Helmet* to dominate the later poetry, particularly *The Tower* and *The Winding Stair and Other Poems*. Yeats's attraction to Georgian Ireland, according to

Donald Torchiana, stemmed from the heroic examples of Swift, Grattan, Burke, and Berkeley and the notion that they might provide models for enlightened public opinion in Ireland.[30] Yeats insisted, as we have seen in the divorce speech, that the Protestant Ascendancy constituted a legitimate aspect of Irish society and that Swift and the others were quintessential Irishmen who "found in England the opposite that stung their own thought into expression and made it lucid."[31] This proved to be the crucial plank in Yeats's platform for expanding the Irish poetic tradition. These great men wrote and thought as Irishmen, and in their particular nationalism Yeats found his proper heritage:

> I declare this tower my symbol; I declare
> This winding, gyring, spiring treadmill of a stair
>   is my ancestral stair;
> That Goldsmith and the Dean, Berkeley and Burke
>   have travelled there.
>
> (YP., 237)

Yeats's interest in the Ascendancy tradition grew as he became more committed to autobiographical poetry as a response to the isolation of Protestant Ireland during the establishment of the Free State in the 1920s. The mythologizing of the Protestant Ascendancy in the later poems stresses heroic solitude and traditional civic virtues, providing Yeats with exempla against which to measure the modern world and find it wanting; the mythologizing also allowed him to shape his evolving poetics by informing the public voice of the later poetry with the values of the landed gentry: ceremony, custom, manners, eloquence, cold intellectual passion, and appreciation for the arts. Yeats's use of the Ascendancy tradition in the later poetry, then, resembles the strategy in the early poems which drew upon Celtic materials and folklore; Ascendancy values established an important literary context but quickly became dependent upon the poetry itself. This development not only sets Yeats apart from other Irish poets but also testifies to his greatness as an artist.

His poetry breathed life into the tradition, inverting the usual practice among poets who rely on systems and structures to vitalize their work

This curious circumstance can be seen in Yeats's evolving identification with Protestant Ireland. As the youthful promoter of the Revival, Yeats did not exalt the Ascendancy;[32] rather he turned to it as he matured poetically and as he became more alienated from the new Irish Free State.[33] The tradition of Protestant Ireland and its great heroes became increasingly important for Yeats because they provided a continuity that shored up his ever-widening disdain for middle-class Catholic Ireland. His gathering of the Gregorys, Hugh Lane, John Synge, Shaw-Taylor, Parnell, and others both established aristocratic values in modern Ireland and stressed the connection with an Irish past, particularly as that past was manifested in an ongoing literary tradition. For the sake of his public voice and poetic strategy, Yeats read the past as he needed to, dramatizing aspects of eighteenth-century Irish life and connecting himself to that age in the process. In "The Seven Sages," for example, he superimposes upon the intellectual thought of Georgian Ireland a distinctly antimodern feature.

The Fifth:	Whence came our thought?
The Sixth:	From four great minds that hated Whiggery.
The Fifth:	Burke was a Whig.
The Sixth:	Whether they knew or not,
	Goldsmith and Burke, Swift and the Bishop of Cloyne
	All hated Whiggery, but what is Whiggery:
	A levelling, rancorous, rational sort of mind
	That never looked out of the eye of a saint
	Or out of drunkard's eye.
The Seventh:	All's Whiggery now,
	But we old men are massed against the world.

(*YP.*, 241)

These voices repeat Yeats's familiar attack upon modern democracy, but they establish important authority by locating the origins of this attitude in the great Protestant thinkers of the eighteenth century. Since Yeats found the basis for this anti-modern stance in Irish history, he was able to identify easily the special role Ireland had to play against the leveling wing of the modern age. Ireland, with its living folk tradition and its aristocratic eighteenth-century heritage, was, for Yeats, unique among world cultures and, he felt, must fulfill its antimodern destiny:

> We Irish, born into that ancient sect.
> But thrown upon this filthy modern tide
> And by its formless spawning fury wrecked,
> Climb to our proper dark, that we may trace
> The lineaments of a plummet-measured face.
>
> (*YP.*, 337)

The dramatic public authority so evident in "We Irish" builds on many other poems to make its impact, all of them collectively defining the notion of "Irish" as something limited and specific in this context. Behind these lines stands the sense of an Anglo-Irish past sketched out in "The Tower" as the poet writes his will; or of the lonely isolation and concentrated control of "The Fisherman" who seeks out a high, difficult stream into which to cast his fly; or of the glory and greatness implied in "Ancestral Houses" from "Meditations in Time of Civil War"; or of the ceremony and custom informing the various poems describing Coole and developed so movingly in "A Prayer for My Daughter." In no sense does the phrase "We Irish" suggest the collective nation of Ireland. Yeats's ideas of community were long since fixed; he had abandoned his cultural ideal of unity much earlier and even had gone so far as to identify the majority culture of the new Ireland as part of the "filthy modern tide." He reflects on his ideas of nationality in literature in a 1910 journal entry, contrasting his own idealistic view of a unified, imaginary Ireland with the common man's practical view.

> Am I not therefore un-national in any sense the common man can understand? He means by national a mob held together not by

what is inferior, delicate and haughty, but by law and force which they obey because they must. I must therefore be content to be but artist, one of a group, Synge, Lady Gregory—no, there is no other than these—who express something which has no direct relation to action. We three have conceived an Ireland that will remain imaginary more powerfully than we conceived ourselves. The individual victory was but a separation from causal men as a necessary thing.[34]

Yeats's attitude toward the common man informs his well-known antimodern stance in section 5 of "Under Ben Bulben," in which he advises and instructs future Irish poets to learn their trade, the first part of which was to scorn those then writing. Yeats's contemporaries knew nothing of Ireland's greatness, since their "unremembering hearts and heads" were "base-born products of base beds." The specific identification of these misshapen poets is not clear, but if we recall Yeats's attitude toward middle-class Catholic Ireland, we can presume that he would have included among the accused Austin Clarke and Patrick Kavanagh. The identification is not important, of course, since it is really the tendency here that is of interest to us. Yeats not only felt compelled to elegize the Ascendancy so that its loss appeared as a great cultural tragedy but he also aggressively attacked those poets from the new Ireland whose Catholic majority now dominated the Protestant classes. These poets from the working and merchant classes could never know the refinement, learning, and custom of the great Anglo-Irish families.

Yeats prescribes as well as criticizes in "Under Ben Bulben," urging Irish poets toward traditional subject matter and away from the tendency to depict the common experiences of modern life. The famous prescription demands a restricting of focus—"Cast your eyes on other days"—which would reflect a heroic aristocracy and a society of peasants and gentlemen, lords and ladies. The important meaning behind these well-known lines equates the source of poetic inspiration with an idealized version of the past. The Yeatsian formula for future Irish poetry was drawn deliberately from conservative romanticism rather than from modernism.

The interesting feature of Yeats's declaration to future poets is its impossibility, both because of the sociocultural changes in Ireland which would make Yeats's future poet obsolete and because his advice directs the poet precisely back to Yeats country, to descriptions of an imaginary structure which he himself had made it impossible to reconstruct. The majesty and irony of his use of the Ascendancy tradition reside in its elegiac note and its isolation from the real Ireland.

> Here, traveller, scholar, poet, take your stand
> When all those rooms and passages are gone,
> When nettles wave upon a shapeless mound
> And saplings root among the broken stone,
> And dedicate—eyes bent upon the ground,
> Back turned upon the brightness of the sun
> And all the sensuality of the shade—
> A moment's memory to that laurelled head.
>
> (YP., 243)

Masterfully, Yeats is at once creating, celebrating, and elegizing the Ascendancy tradition.[35] He declared himself and his few friends to be "the last romantics," writing of things never to be known again. The themes of the later poems refuse to recognize the emerging life of twentieth-century Ireland, the rising middle class, and the tribe of Daniel O'Connell and De Valera. To write of this Ireland would be to cut against the Yeatsian grain. And it was against this grain also to write as poets did who were "determined to express the factory, the metropolis, that they may be modern . . . [defending] their type of metaphor by saying that it comes naturally to a man who travels to his work by tube."[36] This comment of Yeats about W. H. Auden's generation describes, unknowingly, the direction Irish poetry was to take in the 1950s and 1960s. The treatment of common subjects and of ordinary experience neglected the wider perspective offered by history and, in Yeats's view, prevented the development of the heroic.

Out from Under the Upas Tree

It is this focus upon the past and the mythologizing of history which had made Yeats such a severe patriarch for his tribe. Not only have post-Yeatsian poets had to overcome his tampering with the jury, declaring certain subject matter unacceptable, but they have also had to effect a revision of his myth about Protestant Ireland, a task made difficult, if not impossible, by the Yeatsian poetic achievement. The younger poets have seen their way out of this dilemma through direct confrontation with the master on his own high ground. They have declared that Yeats's view of Ireland is self-serving romanticism, bred out of bitter but self-imposed isolation; they have then opted in their own poetry for the treatment of Irish reality, a scrutiny of the common experience of life as lived by most of the people. Once the Yeatsian tradition could be shown to be both limited and specious, particularly in its insistence upon continuity, then the younger poets could offer their own treatment of Irish experience as innovative and, more important, as authentic.

The demythologizing of the Yeatsian poetic tradition has become a regular and important act for almost every Irish poet who had followed Yeats. Clarke, commenting upon the famous advice in "Under Ben Bulben," suggests that Yeats's public poetry assumes backward-looking poses that

> . . . reveal the poet's life-long delight as an artist in attractive and striking gestures and his characteristic antinomianism. But they [the lines from "Under Ben Bulben"] recapitulate a past phase rather than prepare the future.[37]

In a more general vein, Kavanagh has suggested that Yeats attempted to create an Irish tradition only to find himself separated from it in the end and "uneasy that he [didn't] belong."[38] Seamus Deane, one of the staunchest critics of Yeats's patrician version of history, has attacked the very values postulated by the Ascendancy tradition. Far from being aristocratic, Deane has argued, the Anglo-Irish were actually people of no lineage who inherited their status simply by fighting on the winning Hanoverian side against the Jacobites. The late seventeenth- and early eighteenth-century Gaelic Irish of noble ancestry never have thought of the Ascendency as aristocratic. Nevertheless, Deane has charged, Yeats changed the modern understanding of Irish aristocracy in his glorification of the Anglo-Irish: "Since Yeats . . . a literary image has emerged which preempts most others—It is the image of the hero surrounded by the mob, of culture environed by Philistinism, of civility swamped in barbarity."[39] While Deane may be guilty of his own historical extremism, he nonetheless reflects the sentiments of the Catholic poet or intellectual faced with the effects of Yeatsian mythmaking upon the direction of Irish culture. Deane's view also suggests an interpretation of Yeats's inventive reading of Irish history which qualifies considerably the notion of continuity within the tradition.

Yeats's separation from Irish culture receives further attention in Thomas Kinsella's essay on literary traditions in Ireland. For Kinsella, Yeats's Ascendancy tradition constitutes a brilliant metaphoric structure that sustains the public voice of the later poems.

> He yokes together Swift and Burke, and Berkeley and Goldsmith for his writer, and for his chosen people finds a race of swashbucklers, horsemen, swift indifferent men. . . . Yeats created this brief Anglo-Irish tradition for himself, by special selection and then projected his own values into it. But it is still a coherent entity, at a graceful elegiac height above the filthy modern tide.[40]

The coherence of the poetic attitude coupled with the dramatized personality, Kinsella has suggested, allows Yeats to rise above the pettiness of politcal squabbles: "Yeats bestrides the categories. He had a greatness capable, perhaps of integrating a modern Anglo-Irish culture from the main unwashed body."[41] Despite its majestic, self-contained coherence, however, the Yeatsian poetic myth does not reflect modern Ireland. Moreover, in his insistence upon the superiority of Anglo-Irish tradition,

Yeats promoted an exclusive and singular vision of Irish society which denied Catholic Ireland and produced, according to Kinsella, discontinuity in the modern Irish tradition.

Both Deane's and Kinsella's view prove interesting not only for what they reveal in Yeats but also for their reflection of the attitudes of post-Yeatsian writers toward continuity in modern Irish poetry. Most of them have had a stake in emphasizing Yeats's isolation in the Irish tradition, as we shall see in some detail in the next chapter. Kinsella's remarks are less combative that most but do point to a typical ambivalence concerning Yeats's legacy, one that combines a recognition of his rightful place in the tradition with an awareness of his separation from its mainstream.

The problem of Yeats became a serious difficulty, then, for those poets who succeeded him. His mythologizing of Irish history and his narrow view of Irish society, which on the surface might have suggested limitations of the poetic vision, were transformed into strengths by the power and stature of the poetry itself. In his restrictive version of continuity and his identification with the Protestant Ascendancy, Yeats stands for the tradition as broken, but no poet following him has been able to ignore his talent and his achievement. Committed to the realistic and psychological treatment of middle-class, Catholic, modern Irish life, post-Yeatsian poets have turned away from Yeats to follow Joyce into the filthy modern tide, but they have never quite lost sight of the Yeatsian heritage over their shoulders. The memorable Yeatsian line, his poetic style, and his public voice make up the legacy. More important, however, is the presence of personality behind the poems, in the imagination inherent in his mythmaking and in the coherence of the poetry—a presence that intimidates and demands the most that future poets can give.

2
Revivalism and the Revivalists

Although Yeats abandoned his early commitment to the Celtic Twilight and moved toward the Protestant Ascendancy, most Irish poets during the early decades of the twentieth century were content to pursue the tenets and the promise of the Irish Literary Revival. So successful, in fact, was Yeats's revivalist propaganda during the 1890s—with its exquisite culmination in *The Wind Among the Reeds*—that the stage was set for modern Irish poetry for almost forty years. The poets who immediately followed Yeats inherited his enthusiasm for the Irish mode and for the Celtic past, but lacked his shaping imagination and his critical depth. Thus with the notable exception of Yeats himself, Irish poetry from 1900 to 1940 remained relatively static, repeating the themes of the Revival and recycling its material and its metaphors.

Part of the reason for this stasis rested with the poets themselves, whose strength resides in illustrating rather than determining the direction of nationalism in Irish writing and whose talent lay in cultivating rather than in breaking ground. But neither of these conditions explains completely why revivalism enjoyed such longevity, especially considering its growing list of detractors, the most prominent being its founder, Yeats himself. The popularity of the Revival persisted for two other reasons, which show contrasting attitudes toward Yeats among two generations of poets.

For the first group of revivalists writing almost in the wake of the publication of *The Wind Among the Reeds*, the impulse to describe and feature the Celtic Twilight was natural enough. Padraic Colum, Seamus O'Sullivan, and other young poets felt that genuine opportunity still existed in the Celtic Twilight mode, in the faery hills and fields of Ireland. Yeats, it is true, utilized Irish materials with great success in his early poems, but he left much Gaelic folklore and peasant life untouched. Irish poets of the early twentieth century believed they could still distinguish themselves by focusing upon native materials and by depicting landscape. Indeed, they were encouraged to do so by their elders and betters, particularly AE, who enthusiastically arranged for the publication of their poems. From the vantage point of literary history, we now judge these reasons to be misconceptions of the vitality of a movement, although we nonetheless can understand the attempts by young writers of the time to take advantage of a literary opportunity.

The second reason, which applies primarily to a later generation of revivalists in the 1920s, touches more complicated matters and runs counter to ideas about poetic progress. The surge in political sentiment following the Easter Rising in 1916, the Anglo-Irish war, the Civil War, and the shaping of the Irish Free State rekindled an interest in national identity and cultural values which sparked literary expression. Young, idealistic poets, buoyed by great social and political expectations, sought to find a new significance in the old legends and myths.[1] But to avoid appearing as imitators, they wished to purify the work of the Revival by becoming even more Irish than their elders. To do so they emphasized their facility with the Irish language and incorporated Gaelic prosody into their verse, thereby claiming to be more authentic than any of their predecessors, especially the great Yeats. In addition, they broadened the conception of the Irish past, drawing upon early Christian and medieval Gaelic sources as well as upon the heroic era favored by Yeats and Lady Gregory.

The insistence upon greater scrutiny of old materials, upon close study of legends in the original language, and upon the wider conception of Irish history seemed a necessary strategy for these young revivalists. For they faced extremely difficult circumstances. They not only risked repeating twice-told tales but also risked incurring the formidable critical scorn of Yeats himself, who, as we have seen, had turned against the new practitioners of the Revival, objecting to their sentimentality, extreme emotionalism, and exaggeration of things Irish. Their response to these objections was to burrow more deeply into the matter of Ireland, to insist more than ever upon the romantic, idealistic, even sentimental treatment of Irish themes and subjects.

It is not surprising, then, given the deliberately nationalistic thinking of these young poets, among them Austin Clarke. F. R. Higgins and Padraic Fallon, that Yeats withheld his support and encouragement. He found the poetry of these younger writers to be too restricted by its material. For Yeats, subject matter could never be more important than poetry itself. In fact, in Yeatsian practice the informing schemes and fictions gained their vitality from the achievement of the poems. As we have seen from his remarks to AE about overcoming weaknesses in poetic expression, Yeats placed great importance upon the fact that poetry should be unfettered. Moreover, he was not patient with poetry that emphasized and exploited the poetic vices he had exorcised from his own writing. Throughout the 1920s and 1930s Yeats withheld praise and encouragement from the poets who, he felt, imitated rather than created. In 1932, when he was selecting members for the Irish Academy of Letters, he wrote to Olivia Shakespear about the young Austin Clarke.

> An Irish poet Austin Clarke has just sent me a romance called *The Bright Temptation* which you should get from a library. . . . Read it and tell me should I make him an Academician. I find it difficult to see, with impartial eyes, these Irish writiers who are as it were part of my propaganda.[2]

Yeats dubbed such writers his "fleas" and spurned their orientation, their background, and their affiliation with the New Ireland, which he disliked and disdained. These young revivalists, in their turn, looking for a means by which to reflect the intense national feeling of their day, struck back aggressively. First they reaffirmed their interest in a distinctively Irish mode in poetry, and then, in an act of creative and bold interpretation, they criticized Yeats's Ascendancy poems for drifting away from genuine Irish poetry, thereby endangering his authenticity and his strength.

The most extreme version of this position occurs in the criticism of Daniel Corkery, who defined Anglo-Irish literature as the expression of the three main forces in Irish life: religion, nationalism, and the land. For Corkery, those who placed these forces at the heart of their work and could portray them with a deeply felt sensitivity had a true Irish consciousness, which reflected the emotional identity of the majority of Irish people. The crucial word in Corkery's argument is "majority," a transparent cipher for Catholic Ireland. Anyone unfamiliar with this emotional consciousness, particularly the Protestant Ascendancy writer, could not hope to reflect the Irish experience.

> In the case of writers from the Ascendancy their emotional nature differs from that of the Irish people (differs also of course from that of the English people) and such as it is, is also doubtless thrown out of gear by the educational mauling it undergoes. They are therefore doubly disadvantaged. To become natural interpreters of the nation they need to share in the people's emotional background. . . . The ingrained prejudices of the Ascendancy mind are so hard, so self-centered, so alien to the genius of Ireland, that no Ascendancy writer has ever succeeded in handling in literature the raw material of Irish life.[3]

The interesting feature of Corkery's remark lies not in its critical jingoism, of course, but rather in the implicit need to restrict the definition of Irish literature to benefit the fiction, poetry, and drama produced by the young writers emerging within the establishment of the Irish Free State. Indeed, in his struggle with the Ascendancy writers, Corkery went so far as to denigrate and even deny the achievement of the Literary Revival since it was work essentially by Protestants:

If one approaches "Celtic Revival" poetry as exotic, then one is in a mood to appreciate its subtle rhythms and its quiet tones; but if one continues to live within the Irish seas, travelling the roads of the land, then the white-walled houses, the farming life, the hilltop chapel, the memorial cross above some peasant's grave, impressing themselves as the living pieties of life must impress themselves upon the imagination, growing into it, dominating it, all this poetry becomes after a time little else than impertinence. It is not possible to imagine it as the foundation of a school of poetry in which those three great forces, Religion, Nationalism, the Land, will find intense yet chastened expression.[4]

Corkery faults the literature of the Revival because its rarefied aestheticism denies the simple, natural spirituality of the common, authentic Irish imagination. But in his enthusiasm for the denigration of a Protestant, Celtic Revival removed from ordinary life, Corkery lost his critical grip; those very details which, he claimed, depict the real Ireland are themselves falsely sentimental. "The white-walled houses, the farming life, the hill-top chapel" evoke the same romantic qualities of the Revival that Patrick Kavanagh set out to destroy a generation later.

The extremist position taken by Corkery gives further indication of the imposing and troublesome stature of Yeats for the writers of the 1920s and 1930s. In order to assimilate his eminent achievement, the younger generation had to restrict and contain it within some manageable scope. The reading of Yeats as an Ascendancy poet was the first step. Once Yeats was so limited, even in an argument as circuitous as Corkery's, then new writers could gain recognition for treating only what Corkery termed Irish reality. Thus one critical posture neatly resolved two pressing problems. Isolating the Protestant Ascendancy writers, especially its most eloquent and intimidating advocate, cleared some ground for Catholic writers like Clarke, Fallon, and Higgins.[5] Their poetry, which we shall discuss more completely below, naturally filled the void created by Corkery's kind of ideological criticism.

Curiously, the younger poets of Clarke's generation, the intended beneficiaries of Corkery's criticism, did not stand behind his aggressive apologetics. For one thing, although they applauded Corkery's implicit debunking of Yeats, they disagreed somewhat with his extreme position. More important, however, they were not content to let others do their talking. Sensing as the young Yeats had years before the benefits of debate and general visibility, they spoke out on poetic issues themselves in essays, reviews, and letters, reiterating established ideas about nationalism with occasional but steady attention to Yeats's non-Irishness. Fallon's review of *The Winding Stair and Other Poems* demonstrates the characteristic reading of Yeats as one fallen from Irish grace.

> . . . long ago, who could have foretold that the Wanderings of Ossian [sic] would lead at length to the Tower, to this—The Winding Stair; that the enchanted sleeper would awaken in this midnight, the coldness of the moon about him, his mind, once a disc reflecting a land of sun, now a very moon-metal turning in dark and light. . . . I find myself thinking of him as one of the last delicate lights of a sinking epoch, of a civilization "half-dead at the top"—as a star trembling in the shadows with the horizon coming up.[6]

The meaning behind these lunar references illumines the direction of much of this generation's literary crtiticism; Yeats had to be represented as someone who had rejected the very source of his early poetic strength, Celtic materials and the romantic treatment of Irish themes, in favor of a more abstract and philosophical poetry of limited appeal. Clarke, too, following this line of argument, praised Yeats's early poetry with its emphasis upon Irish myth and dismissed his later work as the last gasp of the Ascendancy tradition, a narrowing of poetic focus leading to an end.

> . . . his later poetry celebrates mournfully the passing of greatness. In his ranging themes he sums up an era and for us his language seems to bring to a poetic and glorious end the tradition of Anglo-Irish eloquence, for it has the vibrant timbre which can be heard in Burke's prose . . . and in that last speech by Grattan in the Irish House of Commons before the Act of Union.[7]

Isolating Yeats on the edge of the poetic tradition allowed these younger poets free rein in the development of Irish materials, especially those aspects of the national mind and character which would have been unknown to Yeats because of his limited knowlege of the Irish language. These writers believed that Irish poetry should reflect the consciousness of the people, who themselves lived close to the land in a primitive, pure relationship with nature. F. R. Higgins has described this quality as something "racial" that would manifest itself in poetry as a pagan property, "a reflection of that ancient memory regarding the poet's peculiar powers of dalliance with the mysterious . . . a Gaelic virility where life is fury, magnificent and yet tender," a treatment of "the terrors and mysteries of nature."[8]

These fanciful combinations show both the limited strength and the prevailing weaknesses of revivalist poetics. In Higgins' enthusiasm to sound an Irish note and to reflect intense national feeling, he showed his commitment to revivalism. The vagueness of his phrases, however, and the bromidic romanticism of "Gaelic virility," which is "magnificent and yet tender," serve not as the manifesto of a new Irish school but as a repetition of the sentimentality and propaganda that stretches back to the Young Ireland movement. Moreover, the desire to set his generation's poetry off from other poets of the Irish mode pushed Higgins rhetorically into excessive claims and extravagant combinations of metaphorical language.

> Not with dreams but with fire in the mind, the eyes of Gaelic poetry reflect a richness of life. . . . The younger poets . . . impose upon English verse the rhythm of gapped music, and through their music we hear echoes of secret harmonies and sweet twists still turning today through many a quaint Connacht song.

> Let us be sun bred not dreamers—but indeed drunkards with fire on the mind and in whose eyes shine the richness of life, the intensity of a dark people still part of the landscape moulding our song with sinew and bone. We indeed know that the only minds begetting literature in our time have their being in the muscles of life.[9]

While understandable, perhaps, from a psychological point of view as the enthusiastic expression of a young poet struggling to be both original and traditional, Higgins' argument remains a frenzied scrambling that goes nowhere. Sun produces darkness; bones, sinews, and muscles move only to distract; and poets become drunkards with brains on fire. Despite its giddiness, Higgins' theory nonetheless reflects the view—held by many of the revivalist poets—that Irish poetry should reflect a romantic view of a peasant society. Moreover, as Higgins' remarks clearly show, this post-Yeatsian generation believed not so much in revising revivalism as in stressing its sentimental side.

The Revivalists: The First Generation

The first beneficiaries of the Irish Literary Revival were themselves part of its initial direction and momentum. Work by Padraic Colum and Seamus O'Sullivan, the "promising successors of Yeats,"[10] was collected along with that of other writers in AE's anthology *New Songs*, whose introduction announced these poets as fresh talents:

> I have thought these verses deserved a better fate than to be read by one or two, not only on account of the beauty of much of the poetry, but because it revealed a new mood in Irish verse. . . . There may be traces here and there of the influence of other Irish poets, but there is no mere echoing of greater voices, while some of the writers have a marked originality of their own.[11]

But AE protests too much, and his apology uncovers the weakness of the volume. The poetry of *New Songs* sounds suspiciously like old songs, especially like Yeats's Celtic Twilight poetry of the 1890s. Whatever originality AE divined in these poems was outweighed by those qualities associated with his own and Yeats's early poetry: "delicate impressionism, shadowy themes, otherworldly longings and subtle wavering rhythms blended with Celtic mythology."[12] Indeed, writing as if they sought identification with the early Yeats, the poets of *New Songs* frequently placed or repeated the word "twilight" throughout their poems. Seamus O'Sullivan's "The Twilight People" is characteristic.

> It is a whisper among the hazel bushes;
> It is a long low whispering voice that fills
> With a sad music the bending and swaying rushes;
> It is a heart-beat deep in the quiet hills.
>
> Twilight people, why will you still be crying
> Crying and crying to me out of the trees?
> For under the quiet grass the wise are lying
> And all the strong ones are gone over the seas.[13]

In his survey of modern poetry, Austin Clarke tried to salvage something from this poem, suggesting that it was connected to the Gaelic poetry of the seventeenth and eighteenth centuries with its hint of oppression and exile. The poem fails on its own, however; its awkward rhythm, its artless rhyme scheme, and its self-conscious mood—with the ubiquitous Irishisms "whisper among the hazel bushes" and "gone over the seas"—undercut whatever merits Clarke, or AE for that matter, saw in it.

O'Sullivan wrote prolifically during the heyday of the Revival, publishing three volumes of poems between 1904 and 1909 and his *Collected Poems* in 1912. Most of his early poetry reflected the fashionable interest in faeries, misty landscapes, and rural themes in the style of the Celtic Twilight. In 1917, however, he produced a book of poems which broke from the usual revivalist practice of rural poetry and, instead, offered observations of city life. One of the best known of these poems is "The Lamplighter," a lyrical description of an urban scene.

> Soundlessly touching one by one
> The waiting posts that stand to take
> The faint blue bubbles in his wake;
> And when the night begins to wane
> He comes to take them back again
> Before the chilly dawn can blight
> The delicate frail buds of light.[14]

Here, in what are supposed to be poetic obervations from *The Diary of a Dublin Man*, the title of which creates expectations of urban poetry, we see the mode of the rural Celtic Twilight engulfing urban subject matter. The shadowy half-light and cultivated fragility in "faint," "wane," and "delicate frail buds of light" dominate the poem. In the urban material O'Sullivan might have found the stuff of real originality, yet he missed the opportunity, content merely to gather city scenes under the same low west-of-Ireland skies.

The Revival's grip on O'Sullivan's imagination severely limited any innovation he might have brought to urban subject matter. Not only do Dublin scenes appear as bricks-and-mortar versions of misty glens and mountains, but they rarely reflect the vitality and diversity of city life. The details of a breakfast room in "Nelson Street" are obliterated by atmosphere:

> There is hardly a mouthful of air
> In the room where the breakfast is set,
> For the blind is still down though it's late,
> And the curtains are redolent yet
> Of tobacco smoke, stale from last night.[15]

A description of the sheep being driven to town becomes a vehicle for melancholy:

> Slowly they wind
> In the grey of the gloaming
> Over the wet road
> That winds through the town
> Slowly they pass,
> And gleaming whitely
> Vanish away
> In the grey of the evening.
> Ah, what memories
> Loom for a moment
> Gleam for a moment,
> And vanish away.[16]

The image of sheep moving through city streets offered O'Sullivan a perfect opportunity to dramatize the clash between urban and rural sensibilities, but the potential was never fully realized. Instead, the poem became simply a revivalist catalog of vague imagery and pale impressions. The constant repetition of certain words builds toward an attempt at meaning in the final lines, in which thoughts vanish "away in the dimness/Of sorrowful years." But the stretching of the conceit—sheep are memories—and the imprecision of ideas—gloaming is dimness is sorrow—indicate the poem's imbalance. The weaknesses in *The Diary of a Dublin Man* are characteristic of O'Sullivan's general use of the Celtic Twilight motif. In the end, revivalism overwhiled the poetry, calling attention to itself.

Padraic Colum, another of AE's anthology poets, contributed widely to the momentum of the Revival, in poetry, in drama, and in fiction. His book of poems *Wild Earth* (1907), produced during the "golden decade" of the movement, rightly deserves to be considered as a primary text of the Revival.[17] Colum's intention in *Wild Earth* was to reflect traditional aspects of Irish rural life, employing the various blends of the folk ballad in English and Gaelic poetry.[18] The rural elements in Colum's poetry were deliberately shaped by literary sources, especially from nineteenth-century folk poetry with its English versions of Irish speech and its creative, free translations from Irish poems as practiced by poets such as James Clarence Mangan and Thomas Davis.[19] In his use of Gaelic poetry, Colum relied heavily on another revivalist text, Douglas Hyde's *Love Songs of Connacht*, for subject matter and for the adaptation of Irish prosody into English. Colum's contribution to the poetry of the Revival involved his attempt to sound an authentic Irish rural note by containing the rich speech of Gaelic-English within the traditional ballad measures.

Colum's interest in the folk tradition represents a tendency in modern Irish poetry to move away from mythological treatment of ancient Celtic materials and toward the use of stories, tales, and songs from the Irish countryside. Eventually—in the poetry of Kavanagh and Seamus Heaney—this tendency would evolve into the realistic treatment of daily routines and life in rural Ireland; in Colum's case, however, it had to pass through what Clarke identified as a "folk phase,"[20] the sentimental and romantic treatment of the simplicity of country life, especially the glorification of the peasantry. Thus while Colum anticipated the importance of the real voice of rural Ireland, his own practice continued the sentimental and romantic treatment of the Irish west.

Early in Colum's career, at the turn of the century when he was influenced by Yeats and nurtured by AE, his poetry reflected only the pale shimmering of the Twilight school:

> Your eyes have not her eyes' deep hue,
> Nor has your hair the gold I wrought
> Out of my dreams for hair of her—
> M Bhron! I thought that dream sheen caught
> From hair of you, from hair of you!
> Pale lips, pale hair, 'tis not your fault:
> A shadow of a dream are you![21]

With the publication of *Wild Earth* four years later, however, Colum began to depict the details of peasant life which would give his poetry a certain individuality. His subject is invariably the solitary, frequently isolated individual who finds deep meaning and joy in simple action or small comfort. The tin-whistle player standing in the mist becomes one with nature as he plays "tunes that are for stretches bare,/And men whose lives are lone." "An Old Woman of the Roads" wants only the comfort of a little house with a turf fire and a stool, having spent most of her life worrying about the adequacy of shelter.

> Och! but I weary of mist and dark,
> And the roads where there's never a house nor bush,
> And tired I am of bog and road,
> And the crying wind and the lonesome hush!
>
> And I am praying to God on high,
> And I am praying him night and day,
> For a little house, a house of my own—
> Out of the wind's and the rain's way.[22]

Although Colum often depicts humble peasants in daily chores or at rest by the fire in thatched cottages, he stops short of realism in these poems, idealizing instead the quiet dignity and simple purity of peasant life. "The Plougher," for example, begins with realistic detail in a silhouette of a farmer and his team etched against a late afternoon sky:

> Sunset and silence! A man; around him earth savage,
>   earth broken;
> Beside him two horses, a plough![23]

But as the voice in the poem ponders the meaning of this image, it slips into the conventional, stage-Irish speech—"Is it praying you are as you stand there alone in the sunset?"—aiming for authenticity, no doubt, but producing cliché.[24]

A similar lack of balance occurs in the treatment of subject matter. The poem explores the fatigue of labor in stark imagery that connects farmer to beast.

> "O man standing lone and bowed earthward,
> Your task is a day near its close. Give thanks to the
>   night-giving god."
>
> Slowly the darkness falls, the broken lands blend with the
>   savage;
> The brute-tamer stands by the brutes, a head's breadth
>   only above them,

Yet this realistic treatment is quickly undercut by a romantic and sentimental afterthought that appears to be imposed from without, as an intrusion of another poetic sensibility:

> A head's breadth? Aye, but therein hell's depth and
>   the height up to heaven,
> And the thrones of the gods and their halls, their
>   chariots, purples and splendors.[25]

The central irony of Colum's poetic career grew out of this particular treatment of subject matter. His blend of folklore and rural life distinguished his work from that of other writers, but also limited its appeal. L. A. G. Strong has argued that the very quality Colum attempted to espouse—simplicity—made it impossible for his work to get serious critical attention.[26] Richard Loftus has stated that Colum's portrayal of the Irish country people is purposefully distorted in order to romanticize the peasant, with unfortunate results for the values in the poetry: "He equates meanness with nobility, subservience with heroism, sentimentality with intense passion, religiosity and superstition with spirituality, ignorance with wisdom."[27] Even Zack Bowen, who regards Colum's poetry as a "beautiful and delightful achievement," admits that the poems are often literal, one-dimensional, and even occasionally sentimental.[28]

The consensus among these critics about the limitations of Colum's poetry indicates the general ambiguity surrounding his place in Irish literary history. He is recognized as having been an important contributor to the Revival whose ideas about the use of native material proved to be of interest to future writers. His belief, for example, that authenticity derived from familiarity with simple, ordinary things—"the birds that sing best in the wood . . . /Were reared with breast to the clay"—is an important assumption behind the work of Kavanagh and of Heaney. Yet Colum's own poetic achievement remains flat and static; his *Collected Poems* (1953) and *The Poet's Circuit* (1961) continue to perpetrate the conventions of the Revival rather than show any real poetic growth. Even as a revivalist poet, Colum seems limited. To look at his *Wild Earth* as an early Revival text is to see that it lacks the innovation that might have distinguished it from convention. To choose to represent the communal mind, one critic has warned, is to risk losing the quality of inventive uniqueness, is to deal in types rather than individuals, to present familiar situations using standard descriptions and imagery.[29] In Colum's particular form of revivalism, there was, ironically, the danger of stagnation: the Revival, invented to sustain poetic life, began to restrict it by demanding loyalty and homage in the form of convention.

Some relief from cliché and convention does come from two Revival writers whose literary reputations were established not in poetry but in drama and fiction. Playwright J. M. Synge and novelist and story-writer James Stephens both produced collections of poems which reacted against revivalism and turned away from the Celtic Twilight, anticipating the direction of Irish poetry in the 1940s and 1950s. Synge describes this new direction in a preface to his poems written in 1908:

> . . . when men lose their poetic feeling for ordinary life, and cannot write poetry of ordinary things, their exalted poetry is likely to lose its strength of exaltation, in the way men cease to build beautiful churches when they have lost happiness in building shops . . . it is the timber of poetry that wears most surely, and there is no timber that has not strong roots among the clay and worms . . . the strong things in life are needed in poetry also, to show that what is exalted or tender is not made by feeble blood. It may also be said that before verse can be human again it must learn to be brutal.[30]

The key words and phrases "ordinary," "strong roots among the clay," "strong things in life," and "brutal" suggest the turn away from the delicate dreaminess associated with revivalism toward the bare experience of life itself as a fit subject for poetry.

Synge's manifesto in his preface underscores his intention to depict the raw energy and strangely beautiful life of rural Ireland in his plays, particularly *Riders to the Sea* (1904) and *The Playboy of the Western World* (1907). His poems, though few in number, treat the same ordinary, "strong things in life" with a candor that could be called brutal. Synge was interested in a poetry of life, particularly life as it was lived in the rugged west of Ireland; he was also interested in rescuing poetry about peasants from the sentimental practice of revivalism. Occasionally, his desire to return folk poetry to the primitive carried him to extremes, as in the description of a beating in "Danny":

> Then some destroyed him with their heels,
> Some tramped him in the mud,
> Some stole his purse and timber pipe,
> And some washed off his blood.

> . . . .
> And when you're walking out the way
> from Bangor to Belmullet
> You'll see a flat cross on a stone,
> Where men chocked Danny's gullet.[31]

While this poem is brutal in a literal sense, it does not depict completely what Synge meant by making poetry brutal again. Robin Skelton, Synge's editor, has argued that brutality was not necessarily a subject for Synge but rather a poetic idea, "the violent juxtaposition of literary with colloquial language," in which the vernacular undercuts the literary language, contradicting it.[32] Skelton has pointed to "Queens" as an illustration of this effect, in which the panegyric style and certain poetic conventions—such as the use of the catalog—are qualified and subverted by antiromantic detail and common speech.

> Queens of Sheba, Meath, and Connaught
> Coifed with crown, or gaudy bonnet;
> Queens whose fingers once did stir men,
> Queens were eaten of fleas and vermin,
> . . . .
> Queens who wasted the East by proxy,
> Or drove the ass-cart, a tinker's doxy.
> Yet these are rotten—ask their pardon—
> And we've the sun on rock and garden;
> These are rotten, so you're the Queen
> Of all are living, or have been.[33]

Synge's contribution to Irish literary history derives from his willingness to treat the real passions and experiences of life at a time when most Irish poets were echoing the mystical, fanciful dreaming of the Celtic Twilight. In "The Passing of the Shee," for example, Synge prefers experience to dream:

> Adieu sweet Angus, Maeve, and Fand,
> Ye plumed yet skinny Shee,
> That poets played with hand in hand
> To learn their ecstacy.

> We'll stretch in Red Dan Sally's ditch
> And drink in Tubber fair,
> Or poach with Red Dan Philly's bitch
> The badger and the hare.[34]

In direct opposition to the poetic practice of the Revival, this poem offers a criticism both of art and of life. The exuberance, vitality, and recklessness embodied in the secod stanza stand in sharp contrast to the literary values of the first stanza with its feeble spirits. Indeed, the general vitality of the poem, with its emphasis upon stretching, drinking, and poaching, counters the static nature of the contemplative and imaginative world of the Celtic Twilight poets recalling their gods.

Synge's interest in the exuberant life as a poetic subject led him naturally to a lively and earthy use of language. Critics have praised the vigor of speech in the plays and the colorful colloquialisms in poems such as "Patch-Shaneen," "Beg-Innish," and "Danny." The famous and frequently quoted lines from "The Curse" show Synge's ability to adapt the traditional Gaelic curse and satire into English, retaining the vigor and the spirit of the original:

> Lord, confound this surly sister
> Blight her brow with blotch and blister
> Cramp her larynx, lung, and liver
> In her guts a galling give her.[35]

These poetic qualities suggest continuity with certain aspects of Gaelic poetry and, when coupled with Synge's critical remarks about poetry, represent an important corrective to revivalism, one that even Yeats shrewdly heeded.[36] In the insistence upon showing the rough and severe yet vital side of peasant life, Synge anticipated the poetry of the 1940s and 1950s, particularly Patrick Kavanagh's.

Yet despite all of these innovations, Synge's direct impact upon the direction of twentieth-century poetry remains minimal. His major contribution to modern literature comes in drama; his one book of poetry is a very small one. Because they represent a minimal portion of his writing, the poems, along with the famous preface, tend to be read primarily as commentary on the plays.

Unlike Synge, James Stephens wrote a good deal of poetry as part of a literary career that included drama, criticism, folktales, short stories, and two famous prose fictions, *The Crock of Gold* (1922) and *The Charwoman's Daughter* (1928). A number of Stephens' poems easily fit the revivalist mold, particularly those celebrating the green world of the Irish countryside and involving the fanciful and sentimental treatment of nature. Occasionally in these poems he looks back to the Celtic Twilight.

> There was no day;
> Nor ever came a night
> Setting the stars alight
>
> To wonder at the moon:
> Was twilight only, and the frightened croon
> Smitten to whimpers, of the dreary wind
>
> And waves that journeyed blind . . .
> And then I loosed my ear—Oh, it was sweet
> To hear a cart go jolting down the street.[37]

But often Stephens' energies were directed outward, away from the conventions of the Revival toward a more exuberant and varied portrait of life. In *Insurrections* (1909), a book of poems about Dublin, he attempted an urban pastoral, lyrically depicting city scenes. Most of these verses he would later suppress, excluding them from his *Collected Poems* (1954), but the very attempt at this new form indicates Stephens' innovative imagination.

Reincarnations (1918) collects some interesting free translations of Gaelic poetry of the sixteenth through the eighteenth centuries, some of which are among Stephens' most memorable poems. Inspired and influenced by Douglas Hyde's *Love Songs of Connacht*, these poems display the earthy colloquial eloquence of the Gaelic tradition. They reflect the vitality and primitive emotion of the originals and draw away from the romantic practices of the revivalists. "Righteous Anger," or—as it is called in *Collected Poems*—"A Glass of Beer," utilizes the ancient Irish art of cursing in the verbal lashing of a woman innkeeper who refused the poet a drink: "May she marry a ghost and bear him a kitten, and may/The High King of Glory permit her to get the mange." "Blue Blood," a translation from Dáibhí O'Bruadair, the seventeenth-century satirist, captures the rough country talk in coarse imagery:

> The good men of Clare were drinking his health in a flood
> And gazing, with me, in awe at the princely lad
> And asking each other from what bluest blueness of blood
> His daddy was squeezed, and the pa of the da of his dad?
>
> We waited there, gaping and wondering, anxiously,
> Until he'd stop eating, and let the glad tidings out;
> And the slack-jawed booby proved to the hilt that he
> Was lout, son of lout, by old lout, and was da to a lout![38]

"What the Tramp Said" gives yet another version of the hard life of the country experienced by a traveler.

> Why should we live when living is a pain?
> I have not seen a flower had any scent,
> Nor heard a bird sing once! The very rain
> Seems dirty! And the clouds, all soiled and rent,
> Toil sulkily across the black old sky.[39]

Despite the freshness produced by these vital poems, Stephens did not commit completely in his poetry to this innovative direction, indeed, it represents only a portion of his overall achievement, most of which remained attached to the legacies of the Revival, particularly Irish folklore, faery stories, and legend. Like Synge, however, Stephens demonstrated a vitality and realism that indicate a sense of the limitations of revivalism, even though he never completely left the revivalist mode. In that poetry of his which we can call antirevivalist, his nonetheless anticipates a concern for continuity, connecting the seventeenth- and eighteenth-century Gaelic tradition with twentieth-century Irish poetry. In this sense alone he became an interesting link to the work of Clarke, Kavanagh, and Kinsella at mid-century.

The Revivalists: The Second Generation

The extraordinary feature of revivalism was its longevity. It outlasted Yeats and, in its continued use of shadowy themes, misty landscapes, and the romantic treatment of the Irish peas- ant, outlasted even Colum, O'Sullivan, and the other poets collected in AE's anthology. It flourished into the 1920s, claiming new followers among younger writers who, living in an age of intense national feeling and cultural sensitivity, found its poetic formula irresistible. This new generation of poets, in its turn, rediscovered the Celtic materials, but with two important differ- ences. Most of the younger writers were students of the Irish language, an experience that was not lost on them. Whatever their level of proficiency in Irish, they argued that contact with the language established an affinity with Gaelic sources and ancient Irish culture which Yeats and AE could not have had. The other difference resulted from historical accident: the new generation inherited the literature of the Revival as well as the older Gaelic and Celtic traditions. As a result its members had the advantage of both receiving and criticizing their recent poetic heritage. Thus when they wanted to, they could act as revisionists.

This second generation of poets, then, is rightly identified as revivalist not only in its perpetuation of romantic Ireland and in its choice of the old myths and the Celtic Twilight for subjects and themes but also for its purification of Irish material. Three of these younger writers—Austin Clarke, F. R. Higgins, and Liam O'Flaherty—claimed themselves to be a "new school" of Irish writing, building upon stories and poems from the Irish language and adapting Gaelic prosody into English. They claimed originality in their treatment of the religious life of the peasantry, something with which their Protestant elders were not familiar. In addition, they sought technical innovation in the adaptation of Gaelic versification to English poetry, particularly alliteration and internal rhyme. Despite these pretenses, however, the new school remained too much like the old to expand the frontier of Irish poetry. Thirty years after Yeats had celebrated the Celtic Twilight, poetry decribing misty landscapes and retelling Irish legends could hardly expect to startle and surprise. Nonetheless, it is precisely in their reluctance and, in some cases, their inability to shake the influence of the Revival that these younger poets compose an interesting phase in the development of post-Yeatsian poetics.

In 1917, twenty-one-year-old Austin Clarke published his first poem, "The Vengeance of Fionn," a long narrative in epic style based upon the Diarmuid and Grainne legend. For the next fifteen years Clarke would follow Yeats's earlier lead, devoting himself to the retelling of Irish myth and legend, recreating an Ireland of the imagination. He sought to avoid a direct collision with Yeats by turning to medieval Ireland, when pagan and Christian experience cultures battled for survival. Applying his own Catholic experience to his knowledge of Irish history, Clarke invented what he termed "the Celtic Romanesque," a romantic version of medieval Ireland with roving scholars, randy church clerks, and vital Gaelic chiefs and queens.

Clarke's preference for medieval subject matter instead of the more familiar Celtic legends of folk materials hardly camouflages the revivalist direction of his early work, however. A nostalgic version of rural life forms the basis of the romanticism in these poems. "The Scholar," a free translation from the Gaelic, shows interesting use of Gaelic prosody in the rhyme scheme and alliteration, but presents the idealized version of the pastoral which we have come to expect from revivalist poems.

> Summer delights the scholar
> With knowledge and reason.
> Who is happy in hedgerow
> Or meadow as he is?

> Paying no dues to the parish,
> He argues in logic
> And has no care of cattle
> But a satchel and stick.
>
> . . . .
>
> When midday hides the reaping
> He sleeps by a river
> Or comes to the stone plain
> Where the saints live.[40]

Clarke's pleasant version of the scholar's life nicely contradicts what we know of the wandering scholars in Ireland, particularly in the sixteenth through the eighteenth centuries, when most mendicant teachers were impoverished fugitives wanted by the crown.

The mystical beauty of the Celtic Twilight also appears in Clarke's early lyrics, frequently in attempts to build a particular emotional effect. Misty landscapes, pale, tides, and showery breezes dominate the weather in his early epics, and the visionary beauty of "Aisling" from *Pilgrimage* (1929) suggests his interest in the supernatural:

> Coil of her hair, in cluster and ringlet
> Had brightened round her forehead and those curls—
> Closer than she could bind them on a finger
> Were changing gleam and glitter. O she turned
> So gracefully aside, I thought her clothes
> Were flame and shadow while she slowly walked,
> Or each breast was proud because it rode
> The cold air as the wave stayed by the swan.
>
> (CCP, 174)

To his credit, however, Clarke eventually sensed the inevitable consequences of this kind of poetic practice and turned instead to a more realistic consideration of contemporary Ireland and a treatment of his own identity within modern Irish society. In so doing, he freed himself from what Samuel Beckett in a 1934 essay calls "antiquarianism"—the slavish imitation of the practice of the Revival[41]—and developed into a major post-Yeatsian figure, a poet of individual achievement who reflected the urban, Catholic consciousness.

Two of Clarke's contemporaries were not so fortunate, however. Both F. R. Higgins and Padraic Fallon, though in different ways, struggled throughout their work with problems of imitation and influence, and rarely sounded any distinctly individual note. Higgins began writing pastoral poetry in the revivalist manner, and eventually, under Yeats's tutelage, developed an interest in the ballad. In 1935 Higgins and Yeats coauthored a series of broadsheets with Cuala Press which contained several poems in the style of the folk song or street ballad. The results of their collaboration shaped Higgins' last book, *The Gap of Brightness* (1940). Fallon did not know Yeats, but in the treatment of the Galway countryside which dominates his poetry, the younger writer meditated on the historical presence of Yeats, Lady Gregory, and others connected with Coole. In fact, many of Fallon's poems are obsessed with Yeats, sometimes as a subject, at other times, less directly and more subtly, as a voice behind the lines, the tone giving authority to the diction. In both Higgins' and Fallon's cases, the connection with a powerful poetic predecessor misled the individual talent, eventually depriving the poet of his own voice and expression.

Higgins' early poetry, published in *Island Blood* (1925) and *The Dark Breed* (1927), grew out of the Revival and brought praise from reviewers who were looking for new poetic talent. The setting for almost all these poems is Connemara, which Higgins featured as a beautiful and mystical locale. But aside from the naming of locations—"O watch the grey skies shudder on the cold Twelve Pins/While the sea round Connemara moans"—the description of landscape is so general in these books as to be conventional. The vague references give no real indication of place and offer instead only those general images associated with the Celtic Twilight and perpetuated by Colum and O'Sullivan.

> The soft rain is falling
> Round bush isles,

> Veiling the waters
> Over wet miles
> And hushing the grasses
> Where plovers call
> While soft clouds are falling
> Over all.[42]

These lines typify the young Higgins' dependence upon revivalist motifs. Establishing mood in these early poems seems to be the poet's priority as he continually presents the heaviness of the sky, the settling of the clouds, and the descending of the mist. Unfortunately, the image-making often becomes so incongruous as to obscure meaning—the rain "hushes the grass" in one poem; elsewhere, "shiny blackberries/Sweeten the rain." The poetry is also marred by catalogs of Irishisms—"Curragh," "sheiling," "sulleys," "hazel roots," "salmon weirs"—and a sprinkling of Irish names appears throughout. These devices are used not to develop individual poems but to adorn them, to gain them a distinctively Irish look. Despite these flaws, some critics have praised Higgins' talent for language and for his experiments with Gaelic assonance and rhyming. Even a recent critic, Richard Fallis, who admits that Higgins relied too much on revivalism, has praised his ability to "put words together as no other Irish poet of his time except Yeats."[43]

For most readers, however, Higgins' talent did not impress. Samuel Beckett attacked the propensity in Higgins' poetry for "the Celtic drill of extraversion," his stock Irish responses of "lilting and lisping," the accumulation of "By Gods," and his idealization of nature, the latter seen at its most preposterous in an address to a blackthorn stick: "And here, as in green days you were the perch,/You're now the prop of song." In a letter to Thomas McGreevy, Denis Devlin also condemns Higgins' idealism, complaining of his ignorance of the real world and his retreat into charming lyrics with experiments in assonance.[44] Patrick Kavanagh has identified insincerity as Higgins' real weakness: "He most desperately wanted to be what mystically, or poetically, does not exist, an 'Irishman' . . . all this was essence of insincerity, for sincerity means giving all oneself to one's work, being absolutely real. For all his pleasant verse Higgins was a dabbler."[45] The same tendency that offended Kavanagh's sensibilities also struck Richard Loftus in his discussion of Higgins' place in twentieth-century Anglo-Irish poetry. The central deficiency in Higgins' work is its reliance on convention, particularly in the portrait of the peasant. Higgins' poetry, Loftus argues, "conforms to the established pattern for Irish writers," his landscape is romanticized, and the peasant characters who appear in the poems "are not to be regarded as individualized human beings but rather as racial types, as living symbols of the ancient Gaelic race."[46]

The charges against Higgins' poetry in these critical responses seem to be borne out unwittingly by Higgins himself in an unpublished essay on Irish poetry, which identifies as strengths those very elements that the critics cite as weaknesses. Suggesting that as a result of his Gaelic heritage the Irish poet retains "a pagan property," Higgins argues that truly Irish literature may be really created by those who are ignorant of the Irish language, but have instead "a Gaelic consciousness . . . a mind saturated with the country memory."[47] His prescription for this kind of poetry is itself shot through with romantic clichés, suggesting that Higgins as critic was no less conventional than Higgins as poet: "a life unspoiled by modernism—still virile, stern and rockfast with its roots drinking nature, through the existence of a simple people. Pure song bred among bush rocks can weather the mind better than literary affectations."[48]

As much as Higgins' revivalism blurs his theory, something even more damaging appears in his poetry, particularly in his later work, causing him to remain underdeveloped, a writer who never struck his own distinct chord. In many of the poems of the 1930s, one detects the unmistakable presence of Yeats looming behind the poetry, reminding us not of Higgins but of his debt to a master. Yeats's "Sailing to Byzantium" informs Higgins' "East of Hy Breasil," where an island city is constructed to resemble Yeats's holy city.[49] In "Wet Loveliness," Yeatsian language is present in the phrases "outstalking foamful things,"

"frail throat," and "on secret waters, where slow moon flows,"
and especially in the poem's final quatrain:

> And where the rushes show no whiter stems—
> When star-time floats, when bright fish leap and lie
> Curling the nets of grass with quarter moons—
> She wades and drips out, lit with naked air![50]

Higgins' final book, *The Gap of Brightness*, shows the direct
influence of Yeats more clearly, in "Song for the Clatter Bones,"
for example, Higgins' imitation of the earthy sexuality found in
the Crazy Jane poems.

> God rest that Jewy Woman
> Queen Jezebel, the bitch
> Who peeled the clothes from her shoulder-bones
> Down to her spent teats
> As she stretched out of the window
> Among the geraniums, where
> She chaffed and laughed like on half daft
> Titivating her painted hair.[51]

In the title poem, "The Gap of Brightness," Higgins dutifully
casts his eye on other days to seek poetic inspiration.

>   . . . when Owen Roe's
> Lightheaded and footless music
> Tricked there
>
> . . . .
> There Carolan's laugh was a tinkle of glasses;
>   . . . while Raftery sat
> Stroking a sad-faced fiddle
> To woo those home spun lines.[52]

The litany of past poets and artists prepares for the unabashed
Yeatsian posturing in the closing lines: "On greater peaks we'll
gaze . . . /Where eagled minds have stood."

The critical consensus on Higgins—that he was conventional
rather than original—misleads us, I believe, into thinking that
he was an uninteresting post-Yeatsian Irish poet. To be sure,
Higgins is not remarkable for his imitation of the Celtic Twilight

nor for his perpetuation of the Revival; his attempts to reflect a
Gaelic consciousness are repetitive and even unfashionable. It
is rather what he could not accomplish that makes him interesting, his inability to achieve on an individual level what Lionel
Trilling has called authenticity, a reference to oneself, a conviction of the relationship between art and audience.[53] Higgins'
difficulty in his early poetry stemmed from his willingness to
write what the audience wanted to hear: sentimental
nationalism left over from the Revival. In his later poetry, the
importance of the audience remains but shifts slightly under the
tutelage of Yeats who wished to produce ballads for "the people
of Ireland."[54] Higgins never wrote for his own inner ear and, as
a result, never felt the conviction of his own expression.

The example of Higgins, who squandered the potential for
authenticity in order to be a popular poet, shows the debilitating
effect of tradition and a strong mentor. It is especially note-
worthy that Higgins and Clarke were exact contemporaries who
consulted each other on literary matters in the 1920s and early
1930s, but whose careers, even by 1937, were headed in two
radically different directions. Higgins was being drowned out
by the master's voice; Clarke rejected revivalism and, as we shall
see in a later chapter, turned to most un-Yeatsian poetics.

Padraic Fallon's achievement ranks higher than Higgins',
because even in his early poetry he fought against the seductive
mode of the Celtic Twilight and the sentimental idealization of
the peasant. There are echoes of other writers in the early
work—we hear, for example, the voice of Synge behind the
poem "The Waistcoat":

> O tell me what lazy Peeler
> Thumbing his girth will dare them
> Now money that ripens like rain on ropes
> Runs down their hasty fingers?
>
> And what fat terrified son of the devil
> That tends a till won't pull back porter
> All night for men whose eyes make knives
> Of the lights that worm through his bottled windows?[55]

There are also the sprinklings of "black shawled women," saints, hermits, and pilgrims near holy wells, island men with their pipes, curraghs on the beach, and the occasional reminder "of stone and mist and water." But even with these revivalist relics, one senses in Fallon what Higgins never gives: an individual expression, a lively use of language, fresh treatment of peasant life, and a new subject matter—poetry itself, or, more specifically, the problem of writing poems.

Much of Fallon's poetry draws upon life in Galway, but his treatment of the landscape and peasant life reverses the sentimental view given by the revivalists. Instead, he portrays rural life realistically, showing its harshness as well as its beauty. The details of peasant existence in these poems remind us of the labor that attends it, ploughing, threshing, loading hay, harvesting potatoes, and, in the background, the fierce elements—the rain, the mud, the clay, and the cold wind in the face of the farmer and his team. There is meaning here beyond the drudgery, however, in an acceptance of the rhythms of nature and in a gratitude for the simple things, as in the moment in "Deluge" when winter's grip is finally loosened:

> And then one day
> In a lane no wider than your hand a woman
> Leaned out of a fug
> Of food and napkins and found an air so mild
> She hung the goldfinch out,
> Loitering while the little bird perked up and sang
> To gossip with another window over the way.[56]

The quick, sudden moment occurs often in Fallon's poetry, frequently as counterpoint to a more obvious, lengthy condition. The breaking of winter is described again, as coming in a glimpse of sunlight, in "River Lane":

> Noon, and in the spare woodwork
> of December, low
> As lilac blooms suddenly the sun.[57]

The treatment of rural subjects often becomes part of a larger, more engaging theme, that of poetry itself or the difficulty of the poetic process. In this aspect of his work, Fallon pushes the concept of tradition in an interesting way, placing himself among other post-Yeatsian Irish poets who questioned the difficulties of inheritance and the burden of the past. The subject of art, as it manifests itself in a particularly self-conscious way, becomes an important theme in many poems, and Fallon's treatment shows diversity and understanding. In the impressive poem "For Paddy Mac," for example, Fallon demonstrates an acute critical sense about the tendentiousness in Irish writing which undid Higgins.

> Once, so long ago,
> You used to probe me gently for the lost
> Country, sensing somehow in my airs
> The vivid longlipped peasantry of
> Last Century.
> ·
> Bunkum, Dear P. The thing was gone, or
> Never was. And we were the leftovers,
> Lord-ridden and pulpit-thumped for all our wild
> Cudgels of Gaelic.

The astonishing and abrupt change in direction and rhythm at "Bunkum, Dear P." is arresting and demands that we listen to the counter-truth that follows in the decription of peasant life from which Fallon's poetry sprang:

> . . . the homespun fellows
> Selling their spades on hiring days,
> For a year and a day the dear flesh off their bones
> From penury to slavery
> ·
> That was my country, beast, sky and anger: . . .
> No poets I know of; or they mouthed each other's words;
> Oh, maybe some rags and tatters did sing.
> But poetry, for all your talk, is never that simple.[58]

The poem progresses on one level as an implicit critique of the revivalist direction of Irish poetry and on another as an indirect criticism of Yeats. Fallon's insistence upon scrutinizing not only present days but also the hard side of rural life, the life lived by the majority of country people, posed a neat antithesis to Yeats's scheme of Ascendancy living—hard-riding country gentlemen and subservient peasants who knew and, by implication, loved their place.

While "For Paddy Mac" falls short of a stated manifesto, it nonetheless shows remarkable perception and a willingness to deal frankly with the problem of voice facing all the poets of Fallon's generation. This concern surfaces elsewhere in his poetry with different results. In "Odysseus" the worry about self-expression proves so compelling that it overtakes and obscures the central focus of the poem, the treatment of Odysseus' adaptability. In Fallon's version, the master of disguises embodies the poet in search of his own voice. That Fallon sensed personal significance in the Odyssean dilemma is clear from the poem's perilous echoes in thought and idiom of Yeats's "A Coat":

> Last year's decencies
> Are the rags and reach-me-downs he'll wear forever,
> Knowing one day he'll sober up inside them
> Safe in wind and wife and limb,
> Respected, of unimpeachable behavior.[59]

Donald Davie has argued that the character of Odysseus, who figures in so many of Fallon's poems, represents a shifting poetic mask that allowed the poet to adopt many disguises and to take risks with the voices of others.[60] Yet as Fallon goes on to tell us in "Odysseus," the price is often painful, and perhaps too extreme. For even if the poet "puts on" other voices in the hope of finding his personal one, he may discover in the end that he is left unsure of it. Fallon's awareness of this pressure upon poets is evident in the poem's final lines about Odysseus' homecoming, where proof of his individuality dominates all else:

> Meanwhile he goes forward
> Magniloquently to himself; and, the fit on him,
> Pushes his painful hobble to a dance.

. . . .
His dog will die at the sight of him,
His son want fool-proof, and his lady-wife
Deny his fingerprints, but he
With his talent for rehabilitation
Will be his own man soon, without ecstasy.[61]

Unfortunately, despite this awareness and the achievement of a few very good poems, the impression left by the bulk of Fallon's work denies that he was his own man. Throughout *Poems* (1974) we see examples of a preoccupation with Yeats, a willingness to accommodate the urge felt often by so many of Fallon's generation, to cut the master down to size. As a result the poetry displays what Seamus Heaney has called "an ambitious wrestling with the dead, an attempt to establish territorial rights in a territory already possessed and repossessed," a struggle that Fallon ultimately lost.[62] Too often in these poems Yeats's presence overwhelms the style and the thought to allow "the great ventriloquist" behind the lines to enter through Fallon's voice. "Johnstown Castle," for example, opens with an attempt to expose Yeats's fanciful ideal world:

The summer woods refuse to meet
us on the level we know. We have evolved
too much mind for them, and picked up feet
that solve things differently, like birds.

But as the poem develops, Fallon's confrontational tactics lead to a breakdown of style in both language and rhythm.

An ornamental water
Should be backed with mercury that the sculptured swan
May be an ideal swan forever.
Here one shiver shows the mud
And I am glad because a swan
can turn up his end and shatter mood
And shatter mirror,
Till the woods massed in an architecture shake
Because a real swan mucks up a lake.[63]

It is as though Fallon's struggle became too much for him, and he yielded to Yeats's shade, either by allowing the intrusion of the latter's voice or by loosening his own concentration upon the poem's design, permitting it to drift toward parody—in this case of the ideas and the imagery in "Coole Park, 1929" and "Coole Park and Ballylee, 1931."

"Yeats's Tower at Ballylee" reveals even more completely Fallon's straining in the struggle with his chosen precursor. The poet-narrator visits Yeats's tower on a rainy day, and as he moves through the rooms and climbs the stair he meditates not only on the place but also upon the poetry trapped everywhere in the surroundings, infecting the visitor himself.

> I turn from the arty chimneyplace where glass
> Has the pale wash of dreamy things and climb
> Through a rude and navel arch, . . .
> And the narrow stairway leads me to the place
> Where he worked at the great table
> Or lifted his tall height to pace
> The enormous floor of his own fable;
> Did he wear iron then, I wonder,
> Or when the shadows stole the candle-light
> Imagine himself all constellated night?
> Il Penseroso in the magic chamber?

Fallon's control up to this point in the poem is evident in the description of the building and aspects of Yeats's life, which establishes a mood. But as the poet attempts to shift from description to a confrontation with Yeatsian practice, a change that is essential to the poem's direction, the voice falters, the focus blurs, and the language loses its poetic quality.

> The higher we clamber up
> Into ourselves the greater seems the danger;
> For wider the vision then
> On a desolate and more desolate world
>
> Where the inspirations of men
> Are taken and hurled
> From shape into evil shape;
> With the good and the grace gone out of them
> Where indeed is there hope for men?
> So every civilization tires at the top.[64]

As a result, the critique of Yeatsian practice midway through the poem overshadows the personal meaning that emerges in the final stanzas. The balance between these two elements becomes precarious, until in the last lines of the poem, the language and style give way, causing the final discursiveness.[65] The personal vision that the younger poet claims to experience comes not only within a Yeatsian context but in an expression reminiscent of the rhetorical manner of Yeats's public poetry, the very tone Fallon wished to avoid. The declarative stance and the rolling diction owe everything to Yeats and deny Fallon, ironically, his own voice.[66]

> This tower where the poet thought to play
> Out some old romance to the end caught up
> The dream and the dreamer in its brutal way
> And the dream died here upon the crumbling top. I
> know the terror of his vision now:
> A poet dies in every poem.[67]

Yeats and his circle figure in a number of other poems, partly because, as we have seen, Fallon wished to clear some poetic ground for himself, and partly because Thoor Ballylee and Coole, with all of their literary ghosts, have become associated with the Galway countryside that permeates Fallon's poetry. "Yeats at Athenry Perhaps" speculates on Yeats passing through Fallon's village, but reserved, aloof:

> Why muddy a feathered foot when a great house waited
> Over in Coole among the trees
> (He liked his heraldry alive, well baited)
> With all the amenities for Muse and man,
> Leda's kingbird on a lake, a lawn
> For Juno's peacock, tranquil as a frieze.[68]

"On the Tower Stairs" features Lady Gregory and her ceremonious gatherings, which Yeats had dramatized:

> Her trumpeted house is gone, entirely razed;
> But he did raise up another

There on a totem pole in which the lady is
Oracular and quite composed
To outlast everything, live on forever.[69]

Fallon's insistence on this continual treatment of Yeats and his circle—he made his formidable predecessor the subject of no less than ten poems—works against the younger writer's own development in another way, namely by reminding his reader of the importance of Yeats's presence to Fallon's poetic strategy. Other poems such as "Wexford to Commodore Barry" or "River Lane," which treat other subject matter but are indebted to Yeatsian style or diction, can be included among the evidence to suggest Fallon's capitulation to Yeats.

There is much to admire in Fallon's poetry, in his portrayal of rural life with its blend of Catholic and Irish folk traditions, and in his ambition and anxiety about the making of poems. In the final consideration of his *Poems*, however, he remains an interesting minor figure in twentieth-century Irish literature. His successful resistance to the excesses of what in the poetry of Colum, O'Sullivan, and Higgins we have called revivalism is overshadowed by his obsessive desire to deny Yeatsian values, creating an imbalance in the poems. And while Fallon's poetic instincts hinted at a mature individual style, something we find in the later poetry of Clarke and Kavanagh, he diminished his own poetic presence by not cultivating fully his own voice. His importance to modern Irish poetry lies, ironically, in the central weakness of his work: he wrote realistically about rural Ireland but was finally unable to resist Yeats's powerful gravitational force. Thus Fallon appears as a transitional figure; his career implies rather than embodies the movement away from the Revival toward the more realistic treatment of twentieth-century Ireland found in the work of Joyce and in the poetry of Clarke, Kavanagh, and those who followed them.

3

"Non Serviam": James Joyce and Modern Irish Poetry

Unlike his predecessor fifty years earlier, the Irish poet at mid-century did not want for tradition; indeed, he found it in great abundance all about him. The difficulty came rather in continuity, "the recognition," as Thomas Kinsella has said, "of the past in ourselves," and the attempt to identify with tradition.[1] One aspect of this tradition, revivalism, seemed easily expendable, since it had worked itself into a cliché, becoming an exhausted convention and the by-product of another era. The Ascendancy tradition, on which Yeats directed future poets to cast their eyes, also could be rejected; while offering a conservative critique of the Revival, its exclusive view of Irish culture alienated most lower- and middle-class Catholic writers. Yeats himself, an essential participant in the modern Irish literary tradition, similarly proved to be an unacceptable model for younger writers seeking their own light of day, but was more problematic and less easy to ignore. A major writer always presents special difficulties for those who follow him, not only as the powerful precursor whose work intimidates and threatens younger generations[2] but also, perhaps even more profoundly, as an immediate part of an already burdensome sense of the past.[3] Moreover, the close proximity of a great talent can produce a subtle influence more difficult to describe or analyze, one that Stephen Spender has identified as "the felt presence of one poet in the sensibility and attitudes of other poets."[4] Poets are more likely to feel this quiet kind of influence in a small country like Ireland where attempts to establish a literary tradition have been so conscious. Paradoxically, however, these attempts at tradition-building also offered a new generation of Irish writers the means to ease, if not to nullify, the anxiety of influence. They saw in Yeats's later poetry, for example, the insistence upon defining the Irish literary tradition in a particularly narrow way which allowed them to reject Yeats on ideological grounds and to look elsewhere for a father figure who might provide continuity.

Irish poets found that figure in James Joyce, a surprising choice, perhaps, when one considers his early exile from Ireland and his eventual preference for the novel. Yet Joyce seems to have been a natural father figure on many levels. His employment of lower- and middle-class life as the marrow of his art deconstructed Romantic Ireland, as Denis Donoghue has rightly claimed,[5] opening the possibility for others to deal realistically with Irish life. Joyce's treatment of Catholic and urban experiences in particular offered writers new possibilities. Also, his self-imposed exile was viewed as a heroic solution to the writer's plight in a restrictive Irish society that was puritanical and backward. Finally—and most important, certainly, for Irish poets— Joyce's great achievements came in prose and for that reason did not impose upon Clarke, Kavanagh, Kinsella, and others as directly as Yeats's poetry did. In fact, these younger writers chose to see in Joyce's work the expression of their own experiences and the embodiment of the artist's struggle in the modern world.[6]

"Filthy Streams"

Joyce's alternative to the Irish Revival appeared early in his career in summary form in "The Holy Office," a witty, satirical broadsheet composed in 1904 and circulated in Dublin in 1905. In a clear parody of Yeats's "To Ireland in the Coming Times," the poem announces Joyce's intention to travel a different road— "But I must not accounted be/One of that mumming com-

pany"—and ridicules the practitioners of the Revival, among
them Yeats, Lady Gregory, Synge, Gogarty, AE, Colum, and
Seamus O'Sullivan. The disrespectful stance involved more than
simple levity aimed at toppling the Olympians; it also paved the
way for an Irish declaration of literary independence. Bringing
"the mind of witty Aristotle" to focus upon the low life of
Ireland, Joyce announces that he will embrace life in all its
forms, recognizing its corruption; he will not turn his back on
the distasteful to wrap himself in romantic dreams, even though
others may reject and criticize his stance.

> That they may dream their dreamy dreams
> I carry off their filthy streams
> . . . .
> Thus I relieve their timid arses,
> Perform my office of katharsis.
> My scarlet leaves them white as wool.
> Through me they purge a bellyful.[7]

The references to Aristotle's notion of catharsis with its implication of purgation or purification implies Joyce's intention to
transform the fallen world rejected by other writers. In the context of Irish literature, he opted for the treatment of actual experience, which he viewed as reality: "Life we must accept as we
see it before our eyes, men and women as we meet them in the
real world, not as we apprehend them in the world of faery."[8]
Aristotelian catharsis also implies the fall of the tragic hero,
whose action would purge the audience's feelings of guilt, pity,
and remorse. The idea of poet-hero surfaces in the final lines of
the poem in an isolated figure who is willing to suffer for his
ideals and cleanse the reading public in the process. Vulnerable
yet assertive, the hero contrasts with Yeats and the revivalists,
"that motley crew" that hates his strength:

> Where they have crouched and crawled and prayed
> I stand the self-doomed, unafraid,
> Unfellowed, friendless and alone,
> Indifferent as the herring-bone,
> Firm as the mountain-ridges where
> I flash my antlers on the air.[9]

One need not look far to see the importance of the isolation in these lines. Developed and dramatized, it would become the fabric of Stephens' garb in the final chapters of *A Portrait* and in *Ulysses*. But in 1904 it served as the defiant pose of a literary young man struggling to find his own voice; it was the platform from which he could attack the impulse of the herd to group and move together.

In a series of reviews written between 1902 and 1904, the "unafraid and unfellowed" critic justifies his heroism by standing alone against the momentum of literary taste. He declares that nationalism in poetry too often discourages invention, producing an expression that "the writer has not devised, he has merely accepted."[10] In "The Day of the Rabblement," Joyce warns that in joining a national movement the artist risks "the contagion of its fetishism and deliberate self-deception."[11] Reviewing Lady Gregory's *Poets and Dreamers* (1903), he condemns the use of folk material and squeezes in a deft comparison that damns Yeats with faint praise: "In fine, her book, wherever it treats of the 'folk,' sets forth in the fulness of its senility a class of mind which Mr. Yeats has set forth with such delicate scepticism in his happiest book, 'The Celtic Twilight.'"[12] In a review of Stephen Gwynn's *Today and Tomorrow in Ireland* (1903), Joyce takes the opportunity to expose the paucity of imagination in all the Revival writers save Yeats.[13] Furthermore, he raises the question of motivation. In "A Mother," a story from *Dubliners* (1914) which demands to be read against the background of the Revival, Joyce shows the inevitable result of the artist trading in the public marketplace. Yeats's mistake was to imagine that his literary movement could become truly popular and raise the cultural level of Ireland. Instead, as "A Mother" indicates, the movement lost out to the pecuniary motives of the mob. Mrs. Kearney, the mother of the title, who is determined to exploit the Irishness of her daughter's name, Kathleen, now that "the Irish Revival (has begun) to be appreciable," arranges Irish language lessons and helps to organize a concert of Irish music. She withholds her daughter from the performance, however, when her fee, due in advance, is unpaid. Mrs. Kearney and Mr.

Holohan, the concert director, argue over the money, until in the end Kathleen does not play. Art and artistic values are the victims of commercial exploitation and the shallowness of a merely fashionable interest in Irish culture.[14] Joyce's strategy exposes the fickleness of the crowd and emphasizes the isolation of the true artist.

The muscle-flexing here looks two ways at once, of course, toward the narrow-mindedness of national literature and toward the justification and promotion of Joyce's own literary ideals. The audacity of the critical stance in these early pieces becomes more astonishing when we remind ourselves that at this stage in Joyce's career there were little more than ideals behind the pronouncements; his first book, *Chamber Music*, would not appear until three years later, in 1907, and "A Mother," written in 1905, was not in print until *Dubliners* appeared in 1914. Yet given the hindsight enjoyed by the poets of Kavanagh's and Kinsella's generations, it was this audacity as much as the ideas of the young, unpublished Joyce which made his authority so great. His criticism of the Revival came as early as 1902, when so many young writers were joining its ranks. Joyce refused to serve, however, and established himself as the first important Irish writer to recognize the limitations of revivalism; as such he stands for its primary antithesis.[15]

Joyce's importance for post-Yeatsian poetry is more than a simple matter of a stance antithetical to the Revival, however. Yeats, after all, had rejected revivalism and shared many of Joyce's views about the tyranny of puritanical Ireland, as we have noted. But Yeats lacked Joyce's consistency on the matter, as a reading of the later poems will show; he romanticized the noble and the beggar-man and clung to heroic figures from myth. Indeed, Joyce himself recognized a "treacherous instinct of adaptability" in Yeats's poetics.[16] Moreover, Yeats rejected the Revival in favor of the Ascendancy tradition, an ideology repugnant to Catholic poets. Joyce, on the other hand, tapped the mainstream of modern Irish life, the rising bourgeoisie, and treated it realistically, becoming, in Thomas Kinsella's phrase, "the first major Irish voice to speak for Irish reality since the death of the Irish language."[17]

Joyce's importance for poets who followed him, then, lay in the potential poetic meaning inherent in his subject matter; it declares lower- and middle-class life to be fit material for literary treatment. It also suggests continuity with the dying Gaelic poetic tradition of the eighteenth century, which also treated the harsh realities of Irish life, focusing on the downtrodden and dispossessed Gaelic families. Joyce's pioneer effort in holding a mirror up to modern Irish life gave the poets of the 1940s and 1950s an alternative to Yeats's directive in "Under Ben Bulben," an alternative that was to prove both helpful and familiar. Austin Clarke recognized in *A Portrait* his own youthful experiences with Jesuits; Patrick Kavanagh saw in Joyce's special use of locale a strategy he could adapt to treat rural Ireland;[18] and Kinsella read Joyce as the writer who made urban literature possible.[19] The antiromanticism implicit in Joyce's treatment of Dublin's mean streets not only provides an antidote to Yeats's romantic Ireland but also shows to what extent ordinary experience might be used for art.

"From dewy dreams, my soul, arise"

Ironically, Joyce's aggressive critical stance against the Revival did not save him from its influence on his own poetry. The early poems, written from 1902 to 1904 and eventually published in *Chamber Music*, look back to the 1890s more than ahead to the great modernist prose of *Ulysses*. Throughout these delicate and sentimental love poems we read the imagery of the Celtic Twilight and hear the rhythms of revivalism:

> The twilight turns from amethyst
> To deep and deeper blue
> The lamp fills with a pale green glow
> The trees of the avenue[20]

We also sense the mood of dreamy emotion and fragile beauty in words such as "pale," "soft," "drowsy," "sweet," "dainty," "dewy," and "shadowy." The languishing and suffering voice of the lover in these poems reminds us a good deal of the persona in *The Wind Among the Reeds*, a volume Joyce knew well and greatly admired:

> Gentle lady, do not sing
>   Sad songs about the end of love;
> Lay aside sadness and sing
>   How love that passes is enough.
>
> Sing about the long deep sleep
>   Of lovers that are dead, and low
> In the grave all love shall sleep:
>   Love is aweary now.[21]

Although the twilight mood predominates, other voices besides Yeats's echo in Joyce's lyrics; Tennyson's voice from "The Lady of Shalott," for example, is apparent in poem 5:

> I have left my book
>   I have left my room,
> For I heard you singing
>   Through the gloom,[22]

Oscar Wilde is here as well, particularly in the subtle rhythm of many of the quatrains, as is Shakespeare, whom Harry Levin has seen behind poem 26, "Thou leanest to the shell of night."[23] That there are other literary ghosts besides Yeats who haunt these poems is not surprising, of course, considering how widely Joyce read and how willingly he borrowed. What is surprising, perhaps, is how little his bold critical pronouncements against revivalism affected his own poetic practice.

Had Joyce written nothing else, it is safe to conjecture that his influence upon modern Irish poetry would be nonexistent. *Chamber Music* smacks too much of the 1890s, and while it cannot be called purely revivalist, since it neglects both heroic Irish myth and peasant folk tradition, it nonetheless shares many of the qualities of Celtic Twilight introduced by Yeats and AE and repeated by O'Sullivan and Colum. Even *Pomes Penyeach*, published in 1927, does not indicate a great poetic talent, nor with one or two exceptions do we sense any significant development in poetic style which would compare with the great achievements in prose. In most of the poems Joyce seems to have been content to strive for the effects of rhythm and sound attempted in *Chamber Music*. Alliteration and assonance dominate the music of these later poems:

> Wind whines and whines the shingle
> The crazy pierstakes groan;
> A senile sea numbers each single
> Slime silvered stone.[24]

Consistent variations in rhythm suggest how consciously Joyce worked toward the sound of the poem:

> Rain on Rahoom falls softly, softly falling,
> Where my dark lover lies.
> Sad is his voice that calls me, sadly calling,
> At grey moonrise.[25]

In two of these later poems, however, Joyce's literary attitude and treatment of experience resemble more closely the bold sensibility behind *A Portrait* and *Ulysses*. The first, "Gas from the Burner," attacks George Roberts, the manager of Maunsel and Company, who initially agreed to publish *Dubliners* and then decided against it. In the process of lampooning Roberts, Joyce uses the opportunity to expose the close-mindedness of the Irish publishing world and the hypocrisy of the literary enclave. The basis of the attack centers upon a clash of literary ideologies, the mythical dream world of the Revival against Joyce's insistence upon reality, including actual names and places. The conflict surfaces satirically in the persona of Roberts, who admits a willingness to publish Lady Gregory's and Colum's folk art, but refuses to publish Joyce's hard-hitting stories:

> But I draw the line at the bloody fellow
> That was over here dressed in Austrian yellow,
> Spouting Italian by the hour
> To O'Leary Curtis and John Wyse Power
> And writing of Dublin, dirty and dear
> In a manner no blackamoor printer could bear.
> Shite and onions! Do you think I'll print
> The name of the Wellington Monument,
> Sydney Parade and Sandymount tram,
> Downe's cakeshop and Williams's jam?[26]

The satirical strategy is an old one, reminiscent of another great Dubliner, Jonathan Swift; Joyce allows Roberts to narrate the poem, saying more than intelligence would allow and in the process exposing not only his own shallowness but, by implication, that of the Revival as well. But the attack on Roberts and the revivalists is only part of the poem's meaning. Beneath the satirical strategy, Joyce repeats the literary manifesto first proclaimed in "The Holy Office": he will treat Irish experience realistically, for better and for worse, portraying life as it appears in its glory and in its corruption. As a realist, he will demand details, since they establish authenticity; he will depict as accurately as he can the particulars of everyday life and will reproduce as closely as possible the setting of Dublin, naming names when he must.

The second later poem, "Tilly," eschews romantic treatment of rural life by insisting upon the realistic portrayal of the drudgery of herding cattle.

> He travels after a winter sun,
> Urging the cattle along a cold red road,
> Calling to them, a voice they know,
> He drives his beasts above Cabra.
>
> The voice tells them home is warm.
> They moo and make brute music with their hoofs.
> He drives them with a flowering branch before him,
> Smoke pluming their foreheads.

Boor, bond of the herd,
Tonight stretch full by the fire!
I bleed by the black stream
For my torn bough![27]

In its criticism of the "brute music" of the herd, the poem's antiestablishment direction is clear; indeed, one critic, Robert Scholes, has read "Tilly" as a gloss on Irish literary history, on "The Day of the Rabblement," and on the notion of the artistic hero set forth satirically in "The Holy Office" and dramatically in *A Portrait:*

> . . . the boor with the flowering branch driving the herd [is] another of Joyce's characterizations of the stay-at-homes of Irish literature who cater to the rabblement (as Joyce accused Yeats's Irish Theatre of doing in "The Day of the Rabblement"), flourishing the garlands they have usurped from the true poet, who has been banished for trying to create the conscience of his race.[28]

Scholes has squeezed much out of this poem, so much that he has neglected, I believe, the last two lines of the poem—"I bleed by the black stream/For my torn bough!"—with their Shelleyan, self-conscious suffering that nearly upsets the poem's balance.

The intrusion of emotion upon the carefully controlled form suggests that Joyce's poetics had remained essentially undeveloped since *Chamber Music*. The same tension between sound and sense so apparent in the early poems mars most of *Penyeach*. Only in "The Holy Office" and "Gas from the Burner," nonlyrical pieces that were excluded from both volumes, and in the touching "Ecce Puer," which simultaneously mourns a dead father and celebrates a newborn grandson, do we sense the perspective and breadth of style which we term Joycean.

Because of the degree of narrowness in poetic range, *Chamber Music* and *Poems Penyeach* contributed very little to the future of modern Irish poetry. Those few poems that startle or interest us do so as a result of their ideas rather than their poetic effects. Joyce's poetry reminds us too often of those very literary trends he condemned and rejected in his criticism. The real and long-lasting Joycean influences on post-Yeatsian poetry come from those texts that declared Joyce's genius, *Dubliners, A Portrait,* and *Ulysses.*

The Created Conscience of Race

In his famous exchange with the publisher Grant Richards over the fate of *Dubliners,* Joyce writes prophetically about the effects of his work, particularly on Irish poetry: "I believe that in composing my chapter of moral history in exactly the way I have composed it I have taken the first step towards the spiritual liberation of my country."[29] The immediate aim of these remarks was to reveal the artistic intention behind the stories in *Dubliners,* that they were realistic portraits of life in Dublin and necessarily demanded the "ashpits, weeds, and offal" of city life. Such realism would counter the fabulous and romantic accounts of Irish life and, at the same time, present a "nicely polished looking-glass" wherein Joyce's fellow citizens could see themselves and their world. The long-range effect, however, went beyond an apologia for an aesthetic of fiction. Supported by his stories and novels, Joyce's critical remarks indeed liberated a number of middle-class Catholic writers, providing them with both the authority and the example they needed to write from experience and from the heart.

By far the most expansive liberation came with *A Portrait,* which in its development as a *Bildungsroman* explored the theme of Irish identity as no other book had done before. Austin Clarke, student at Belvedere a generation after Joyce, recognized in Stephen Dedalus' experiences tensions common to any Irish adolescence. Commenting on Joyce's fiction in an essay written in 1930, Clarke praises *A Portrait* for its authenticity, particularly the way in which it pits the individual against authority, Irish style.

In that astonishingly frank portrayal of the adolescent mind we see sensitive youth struggling through the terrors of religious unbelief to act, and no detail of the clash between immature idealism and the ugliness of matter and sexual development is spared us. Here are the tortuous agonies of the half-medieval Catholic mind which we find in Huysmans. Against a drab Dublin background Stephen Dedalus pursues his thoughts and dreams.[30]

This analysis illuminates more that Joyce's fiction, however; Clarke's reading of *A Portrait* has autobiographical significance and explains a good deal about the Joycean themes in his own writing. Indeed, *A Portrait* so impressed Clarke in its vivid descriptions of certain experiences that he admitted the book "completed" his own memories of adolescence.[31] This extraordinary notion that a novel could complete one's feelings is perhaps the absolute compliment to the novelist; it is also the candid admission by an artist of the extent to which his imagination is occupied by another, reminding us of Jorge Luis Borges' statement "that each writer creates his precursors.[32]

For Clarke, and for others of his generation, Joyce's startling originality came in the treatment of Irish Catholicism, producing a cathartic effect that eventually would surface in post-Yeatsian poetry. Virtually all aspects of a Catholic youth are explored in *A Portrait*, which caused Clarke to see it as a cardinal text. As a young schoolboy Stephen is attracted to the aesthetics of the Church, to its liturgy and its mysteriously beautiful Latin language. In adolescence, vulnerable and softened by sin, Stephen listens in horror to the sermon on hell and, out of fear, resolves to confess his sins. Here, in the central crisis of the novel, Stephen begins the sequence that will culminate in apostasy. Blinded by fear and guilt, he wanders to a small church in a squalid neighborhood to confession.

His sins trickled from his lips, one by one, trickled in shameful drops from his soul festering and oozing like a sore, a squalid stream of vice. The last sins oozed forth, sluggish, filthy. There was no more to tell. He bowed his head, overcome . . . He knelt to say his penance, praying in a corner of the dark nave: and his prayers ascended to heaven from his purified heart like perfume streaming upwards from a heart of white roses. . . . In spite of all he had done it. He had confessed and God had pardoned him. His soul was made fair and holy once more, holy and happy.[33]

This emotional release is only temporary, however, since Stephen realizes that he has allowed the Church to dictate his happiness. In reaction, he decided to break free of the Church's domination and to become a priest of art. He explores his feeling in conversations with his friend Cranley, admitting that although he is not sure of Catholicism's falseness, he will not obey Church teaching. In the process of his denial, he replaces theological values he has rejected with aesthetic ones to fabricate an artistic posture: "I will try to express myself in some mode of life or art as freely as I can and as wholly as I can, using for my defense the only arms I allow myself to use—silence, exile, and cunning."[34]

The central tension in Stephen's religious denial grows out of the opposition between the freedom of artistic expression and the constraint of Catholic authority. Religion is described as one of the nets which Ireland flings at the soul to keep it from flight. The artistic consciousness, in keeping with the Joycean idea of artist-hero, cannot be guided by any forces other than the imagination and the intellect. Stephen's remarks seem extreme in the context of the novel, but they are modified by Clarke's and Kinsella's comments about the importance of religion in Irish life. Clarke has written widely—in novels, in poetry, and in his autobiography—about the powerful effect religion had upon his imagination, particularly his sense of sin and guilt. Kinsella had described the Catholicism of his youth as "so pervasive that it hardly counted as an influence at all; it was a reality like oxygen."[35]

Another reality that Joyce worked into a powerful artistic expression is what Stephen Dedalus calls "the drab dullness of Dublin." Of crucial importance to the poets following Joyce has been his manner of working with raw material, not as a transformation of the environment—which would be akin to the romanticism of the Revival—but rather as an acceptance of the city as a *paysage moralisé*, a kind of moral and spiritual setting for those who live there. It is unnecessary to trace the various examples of torpor, pettiness, and timidity in the characters whom Joyce portrays in *Dubliners*, since these features have been noted by critics and scholars since the stories appeared as a collection in 1914. For the Irish poet of the 1940s and 1950s, particular incidents, settings, or characters seemed less important than Joyce's general purpose: to present "in a style of scrupulous meanness" a chapter of moral history with Dublin as a center of paralysis.[36] In his choice to take the material for his art from among the lives of average Dubliners, granting artistic stature to the ordinary, Joyce broke ground as no other modern Irish writer had done before him, and in the process he raised the consciousness of those who followed him. He demonstrated emphatically that the artist could garner inspiration from a life that, according to Yeatsian poetics, was without meaning; he encouraged writers by his example to sense in negative attitudes about nationality and religion a positive artistic potential.

What stunned Clarke and what subsequently moved Kavanagh, Kinsella, and other Catholic writers was Joyce's controlled forging of oppressively negative experiences into artistic triumphs. The humdrum of the Dublin streets, the shabbiness of lower-class neighborhoods, and, most important, the intrusion of the Church and particularly the clergy upon intellectual and moral development could be transmuted by the relentless imagination of the artist. Subject matter alone, then, did not determine Joyce's importance as the great liberator, although his treatment of middle-class Ireland, what Kinsella has called "the eloquent and conniving and mean-spirited tribe of Dan," represents its own form of liberation for Irish poetry.[37] The younger writers were also impressed and influenced by Joyce's notion of the artist-hero, especially the evolving character, integrity, and stature of the artist as he struggles to define himself. The crucial conflict in *A Portrait*, the tension over Stephen's choice between religion and art, builds upon the gradual establishment of the artist's independence. Early in the book, when Stephen refuses to cry out when struck unjustly, he assumes a defiance that culminates in the final chapter in his famous refusal to serve that in which he no longer believes. This independence and integrity of imagination resulting from a defiant stance against authority proved crucial to the satirical and critical development of Irish poetry. Thus Joyce not only opened up the Catholic and the urban experiences to those writers who followed him but he offered as well the heroic posture of the artist, transforming ordinary events and commonplace reality while challenging authority and convention.[38]

Surprisingly, Clarke's and Kinsella's generations seemed more interested in the social realism and iconoclasm of the early fiction than in Joyce's more innovative and daring stylistics in the later works. Thus the importance of *Ulysses* for post-Yeatsian poets resides not in the high-modernist manner that so impressed T. S. Eliot but rather in the novel's amplification of those features of Irish life uncovered in *Dubliners* and *A Portrait*. Clarke and Kavanagh read *Ulysses* as a text of Irish literary history, antithetical to both Yeats and the Revival, developing to a more sophisticated degree the themes and subject matter of the earlier works. The downtrodden, trapped, and paralyzed are here in Simon Dedalus, the Citizen, Bentam Lyons, Nosey Flynn, Joe Breen, Gertie MacDowell, Mr. Deasy, and even the energetic Blazes Boylan, all victims in various degrees of the life-consuming, closed-in world of Dublin. Religion continues to be an important subject but does not dominate the later novel as it does *A Portrait*. Bloom muses on the hypnotic and soporific qualities of Catholicism in chapter 5, "Lotuseaters," and chapter 6, "Hades," but the subject occupies his mind only momentarily. Even Stephen's "agenbite of inwit," while framed in religious thought, reflects and grows out of the deep psychological trauma caused by his refusal to pray at his mother's deathbed.

Ulysses also impressed post-Yeatsian poets by reinforcing Joyce's concept of the artist-hero, which stands behind the work as the omniscient intelligence. Indeed, the artist-hero's stature reaches a culmination in *Ulysses* because of the scope of the novel, its enormous ambition, its range of style, and its emphasis on the role of the imagination in the character of Leopold Bloom. Bloom's persistent humanity and curious intelligence sustain him in various skirmishes with those who would defeat him. Throughout his peregrinations he draws consistently in time of crisis upon memories, upon dreams, and upon his irregular learning to ease him through difficulties. Two well-known instances may serve as illustrations. His lively and sometimes preposterous ruminations in the "Hades" chapter set in Glasnevin Cemetery prevent him from following the mawkish and maudlin behavior of his companions among the dead. His most evident act of courage comes in the "Cyclops" chapter, in which, during his debate with the fanatical and myopic Citizen, Bloom's firm insistence upon love over hate establishes his moral superiority. Bloom's difficulties and successes correspond to the struggle of the imagination in transforming an occasionally hostile, frequently oppressive environment, the task that Joyce as the pure modernist placed at the center of his work. This centrality becomes clear when we consider that in a novel where most of the action is mental, Joyce takes care to offer us two responses to experience: Bloom, who can overcome adversity, and Stephen, beset by remorse and self-consciousness, who cannot. Bloom's Ulyssean adaptability and instinct for survival, demonstrated in the play of his imagination, assume an even greater importance in comparison with Stephen's failures.

Aside from these essentially conservative features of *Ulysses*, Joyce's masterpiece did not influence post-Yeatsian poets as we might expect, considering the novel's experimental form, its myriad of writing styles, and its erudition. Nor did the more complex, ambitious, and polemical *Finnegans Wake*, which followed in 1939. Patrick Kavanagh claimed that *Ulysses* was one of the three books he constantly reread and that some of its comic spirit infiltrated his later poetry; Clarke's "Mnemosyne Lay in Dust" demonstrates the technique of association in the play between mind object, so characteristic of Bloom and Stephen. In "Nightwalker," Kinsella adapts similar techniques and also sprinkles his text with important Joycean allusions. On the whole, however, the use of the later Joyce is rare in these poets' work; they seem to have been more attracted to the early works and to have more to emulate in Joyce's general artistic posture and his early quarrels with Ireland and its literary establishment.

The Irish Modernists: Devlin, McGreevy, Coffey, and Beckett

We shall consider the Joycean practices in the work of individual poets more completely in separate chapters to follow. At this stage, however, it would be useful to turn to four Irish writers who worked in the 1930s and whose relatively small poetic output has restrained any developed criticism of their work. More than any other Irish poets of this period, Thomas McGreevy, Samuel Beckett, Denis Devlin, and Brian Coffey were committed to modernism and consciously attempted to develop Joycean techniques in their poetry; two of them, McGreevy and Beckett, were close associates of Joyce during the 1920s and 1930s in Paris. In their deliberate practice of modernism, these four writers offer an instructive comparison to Clarke, Kavanagh, and the young Kinsella, all of whose interest in Joyce primarily involved the treatment of Irish subject matter.

McGreevy, Beckett, Devlin, and Coffey, contemporaries and literary associates, supported one another's efforts during the 1930s to counter the last vestiges of revivalism in Dublin. Attracted both by learning and temperament to European culture, they saw Irish poetry as part of an international movement in modern literature. In defining the problem of their immediate poetic inheritance, they regarded both Yeats and revivalism as false trails. Beckett in his 1934 essay on Irish poetry praises Devlin and Coffey as "without question the most interesting of the youngest generation of Irish poets" and, in the same essay, remarks that McGreevy's poems "may be called elucidations . . . probably the most important contribution to post-war Irish poetry."[39] For Beckett the salient feature of their (and presumably his own), work was "that it does not proceed from . . . that Irish Romantic Arnim-Bretano combination, Sir Samuel Ferguson and Standish O'Grady, and that it admits—stupendous innovation—the existence of the author."[40] Beckett demanded integrity and authenticity rather than imitation; literature, he felt, should become truthful again, and personal. Coffey, too, was concerned about authenticity. In a letter to McGreevy, he expresses dissatisfaction with Yeats's rarefied view of a literary tradition that would exclude "the kind of Ireland our Kerry parents and grandparents belonged to." Coffey saw Yeats as struggling against the pull of Catholic Ireland and, by virtue of his extraordinary gifts with language, creating difficulties for poets who followed him: "The effort to speak my own verses with accents and tones which are such that my father and my mother would not have called artificial has meant that I have had to be careful not to get pulled under by WB. . . . WB's verse is strong and has its own fascinations.[41]

Though we must be wary of the blindness of friendship and the mutual promotion by these four poets of one another's work,[42] the commentary they generated about each other's writing shows the commitment they shared to a Joycean direction in poetry. In another letter to McGreevy, Coffey interprets for his generation the false and true paths of the Irish tradition: "While I think all Irish poets have a craft to learn, I don't think it is best developed in a cast-backwards to other days. . . . And with the example of the Yeatsian and the Joycean Practice in mind . . . I want to raise more accurately (than Stephen D. does) the matter of proper artistic awareness, self-consciousness."[43] Coffey's remarks, and Beckett's, too, aim at the sincerity of art as well as the recognition of the world; the poet's self-consciousness, what Coffey terms awareness and what Beckett calls "existence," forms a part of that world. While Coffey did not develop specifically what he meant by "Joycean Practice," we can infer from his negative allusion to Yeats's "cast your mind on other days" that such a practice would surely have involved a presentation of modern Irish life as it was actually lived.

In supplanting Yeatsian history with Joycean realism, these

four poets resemble the others of their generation. They are unique, however, in their willingness to adopt modernist techniques, which they derived from *Ulysses*. McGreevy and expecially Beckett had close personal associations with Joyce from the late 1920s on, and both were directly influenced by his writing and his ideas. Beckett, who became Joyce's secretary, particularly succumbed to Joycean ways, not only in his writing but also in his mannerisms and dress, even attempting to squeeze into Joyce's smaller shoe size.[44]

McGreevy's poem "Cron Trath Na nDeithe," whose Irish title means the equivalent of *Gotterdammerung*, reminds us throughout of *Ulysses*, both in its wandering motif and in its various stylistic devices to indicate changes in setting and time:

> Ter-ot . Stumble . Clock-clock, clock-clock
> Quadrupedante, etcetera,
> And heavy turning wheels of lurching cab
> On midnight streets of Dublin shiny in the rain![45]

The sound effects here echo Joyce's "Sirens" chapter, and the use of allusion is thoroughly Joycean, mixing high and low culture: old Dublin sheet ballads, lines from opera, from Roman Catholic ritual, and from various literary works including modern German and Spanish literature and an unabashed echo of T. S. Eliot: "So Dublin's rows/Of Michelangelos." So pronounced are McGreevy's modernist echoes that in a note to the poems he feels compelled to alert his readers and disarm his critics, explaining that it is scarcely necessary "since it is obvious, formally to acknowledge the debt . . . to Mr. Joyce and the one or two writers in English who have successfully adapted the techniques of *Ulysses* to their own literary purposes."[46]

Beckett eventually gained worldwide recognition as a great writer, the only one among the four young poets to do so. Like Joyce, however, whom he befriended and assisted periodically from 1928 until 1939, Beckett began his literary career as an aspiring poet and turned to other genres as he matured. His poetry represents only a small portion of his literary output and, like Joyce's, was confined to a relatively short period of his youth. Most of it was written in the 1930s and shows a strong Joycean element. Indeed, so pronounced are the Joycean echoes in these intense lyrics that one reader has speculated that Beckett wrote them to gain favor with Joyce.[47] "Malacoda" uses the familiar Joycean method of allusion to explore the meaning of Beckett's father's death; the title comes from Dante's *Inferno* 21 and refers to a deceitful demon whom Beckett recasts as an undertaker and a grave-digger at a funeral. "Enueg 1" is Joycean in design as well as technique; the protagonist wanders through a section of Dublin, sensing in the physical environment an exemplum of his own mental state, reminiscent of Stephen's mental gymnastics in the "Proteus" chapter of *Ulysses*:

> on the hill down from the Fox and Geese into
> Chapelizod
> a small malevolent goat, exiled on the road,
> remotely pucking the gate of his field;
> the Isolde Stores a great perturbation of sweaty
> heroes,
> in their Sunday best,
> come hastening down for a pint of nepenthe or
> moly of half and half
> from watching the hurlers above in Kilmain-
> ham
>
> Blotches of doomed yellow in the pit of the
> Liffey;
> the fingers of the ladders hooked over the
> parapet,
> soliciting;
> a slush of vigilant gulls in the grey spew of the
> sewer.

The use of subject matter here also draws heavily from Joyce. The references to Chapelizod, the Fox and Geese, and Isolde and the particular environs around the river Liffey are conscious echoes of *Finnegans Wake*, which Beckett knew in the late 1920s as *Work in Progress*. Moreover, the journey of the poet-persona in "Enueg 1" is both internal and external in the manner of both

Bloom and Stephen in *Ulysses*. There is even an attempt to replicate Joyce's blurring of the psychological and the real in the "Circe" chapter; in Beckett's version the mutability in nature mirrors human corruption:

> The great mushy toadstool
> green-black,
> oozing up after me,
> soaking up the tattered sky like an ink of
>   pestilence,
> in my skull the wind going fetid,
> the water.[48]

The modernist techniques in the poetry of Coffey and Devlin reflect a pan-European orientation, and Joycean echoes often come filtered through Eliot or modern French poetry. Devlin, who published translations of St. John Perse, Paul Eluard, and Paul Valéry, was a highly erudite poet who used the Joycean technique of allusion to allow meaning and logic to expand, one reference leading us to another. Devlin's critic Dillon Johnston regards as characteristic the practice in "The Heavenly Foreigner," in which the poet takes the reader from Perse to Yeats and to Shelley.[49] Johnston's reading is helpful in accounting for the many voices in the poem, but he misses what I believe is its clearest echo of Joyce: the fall from innocence, so prevalent throughout *A Portrait* as the necessary condition of artistic consciousness. With Devlin the movement away from innocence comes in the realization of lost love:

> Last night on the golded Bourbon Bridge
> The doom of Adam brought me down to earth
> While the houses with their ruined freight
> Filed down the soft, erotic river.
> I was not guilty, had I but known it!
> . . . .
> Love's earnest gift being frivolously given;
> And as the lucid, pagan music
> Blows with brown leaves over the asphalt,
> Guilt slips off like a wet coat in the hall.

Throughout this poem a tension rises in the form of temptation away from one life, known in childhood, toward another, more mysterious one, represented by the "absolute woman." At the moment of recognition, Devlin's poet-narrator experiences a vision similar to Stephen Dedalus' vision of the girl in the surf:

> How she stood, hypothetical-eyed and metaphor-breasted
> Weaving my vision out of my sight
> Out of my sight, out of my very sight,
> Out of her sight
> Till the sight it sees with is blind with light
> Other than hers, other than mine.[50]

Coffey's use of modernism came primarily by way of Eliot. In the following lines from "Dead Seasons," we hear the clear echoes of "Prufrock" and "The Waste Land":

> I am tired, tired, tired. I will go home now,
> The train clanking through the greasy fog,
> The train clattering between the tenements,
> I shall ask them to shut the window,
> Smoke, smuts, fog pouring in choking me.
> "Will you open that window, open that window please."
> Eyes stare me, black sunken hole,
> Faces of dead men, pearl sweat on the forehead,
> And the little movements of the lips as of worms stirring
> "Will you open that window, open that window please."[51]

The reverberations of Joyce's modernism are here as well, of course, in the focus on the reality of modern living, as they are in a more direct way in "Exile," a poem that deliberately aims for an attitude of urban consciousness:

> We shall go walking down the waking streets
> Through the dustfull golden air that morning bears
> Between the city houses and the spires
> Into the vistas and impassive mists.[52]

Because of their peculiar sense of themselves as Irish poets and their heavy debt of Joyce, these four writers deserve a place in the history of post-Yeatsian poetry. Their poetic output is too slight, however, to enable them to rank with Clarke, Kavanagh, or Kinsella. Even Denis Devlin, the most accomplished and celebrated poet in this group, does not offer the range or depth we see elsewhere in modern Irish poetry. Moreover, perhaps as a consequence of limited productivity, even their modernism seems strained, too willful, and certainly too imitative to demonstrate the sincerity of authenticity that Beckett and Coffey themselves demanded. Nonetheless, even as minor poets, Devlin and his colleagues show an antithetical direction to the Revival and testify further to Joyce's presence in modern Irish poetry.

Reluctant Father

The prominence of Joyce in modern Irish poetry grows out of the needs and the temperaments of a new generation of writers rather than from Joyce's own interests in literary patrimony. Unlike Yeats, who throughout his life actively participated in the literary affairs of Ireland, Joyce remained an exile, cut off from Irish letters, refusing to join the Irish Academy in 1932, and offering little commentary on the work of younger writers.[53] Yet he seems to have been a natural model for middle-class writers whose religious experiences, education, political disillusionment, and poetical opposition to both Yeats and revivalism were reflected in *Dubliners, A Portrait,* and *Ulysses.* In depicting their world, Joyce transformed their experiences, providing these younger poets with new potential. He taught them by example to trust their own cultural orientation and, in the process, unwittingly became a less austere and threatening father-figure than Yeats. In the end it was precisely his reluctance to participate in the affairs of the Irish literati which made him so appealing as a paterfamilias. His exile established symbolic authority from afar, conveniently guaranteeing that he would never be a restrictive presence on the crowded Dublin literary scene. Moreover, his choice of genre gave the same comfort.

The treatment in fiction of religious doubt, alienation from society, and memories of oppressive schooling invited similar treatment in poetry. That was not all; the techniques of realism and the use of the psychological might be adapted for poetry.

While both Joyce and Yeats looked upon Catholic lower- and middle-class Ireland with a critical eye, Joyce looked from within, making his separation the rebellion of one who knew firsthand the conditions that had proved unacceptable. The very forces he repudiated: the Church, the home, the fatherland. Yeats, on the other hand, remained apart from that which he criticized. His Protestant inheritance drew him naturally toward the privileged Ascendancy values; as a result he saw in the English literary tradition as much meaning and importance as in the Irish one he sought to create. Yeats recognized this distance and commented late in his life, in regard to his peculiar cultural perspective, that despite his Irish ancestry and his work for Irish literature, he owed his soul to Shakespeare, to Blake, and to the English language that he spoke and wrote. This ambivalence stood behind his famous remark about his Anglo-Irish perspective: "My hatred tortures me with love, my love with hate" and his well-known repudiation of the younger Irish poets as "Base born products of base beds." While Yeats turned his isolation into a powerful poetic statement, as we have seen, he subsequently removed himself from the mainstream of modern and contemporary Irish literature.

This divided tradition, which Yeats identified and then fought against, Joyce accepted as "the cracked lookingglass of a servant," which—held out by Mulligan in the opening chapter of *Ulysses*—gives back a divided image as Stephen looks into it. This image represents the essential condition of the modern Irish mind and demonstrates why the Revival's promise of mending a broken tradition died so hard in Ireland. An Irish literary tradition proffered a sense of identity which obsessed Irish writers of the early twentieth century and continues to confound contemporary poets like Seamus Heaney and Derek Mahon. Modern poetry in general is haunted by the divided mind, as we sense in Rilke, Eliot, and Stevens, poets who portray man cut off from his past, confused about meaning, and involved in an attempt to reconcile himself to his isolation. In the Irish literary tradition, that reconciliation is defined in cultural and national terms, that is, the struggle for reconciliation becomes embroiled in the question of identity. Yeats's ultimate definition of this tradition not only made it impossible for most writers to follow him but exacerbated the problem, driving a cultural wedge between two elements of Irish society. Joyce, whose understanding of the condition is implicit in the image of the cracked looking glass, recognized the difficulty for the Irish writer who inherited a fractured tradition. In *A Portrait* Stephen confesses to himself that the English tongue is not his own, but this understanding does not drive him into the arms of the Revival. Indeed, in the diary section of chapter 5, he admits a reluctance about the native Gaelic tradition. The old man from the west of Ireland who speaks Irish, smokes a pipe, and lives in a cabin offers no comfort to him: "I fear him. I fear his redrimmed horny eyes. It is with him I must struggle all through this night till day come, till he or I lie dead, gripping him by the sinewy throat."[54] Joyce could not identify with the dying Gaelic culture nor could he accept completely the imposition of an English one; instead, he accommodated both and in a sense mended the fragmentation of Irish literature by insisting upon the reality of the modern condition. By accepting its disjointedness and, more important, by insisting on a personal vision of reality which made cultural and spiritual isolation its subject, Joyce offered the next generation of poets a sense of continuity, and with it the means to widen the poetic tradition Yeats had narrowed.

4

Tradition and Continuity I: Austin Clarke

Austin Clarke appears as the true transitional figure of twentieth-century Irish poetry. His career, begun in 1917, spanned the waning fashions of the Revival, the heightened nationalism of the 1920s, and the more recent social criticism of the new Ireland. Indeed, Clarke's poetic history serves as a barometer of Irish poetry after Yeats. His early poems essentially follow the young Yeats's interest in the retelling of Irish myth and saga; in Clarke's middle years, he attempted to revise Yeats's romantic version of Irish history by emphasizing medieval Ireland; Clarke's later poems incorporate a Joycean perspective in their treatment of ordinary life and their critical view of religion and society. Throughout these changes in subject matter, voice, and poetic technique, Clarke remained consistent on one account: the desire to be a thoroughly and distinctively Irish poet.

The Irish element in Clarke's work, which has drawn both the scorn and the praise of the critics,[1] presented him with the major problem of his poetic career, the solution of which secured his place in modern Irish literature. Clarke's interest in a purely Irish mode in poetry meant, inevitably, conflict with Yeats, who had done it all before and whose shadow would fall across almost everything the younger poet was to write. Clarke's personal struggle in coming to terms with Yeats, in which he had to contend with the master first as an influence and later as the

dominant personality of the Irish literary establishment, determined the important stages of his own development as a poet.

Born in 1896, Clarke grew up during the grand days of the
Revival and was very aware of Yeats's achievement and his
presence as a literary figure. The young Clarke attended some
of Yeats's public lectures and saw his green-and-gold-covered
books prominently displayed in all of Dublin's bookstores.[2]
Clarke's earliest publications, as we noted in our discussion of
the revivalists, were epic treatments of Irish sagas, inspired by
the momentum of the Revival and imitative of the early Yeats.
By the mid-1920s, however, after four different attempts at
heroic poetry, Clarke had realized that the epic mode would not
suffice, both because it resembled too closely Yeats's early attempts at the long heroic poem and because it did not suit
Clarke's own lyrical bent. In the early 1930s he wrote of his
decision to abandon the epic treatment of Celtic legend:

> The thousand tales of Ireland sink: I leave
> Unfinished what I had begun nor count
> As gain the youthful frenzy of those years.
>
> (CP., 179)

Instead, Clarke turned to a treatment of Gaelic and Catholic
medieval Ireland.

Part of the strategy for such a shift in emphasis reflected
Clarke's uneasiness over the strong Yeatsian direction in his
own poetry. The choice of a new poetic terrain—medieval rather
than pagan Celtic Ireland—allowed the possibility of new subject matter without giving up an Irish context and background.
Moreover, in emphasizing this particular era in Irish history,
Clarke hoped to gain an edge on Yeats on two fronts: religion
and the Irish language. Clarke's Catholicism and his familiarity
with literature in Irish not only established the authenticity of
his work but also, in comparison, exposed Yeats's connection
with the Irish tradition as tenuous due to his lack of facility in
Irish. Much of Clarke's literary criticism of this period follows
this strategy. Along with other young writers like Higgins and
Fallon, who were struggling to establish their reputations in the

1920s and 1930s, Clarke stressed repeatedly in his essays and reviews how Yeats, out of touch in his later years with Catholic Ireland, left the mainstream of Irish literature and, as a result, lost his sincerity as a poet. The new generation, the strategy dictated, had to fill the void in order to truly reflect the Irish character.

This maneuvering proved to be limiting and even disastrous for those who followed it, as our glance at revivalist poetry has shown. Yet, recognizing the enormous stature of Yeats and the insecurity of those fledgling writers who came after him, it is easy to understand how desperately the new generation wished to separate itself from its great predecessor. So strong was this desire that it remained with Clarke all his life. Reflecting in his autobiography on his beginnings as a writer, Clarke identifies Douglas Hyde as his primary inspiration, a significant denial of the obvious connection with Yeats. Clarke is careful to disavow Yeatsian influence, recounting how as a youth he read Hyde's *Love Songs of Connaught* and attended his lectures on the Irish language. At one of those lectures Clarke felt an almost vocational call: "Those plain words changed me in a few seconds. The hands of our lost despised centuries were laid on me."[3]

This dramatic recounting reveals the importance of the separation from Yeats and the lengths to which Clarke went to achieve it, even if it meant the distortion of literary history. The Irish scholar and translator Hyde, according to Clarke, was the proper originator of modern Irish poetry since he, rather than Yeats, knew the language and, through it, the culture of ancient Ireland. What Clarke omitted about Hyde adds to the significance of the choice. Apart from translations, Hyde's literary output was hardly prolific, nor could his achievement between 1910 and 1920, when Clarke was reading avidly in revivalist texts, remotely compare with Yeats's. But Clarke's interesting misreading provided its own special comforts. As a poet with less range than Yeats, Hyde did not threaten a new generation of writers; for all his deep knowledge of the Irish language, he served as a safe and comfortable ancestor, one whose literary accomplishments left great room for future poets.

The desire to outflank Yeats and to surpass what he had started caused Clarke and his compeers to see themselves not only as inheritors but also as trustees of Irish Literary Revival, becoming—in Samuel Beckett's phrase—"romantic antiquarians."[4] Some, like F. R. Higgins, turned to the pastoral and the treatment of folk motifs, simply offering, as we have seen, the same warmed-over fare to the established and expectant audience. Clarke chose a different course for different reasons. Acutely aware of Yeatsian practice, he sensed real poetic opportunity in Irish history, especially the medieval period, which Yeats had not touched. Clarke wrote to Seamus O'Sullivan in the 1930s, "Yeats, in transforming himself into a world poet, has left the Irish Revival baby on the doorstep, and the question is what are we to do with it."[5] This wonderfully revealing sentence tells us much about Clarke's poetic survival instincts: that he would insist upon Yeats's defection from Irish literature, that he would prefer the early to the later Yeats, that he identified himself as an inheritor of a tradition he felt compelled to extend and develop. In an essay written in 1935, Clarke damns Yeats with faint praise by suggesting that he abandoned his true poetic nature:

> An important event which cannot be ignored in any discussion of the present state of Irish poetry is the return of Mr. Yeats to the main sources of English literature. . . . Magnificent as the poet's later work is, we have to realize that it is steeped in the rich imaginative associations of English literature. . . . His flightiness belongs to the adventurous, restless Anglo-Irish type of the past, those writers who, lacking cares of their own, were extraordinarily responsive and adaptable to any environment in which they happened to find themselves. . . . If we can eventually express our own scholastic mentality in verse, I believe that our art will lead us, not towards, but away from English art.[6]

Clarke's choice of medieval, Christian Ireland assumed that he might move away from English art without appearing to be slavishly imitative of the early Yeats. The structure of the historical and religious framework would provide what Celtic myths and legends had for Yeats's early poems, but the choice of Gaelic-Catholic subject matter would be original. Clarke could employ the Yeatsian idea of the unit of culture embodied in medieval Ireland and at the same time find fresh metaphors for his poetry. Moreover, by setting his work into a historical framework, he would fulfill another important aim of the Revival, informing the present age of its rich past.

The complete development and treatment of the medieval theme comes in Clarke's novels *The Bright Temptation* (1932), *The Singing Men of Cashel* (1936), and *The Sun Dances at Easter* (1952), and in the verse plays of the 1930s and 1940s, although the earliest attempts appear in the 1929 book *Pilgrimage and Other Poems*. The essential practice in these works was to focus upon the importance of the medieval Church in society in order to show its effect and influence upon individual people. The novels and the plays contrast the beauty of Church ritual and dogma with the depravity of the Church's teaching on sex, usually by highlighting a young, vigorous, and attractive clerk who struggles with his conscience but gives in to vital forces and natural urges.[7] Often, Clarke used the medieval setting as a satirical device to comment upon modern Irish society, anticipating his biting satires of the 1950s and 1960s.[8] Ultimately, he abandoned the historical scheme, judging correctly that it resembled too closely the early practice of Yeats. In fact, Clarke may have sensed its limitations for poetry after the completion of *Pilgrimage*, although he continued to use the medieval setting for fiction and drama well into the 1950s. Not only did he feel the weight of Yeats's hand behind the idea, but he also recognized the restriction of a poetic strategy based on the romantic conception of an Ireland of the imagination, a misty, pastoral land where time stood still.

Pilgrimage demonstrates the most complete development of Clarke's creation of "the Celtic Romanesque," the term he invented to describe his version of romantic Ireland.[9] The titular and opening poem of the 1929 book presents the beauty of landscape and the celebration of Church ritual not as subjects in their own right but as means to create a certain mood.

> Grey holdings of rain
> Had grown less with the fields,
> As we came to that blessed place
> Where hail and honey meet.
> O Clonmacnoise was crossed
> With light: those cloistered scholars,
> Whose knowledge of the gospel
> Is cast as metal in pure voices,
> Were all rejoicing daily,
> And cunning hands and cold jewels
> Brought chalices to flame.
>
> We heard with the yellow candles
> The chanting of the hours, . . .
> And in stained glass the holy day
> Was sainted as we passed. . . .
> Treasured with chasuble,
> Sun-braided, rich cloak'd wine-cup.
>
> (*CCP.*, 153)

Although the balance is sometimes tenuous in *Pilgrimage*—occasionally in these poems, sense gives way to sound—Clarke persevered in establishing his mood. The imagery richly describes the importance of liturgy in the medieval Church and hints at the achievement of scholasticism in Ireland. The trappings of legend and history crowd these poems—Saint Patrick appears, as do hermits, sailors, scholars, queens, visionary women, and characters from folklore and history—and often restrict their originality. Yet there are moments of high achievement here, in Clarke's use of the traditional Gaelic forms such as the Aisling, or vision poem, in the effective use of Gaelic prosody, and in the description of the clash between Christian and pagan Celtic Ireland.[10] A characteristic example is Clarke's reworking of the well-known folk stories about the old woman of Beare; his version, "The Young Woman of Beare," stresses the energetic sexuality of youth with a skillful integration of image and rhythm:

> Heavily on his elbow,
> He turns for a caress
> To see—as my arms open—

The red spurs of my breast.
I draw fair pleats around me
And stay his eye at pleasure,
Show but a white knee-cap
Or an immodest smile—
Until his sudden hand
Has dared the silks that bind me.

See! See, as from a lathe
My polished body turning!
He bares me at the waist
And now blue clothes uncurl
Upon white haunch. I let
The last bright stitch fall down
For him as I lean back,
Straining with longer arms
Above my head to snap
The silver knots of sleep.

                                    (*CCP.*, 165)

Although Clarke achieved lyrical success in many of these poems, he did not feel bound to the Celtic Romanesque as his supreme fiction. He sensed a completion in *Pilgrimage*, as Yeats did in *The Wind Among the Reeds*, and recognized the need to move on to other forms and modes in order to develop as a poet. In 1936 he announced the end of his plan to retell Ireland's sagas and tales and turned instead to the private material of his own religious identity. In a huge poetic leap he moved away from the world of the early Yeats and the Revival to the Joycean preoccupation with the makeup of modern Ireland: nationality, religion, and family. For Clarke the leap was decisive; he forged a new poetic identity and became, along with Patrick Kavanagh, one of the two most important Irish poets of his generation.

Prosody

Before we turn to the new phase in Clarke's poetry, which began with *Night and Morning* (1938), one aspect of his interest in the Irish mode, or "Irish note" as he sometimes called it, deserves special mention. As a student and a hopeful young poet, he became aware of the potential Gaelic prosody held for poetry in English. In his autobiography he writes about the influences of George Sigerson, whose book *Bards of the Gael and Gall* (1925] explores Gaelic rhythm and poetic meter, and of Thomas MacDonagh, whose study *Literature in Ireland* (1916) advocates the use of Gaelic poetic techniques in English in order to produce a truly Anglo-Irish mode.[11]

Clarke took the advice of both of these teachers seriously. Throughout the various stages of his career, he adapted Gaelic poetic devices to poetry written in English, hoping to capture the Irish note in his own poems and to provide a continuity with the rich tradition in Gaelic poetry. Robert Welch has argued that Clarke's lifelong interest in prosody went beyond the merely technical and that he was attempting to convey in English the tone and the emotional quality of the Gaelic originals. Welch quotes from Clarke's early epic, "The Cattledrive in Connaught," to show "the melancholy and recklessness of many a Connacht folk song . . . the musical power of eighteenth-century accented verse."[12]

Clarke's commitment to the use of Gaelic prosody never faltered. In an explanatory note to *Pilgrimage* he explains the use of the Gaelic technique of assonance:

> Assonance . . . takes the clapper from the bell of rhyme. In simple patterns, the tonic word at the end of the line is supported by a vowel-rhyme in the middle of the next line. . . . The natural lack of double rhymes in English leads to an avoidance of words of more than one syllable at the end of the lyric line. . . . But by cross-rhymes or vowel-rhyming, separately, one or more of the syllables of longer words, the difficulty may be turned: lovely and neglected words are advanced to the tonic place and divide their echoes.[13]

Throughout *Pilgrimage*, Clarke consistently utilized this technique, particularly with internal rhyme. The "tonic word" often cross-rhymes with a middle word in the next line, as we note in the title poem "Pilgrimage":

> . . . those cloistered scholars
> Whose knowledge of the gospel
> Is cast as metal in pure voices
> Were all rejoicing daily.

Clarke also attempted variations in rhyming patterns, in half-rhymes—"scholars-knowledge; gospel-metal"—or in the complicated pattern from another poem from *Pilgrimage*, "The Scholar," in which the end rhymes are both half-rhymes—"reaping-river; plain-live"—and perfect rhymes—"river-live"—and the internal cross-rhyme is perfect—"reaping-sleeps";

> When midday hides the reaping
> He sleeps by a river
> Or comes to the stone plain
> Where the saints live
>
> (*CCP.*, 162)

For the budding poet, the deliberate attempt to adapt Gaelic prosody into English forced a respect for technique and discipline which benefited the later poetry; Clarke's mature verse is characterized by its devotion to craft, particularly in language and form. The rhyming techniques continue in the later works as well, although sometimes by calling attention to themselves they force the rhyme scheme and even obscure meaning:

> Goodness of air can be proverbial
> That day by the kerb at Rutland Square,
> A bronze bird fabled out of trees
> Mailing the spearheads of the railings
> Sparrow at nails, I hailed the skies
> To save the tiny dropper, found
> Appetite gone. A child of clay
> Has blustered it away. Pity
> Could raise some littleness from dust.
>
> (*CCP.*, 200)

In this example from a 1955 poem, "Ancient Lights," Clarke abuses the rhyming devices, so that the words echoing throughout the stanza drown out the meaning: "proverbial-kerb,"

"fables-mailing-railings-nails-hailed," "skies-tiny," "clay-away,"
"blustered-dust," "pity-littleness."

Other lapses occur in Clarke's use of rhyme in the later
poetry, an outgrowth of his interest in assonance and cross-
rhyme. The combined use of the French techniques of *rime riche*,
or the use of homonyms, with cross-rhyme becomes very self-
conscious in some of the poetry of the 1960s.

> Freedom
> Waits, feeble, dumb, for
> The gallows rope,
> When we are europed
> From nape to toe-nail,
> Scheduled, natoed.

> He heard
> Far off, phantoms
> Of Buddhist monks
> Still burning, sigh: "Gone!"
> As he left Saigon.
>
> (*CCP.*, 471, 474)

There are other moments in the later poetry, however, when
Gaelic prosody is used more moderately so that it does not
intrude upon the overall design of the poem. When combined
with other elements, the rhyming techniques and internal
echoes provide a formal device that clarifies the poem's direction
and meaning. In the very personal and emotional poem
"Mnemosyne Lay in Dust," for example, prosody facilitates the
expression of intense feeling:

> He tumbled into half the truth:
> Burial alive. His breath was shouting:
> "Let, let me out." But words were puny.
> Fists hushed on a wall of inward-outness.
> Knees crept along a floor that stirred
> As softly. All was the same chill.
> He knew the wall was circular
> And air was catchcry in the stillness
> For reason had returned to tell him
> That he was in a padded cell.
>
> (*CCP.*, 335)

The subtle echos of cross-rhyme in "truth-breath," "shouting-out," and "chill-wall" are used sparingly and mesh with the *abab, cdcd, ee* pattern of imperfect and perfect end rhyme. Despite such controlled moments, the Gaelic element in Clarke's poetry is more interesting in theory than in practice. His persistence in struggling to make Gaelic prosody an essential part of his poetic effort overshadowed the often unbalanced and strained use of the techniques in the actual poems.

Clarke's efforts with Gaelic prosody were so consistent and thorough that he unwittingly liberated future poets from the necessity of such technical experimentation. As John Montague said in a recent interview, Clarke is to be admired for his scholarly approach to the Irish tradition and for his commitment to continuity, but he is especially to be thanked for clearing some ground.

> We now have that example before us, an example, I would have to say is at least a partial failure. I don't think a poet should restrict himself in this way, but historically, Austin probably had to. . . . So Austin trying to make himself into an Irish writer is excellent as a technical example for other Irish writers to follow. . . . But Austin is not a Gaelic writer.[14]

Thomas Kinsella concurs and regards Clarke's use of prosody as important not primarily to the poetry itself but rather to Clarke's overall poetic strategy.

> It has long been an essential vehicle of expression for him, and though it has resulted in a number of poems which remain little more than exercises, it has also helped him to many fine statements, even on fairly urgent contemporary matters. . . . Gaelic prosody is not a very important issue in itself, but it is by means of such devices that a poet seeks, and may find imaginative freedom and ease.[15]

The Break with Revivalism

Clarke's decision to forsake the Celtic Romanesque in his poetry resulted from two important discoveries. One was his growing recognition of the stale qualities in much of the poetry of his generation, including that of his contemporary F. R. Higgins. The other, which grew from self-criticism, was the disturbing understanding that his use of medieval Ireland had failed in at least one of its purposes, to provide the essential distance from Yeats. The separation from Yeats was crucial to Clarke's sense of poetic identity, but involved personal feelings as well, according to Thomas Kinsella. "Yeats himself, one way and another, has been a lifelong fixation, an object of inspiration and emulation, and a cross . . . rejecting him [Clarke] from the *Oxford Book of Modern Verse*; always hypnotising him, even from the grave."[16] Clarke's "fixation" caused him to develop a set of evolving critical responses to Yeats which corresponded to various stages in his own poetic development. In his early, revivalist days, as we have seen, it suited him to sever Yeats from the Revival in order to make his own Celtic Romanesque seem more authentically traditional and Irish. In his later, antirevivalist work, still needing the crucial distance from Yeats, Clarke found it necessary to revise his critical views, claiming that "Yeats never really left the Celtic Twilight" and that the later Yeats "celebrated mournfully the passing of greatness" and was himself the end of an era, a personal symbol of the passing of Ascendancy Ireland. Once Clarke had redefined Yeats in order to dismiss him, it was an easy task to find a new father figure. Joyce, not Yeats, spoke for the new Ireland; a Joycean direction in modern poetry would provide middle-class, Catholic, essentially urban poets like Clarke with a solid framework for self-expression.

Clarke's Joycean context begins with the intensely personal examination of religious doubt in the poetry of *Night and Morning*. The agony of deliberation reverberates throughout the book—the word "pain" appears in almost every poem—as reason clashes with faith.

> . . . yet who dare pray
> If all in reason should be lost,
> The agony of man betrayed
> At every station of the cross?
>
> (*CCP.*, 183)

The doubt that permeates each poem suggests that Clarke had arrived at apostasy, but, like Stephen Dedalus in *A Portrait of the Artist as a Young Man*, the poetic voice is obsessed with the Catholicism it attempts to reject, even to the point of celebrating in rich imagery the Church's symbolism and ritual: "Adoring priest has turned his back/Of gold upon the congregation. . . . "; "This is the hour that we must mourn/With tallows on the black triangle";

> The word is said, the Word sent down,
> The miracle is done
> Beneath those hands that have been rounded
> Over the embodied cup,
> And with a few, she leaves her place
> Kept by an east-filled window
> And kneels at the communion rail
> Starching beneath her chin.
>
> (*CCP.*, 184)

Clarke's common trope in these poems is the waning of the light of reason amid the spreading dark superstition of faith. Indeed, darkness dominates *Night and Morning*; whatever light appears in these poems seems to be refracted through "an east-filled window" or flickers at the ends of holy candles. Yet the poetry does not completely deny faith, nor does it suggest that religion is not an important part of experience. As Donald Davie has remarked, the following lines from "Martha Blake" could have been written only by a poet who had experienced the Eucharist very fervently":[17]

> She trembles for the Son of Man,
> While the priest is murmuring
> What she can scarcely tell, her heart
> Is making such a stir;
> But when he picks a particle
> And she puts out her tongue,
> That joy is the glittering of candles
> And benediction sung.
>
> (*CCP.*, 184)

There is present in these poems, however, clear religious doubt, which grows out of an intellectual posture reminiscent of Stephen's pose in chapter 5 of *A Portrait*; in Clarke's poems, however, the pedantry and arrogance of the intellect are understated. Instead, religious skepticism develops in constant references to the agony of the mind, or the pain of thought, as if the poet is questioning the price of reason. Opposing reason is the irrational and emotional faith of a Martha Blake:

> So to begin the common day
> She needs a miracle
> Knowing the safety of angels
> That see her home again.
>
> (*CCP.*, 185)

The shallowness of such a faith produces doubt in the poetic voice about the promise of religious teaching.

The basis of this intellectual doubt rests upon a combination of scholarly and artistic predilections, again reminding us of the college student Stephen Dedalus. Clarke's protagonist appears in "The Straying Student" as another version of his medieval clerk, a scholar with poetic pretensions; in this poem the young man has been enticed by a female figure who may represent art or reason.[18] Instead of remaining at the seminary at Salamanca to become a priest of God, the clerk heeds the call of a secular angel and embraces worldly knowledge.

> I learned the prouder counsel of her throat
> My mind was growing bold as light in Greece;
> And when in sleep her stirring limbs were shown,
> I blessed the noon day rock that knew no tree:
> And for an hour the mountain was her throne,
> Although her eyes were bright with mockery.
>
> They say I was sent back from Salamanca
> And failed in logic, but I wrote her praise
> Nine times upon a college wall in France.
> She laid her hand at darkfall on my page
> That I might read the heavens in a glance
> And I knew every star the Moors have named.
>
> (*CCP*, 189)

The decision to follow the woman so closely parallels Stephen's encounter with the bird-girl in chapter 4 of *A Portrait* that Joyce's words provide a gloss on Clarke's poem:

> Her eyes had called to him and his soul leaped at the call. To live, to err, to fall, to triumph, to recreate life out of life! A wild angel had appeared to him, the angel of mortal youth and beauty, an envoy from the fair courts of life, to throw open before him in an instant of ecstasy the gates of all the ways of error and glory.[19]

Clarke's break with the church seems clear in *Night and Morning*, yet it is not stated with the Joycean defiance we see in *A Portrait*. Indeed, there is an element of lament present in these poems, despite the overall intellectual denial of faith. In becoming a thinking, questioning, and reasoning adult, Clarke regretted the loss of blind innocence and simplicity he remembered from in his own youth:

> The misery of common faith
> Was ours before the age of reason.
> Hurrying years cannot mistake
> The smile for the decaying teeth,
> The last confusion of our senses,
> But O to think, when I was younger
> And could not tell the difference,
> God lay upon this tongue.
>
> (*CCP.*, 192)

Joycean elements continue to shape the poetry after *Night and Morning*, particularly in the distanced, ironic stance of Clarke's social criticism in the later work of the 1950s and 1960s. The strategy behind these satiric poems follows Joyce's admonition—in "The Holy Office," "Gas from the Burner," and essays such as "Day of the Rabblement"—that the true artist must be separate from the masses and critical of nationalism and national movements. Clarke's Joycean practice exposed the institutions in Irish society as negative forces that made life difficult in Ireland—those elements which Stephen Dedalus labels as nets. Clarke's most common targets are the Church and the clergy, whose Jansenist obsession with sexuality and puritanical stand against birth control make religion a repressive rather than an uplifting force in Irish society.

Clarke frequently attacked the commitment to religious faith in Ireland as appearance—the pomp of bishops, the building of churches, the erecting of statues in harbors and lonely glens—rather than something genuinely felt. The government, too, was often criticized for pretension and show, especially when it appeared to be in collusion with the Church on matters of public policy or even social behavior. In "The Burial of an Irish President," Clarke ridicules the hypocrisy and blind obstinacy of Catholic government officials who would not attend the funeral service for former Irish president Douglas Hyde because it was to take place in Saint Patrick's Cathedral, a Protestant church. Instead, the official mourners waited outside in the dirty alley near the cathedral, a ludicrous picture:

> Professors of cap and gown,
> Costello, his Cabinet
> In Government cars, hiding
> Around the corner, ready
> Tall hat in hand.
>
> (*CCP.*, 250)

The satirical direction in Clarke's poetry ranges widely in these poems, attacking institutions, government policy, religious practice, and, occasionally, individuals who exhibit folly or vice, countering the romantic, sentimental version of Irish life perpetrated by the poetry of the Revival. Indeed, the shift in poetic tone, voice, and subject matter is so dramatic in the later poems that some critics "rediscovered" Clarke as a satirist in them and praised his innovation.[20]

In fact, Clarke was only one of a number of Irish writers in the 1940s who actively sought to debunk the idealism and sentimentality of the Revival; indeed, these writers felt strongly that post–World War II Ireland required criticism as a new nation. Sean O'Faolain and Frank O'Connor led the fight against censorship; Clarke and Patrick Kavanagh criticized the insularity of society; and younger writers like John Montague and Thomas

Kinsella, following the lead of their immediate predecessors, took a realistic and sometimes cynical view of contemporary Ireland. Of course, Yeats himself was critical of the new Ireland, but among younger writers he got little credit for the impulse.

The Joycean direction in Clarke's later poetry grew from a realistic and sometimes satirical treatment of Irish life to more purely literary details, such as allusion and tone. The deliberately urban flavor of this work, for example, particularly in the use of Dublin not only as a setting but also as a cultural force, indicates Clarke's debt to Joyce. The development of characterization and the preoccupation with language, especially the use of puns, also show strong Joycean influence.

The use of Dublin as a setting is so prominent in the later work that Clarke can rightly be called the first real poet of the city in Irish literature.[21] For he not only placed Dublin at the heart of his work, but he wrote with a familiarity and from a perspective that revealed an urban consciousness. Scenes of Dublin life are presented with the Joycean touch in exactness of detail:

> The Liffey
> Frothed and Guinnessed as I came from Store Street.
> ·
> Cornered by a gust at O'Connell Street
> Past the Four Angels, where bus conductors
> Leaned against a bank-door near Forte's
> Saloon, I saw a procession.
>
> (*CCP.*, 430)

There are references to the Georgian buildings on Kildare Street and Merrion Square, to the commercial area surrounding Saint Patrick's Hospital, and to Dublin neighborhoods from the tenements to suburban Templeogue. There are descriptions of famous city landmarks: "the spike upon the gateway/ . . . of Dublin Castle," "sixteen floored Liberty Hall/ . . . Shaming the Custom House," and "The pond/In St. Stephen's Green." Finally, there is a nostalgic memory of the Edwardian Dublin of Clarke's childhood:

                                    Horses,
            Men, going together to daily work; dairy
            Cart, baker's van, slow dray,
            Suddenly in Mountjoy Street, at five o'clock
            Church-echoing wheel-rim, roof-beat, tattle of harness
            Around the corner of St. Mary's Place:
            Cabs, outside cars, the drivers unranked in race
            Greet with their own heat
            Galway Express that puffed to Broadstone Station

                            Champions went by,
            Guiness's horses from St. James's Gate:
            Their brasses clinked, yoke, collar shone at us:
            Light music while they worked. Side-streets, alleys
            Beyond St. Patrick's, floats unloading, country
            Colt, town hack, hay-cart, coal-bell.
                                            (*CCP.*, 238–239)

    Clarke's interest in the life of the city demonstrates further
Joycean influence. In various portraits of selected Dubliners,
Clarke depicts the closed-in, routine existence of modern city
life in a manner reminiscent of Joyce's representation of paralysis
in *Dubliners*. "Martha Blake at Fifty-One" each morning walks
the road "To Mass at the Church of the Three Patrons." The
menial tasks in her daily routine are described in detail, emphasizing the dull habits of her life. "Slowly walking after Mass/
Down Rathgar Road," she begins her day with the practiced
ritual of breakfast, with careful attention to detail: "match to
gas-ring," "half-filled saucepan," a "lightly" cooked egg, with
tea and bread. In a regular pattern she leaves her neighborhood
and journeys to the heart of the city,

                    once a week, purchased
            Tea, butter in Chatham St. The pond
                In St. Stephen's Green was grand.
            She watched the seagulls, ducks, black swan,
                Went home by the 15 tram.
                                            (*CCP.*, 268)

Other characters from the city are presented, each a reflection of the living death, the lonely frustration of emptiness. "Miss Rosanna Ford" describes a lady spinster,

> . . . aloof at eighty-four.
> So indigent she seldom could afford
> Sufficient warmth or food for the cupboard shelf.

Another spinster, "Miss Marnell," gives away all her savings to the Church so that she will die a peaceful, holy death. Father Eddie Bourke in "The Knock" appears as the corrupted but morally righteous clergyman who hopes to persuade the poet to return to the Church.[22]

Joycean echoes are also audible in the description of a Dublin public house, a center of Irish social life. Fittingly, the setting is Davy Byrne's in Duke Street, the habitat of Leopold Bloom:

> Men elbow the counter . . . drink
> Their pints of plain, their chaser, large or small one,
> Talk in the snug, the lounge, nod gravely, wink fun
> In meanings, argue, treat one another, swallow
> The fume, the ferment.

The friendships become inflated, however, the rhetoric hollow, and the sentimentality heavy. The "parting glass" becomes a stagnant act and another example of Dublin paralysis:

> Joyful, self-important,
> Soon all are glorious, all are immortal
> Beings of greater day, hierophants; . . .
> Cordial, benevolent, with anecdotes. . . .
> At bolting time, each thirst becomes enormous,
> Farewelling, farewelling, farewelling, because it must.
>
> (CCP., 277)

Clarke's portraits are much more selective than Joyce's, however, because they are part of a larger satirical strategy; pathetic as their lives may appear, people like Martha Blake surface in

Clarke's poetry to suggest victimization, usually by a demanding Church. Most of Clarke's Dubliners, in fact, are testimony to the abuse of power by Irish institutions. Such portraits, then, validate his satirical treatment of Irish life.

A Joycean presence also appears in Clarke's fascination for wordplay, puns, and diction. Hugh Kenner has commented on the respect for language in Dublin, the powerful tradition of public oratory that existed in the city during the early decades of the twentieth century, and the trivium that was at the core of the city's educational system.[23] As a schoolboy at Clongowes and Belvedere, Joyce was steeped in classical rhetoric, which, as Kenner has pointed out, facilitated his project of transcribing anecdotes, bits of speech, and journalese from his daily experiences in Dublin. Clarke was also educated at Belvedere, and his work demonstrates similar preoccupations with language and rhetoric. The strategy of the public poetry in *Later Poems* (1961), *Flight to Africa* (1963), and *The Echo at Coole* (1968) is essentially rhetorical, sustained by a sense of civic responsibility. The mode is ironic, and the technique frequently demonstrates a manipulation of language through parody and the pun. There is an abundance in Clarke's later poetry of the double focus of language. For example, the Joycean touch shapes the satirical poem "Ecumenical Council":

> What Bishop, Cardinal
> Will come back the same from Rome?
> Good habit should never roam.
>
> (*CCP.*, 247)

"Habit" refers both to the bishop's and cardinal's gowns and to their conduct. "Roam" is an echo of "Rome" in the second line and ironically implies that the conduct of the Irish clergy should never Rome, that is, replace their insular attitudes with the spirit of the ecumenical movement. Toward the end of the poem, "choleric" suggests cleric and "mitre" implies might. Clarke's self-portrait as "a Temple ogre" puns on his Templeogue home; the lines "Forget that honor/Has been lynched" from "Ex Trivio" implicate an Irish prime minister; and in "The Dead Sea Scrolls" the poet reminds fellow Catholics that "No looking back will change our Lot."[24]

Parody is present in Clarke's work only minimally, as in a line from "A Sermon on Swift" which describes the Dean as "a man who did not know himself from Cain." This suggests both that Swift was brutal to his fellow human beings and that he led two existences, one within the Church and one without. "Irish-American Dignitary" parodies the Irish people's capacity to lionize visitors who are remotely descendant from Ireland. The speaker is a Corkman who quickly rattles off the American bishop's itinerary, proud that His Excellency stayed a

> . . . whole day with us
> To find his father's cot, now dust
> . . . .
> . . . so many kissing
> His ring—God love him!—almost missed
> The waiting liner: that day in Cork
> Had scarcely time for knife and fork.
>
> (*CCP.*, 221)

Maurice Harmon has identified a parody of two patriotic songs, "Who fears to speak of Ninety-Eight" and "Easter Week" ("The Song of 1916"), in the opening lines of Clarke's poem "Celebrations."[25] An ironic commemoration of the Dublin Eucharistic Congress of 1932, held in Ireland, the poem grounds its strategy in the multileveled meaning of its language. Professor Harmon's close reading helps considerably in untangling what he calls "the manner of *Finnegans Wake*" in this poem. He illustrates Clarke's practice of employing multiple meanings by examining three definitions of the word "wart"—a political district, one who is under guardianship, and the edge of a lock, which prevents all but the right key from entering. There are, in addition, other examples of multiple meaning. "The yellow-and-white above the green" is an actual description of the papal flag and a metaphorical depiction of Ireland's political status—

Rome over Dublin. "Ageing politicians pray" for themselves and on the people as the "blindfold woman," both justice and Ireland, "condemns her own for treason." The use of language in "Celebrations" and in Clarke's poetry in general, of course, does not come close to Joyce's great achievement in *Ulysses* and *Finnegans Wake*. Joyce's rhetorical proficiency, his manipulation of style, and his puns and parodies are developed to a degree unmatched by any modern writer. It is clear, however, that Clarke's use of poetic language in these later poems displays a high level of wit and a Joycean concern for wordplay.

The Tradition Repaired

In following a Joycean direction in his poetry, Clarke opted for continuity over tradition. He sensed in Joyce's approach to art an acceptance of the bifurcated Irish mind and a recognition of the Irish experience as being essentially a reflection of a culture dominated by both British politics and Roman Catholic religion. Joyce's treatment of those themes not only made use of national inferiority but also, as Thomas Kinsella has argued, identified modern Irish literature as the product of an intrinsically Irish mind reflecting life as it is lived by most of the people. In the acceptance and portrayal of this particular Irish reality, Joyce connected twentieth-century literature with the Gaelic poets of the seventeenth and eighteenth centuries, who wrote of the experiences of a subjected people.[26]

But Joyce provided Clarke with more than poetic strategy and subject matter. With his deep knowledge and inventive use of popular culture, Joyce democratized the Irish tradition, extending it beyond the heroic sagas and the folk material that animated the revivalists to include the literature and songs of the urban middle class. After Joyce's fiction, particularly *Dubliners* and *Ulysses*, the literary tradition in Ireland expanded to embrace popular urban culture, including the novels of Marie Corelli and the sentimental songs of composers such as J. J.

Malloy.[27] Joyce's portrait of bourgeois culture highlighted by Bloom's imperfect knowledge of literature, science, and cultural history, places the fragments of popular art alongside those of epic poetry, Shakespearean tragedy, and grand opera in order to depict the range and taste of the middle-class mind. Joyce's practice offered Clarke and his contemporaries an example of wide subject matter, reflecting the disjointed condition of the modern consciousness. For his part, Clarke followed Joyce's use of popular culture by drawing from a wide array of everyday material, including newspaper articles, advertisements, children's jingles, and street ballads, to capture the incongruous quality of twentieth-century life.[28] As a good Joycean, however, he blended this popular material with more erudite sources, chiefly in the form of allusions to poetry or to literary and historical figures. In the final phase of his long career, in fact he drew less upon middle-class culture and turned instead to the use of more purely literary sources and traditional materials.

There are scattered references to Clarke's sense of inheritance throughout the later poetry, making for a distinct difference in tone and voice from the early poetry through the 1930s. Beginning with *Ancient Lights* in 1955, his tone becomes more conversational and anecdotal; constant references to history and culture appear in these later poems. Clarke alludes to a number of writers, among them the popular nineteenth-century Anglo-Irish novelists Charles Lever and Samuel Lover, Thomas Moore, James Clarence Mangan, and many of his revivalist acquaintances such as James Stephens, Seamus O'Sullivan, F. R. Higgins, AE, and George Moore. He also refers to the many seventeenth- and eighteenth-century Gaelic poets such as Owen Roe O'Sullivan, Brian Merriman, and the harpist Turlough O'Carolan, whose songs Clarke translates in *Flight to Africa*. Most of these, it is true, appear as passing references and remain essentially undeveloped; yet the allusive element in Clarke's later poems occurs with enough regularity to cause a cumulative effect.

With his free translations of O'Carolan and other seventeenth- and eighteenth-century Gallic poets, Clarke offered another version of Irish literary history to set beside Yeats's indomitable Irishry. By connecting the Gaelic bards with the Anglo-Irish writers, Clarke hoped to demonstrate the vitality of the Irish poetic imagination. His insistence upon tradition confirms the great obsession with identity among Irish poets from Yeats to the present; in Clarke's case, however, we sense a shift toward continuity, a desire not only to acknowledge but to link Gaelic poetic tradition with modern literature. It was a bold attempt to outflank Yeats. In "The Echo at Coole," standing in the Gregory garden, beneath the famous beech tree with the many initials of Irish literati cut into its bark, Clarke has what must be called a historical experience.[29] Reflecting upon Yeats, O'Casey, George Moore, Edward Martin, AE, Lady Gregory, Swift, and—from a more distant past—Carroll O'Daly, a fifteenth-century Gaelic poet, Clarke hears the echoes of their ghostly voices in the garden. As he listens to them he is reminded of the echo poem, first of Yeats's use of it in a draft of "A Prayer for My Daughter," and then of O'Daly's Gaelic version. Linking O'Daly with Yeats, Clarke composes his own poem and pays tribute to the important echoes that shaped his own poetic voice:

> "Echo, whereabouts can you hear
> From?"
>> *Here.*
>> "My task in the future, can I know?"
>> *No.*
>>> "Must I still hope, still body on?"
>>>> *On.*
> "Yet how can I be certain my way is right?"
> *Write.*
>> "Tell me what thoughts had Carroll O'Daly,
> Swift,
> Who called on other echoes, lonely as you?"
>>>> *Yew.*
>>> (*CCP.*, 401)

To establish continuity in the Irish tradition, Clarke sought to reclaim both his Anglo-Irish and Gaelic past. The Gaelic element in his poetry, including the adaptation of prosody and the free translations of seventeenth- and eighteenth-century poems and harp songs, remained important throughout his career; even in his final poems he was applying Gaelic rhyming patterns. The Anglo-Irish heritage became increasingly important to him in his old age because of his fascination with its two most prominent writers, Swift and Yeats. Yeats, as we have seen, was a lifelong preoccupation, one that Clarke frequently dreaded. Swift, on the other hand, fascinated him. As a poet frequently at odds with his society, Clarke felt a deep personal identification with Swift as a fellow Dubliner who satirized mankind. Moreover, Clarke's concern for an expanded literary tradition encouraged him to look to Swift as one of his poetic ancestors. In "A Sermon on Swift," one of his last poems, Clarke reveals the personal and the poetic significance he attaches to Swift's life and his work. Early in the poem Clarke announces that he must speak the truth about Swift, since what is known about him, either from Dublin legend or from scholarly commentaries, emphasizes his serious and tragic aspects. Clarke takes issue especially with Yeats, whose romantic vision of Swift dwells on the lacerated heart of his famous epitaph. Clarke's Swift, on the other hand, is a humorous and eccentric character,

> . . . the chuckling rhymster who went,
> Bald-headed, into the night when modesty
> Wantoned with beau and belle, his pen in hand
> Dull morning clapped his oldest wig on.
>
> (*CCP.*, 457)

Not surprisingly, since it corroborated his view of the man, Clarke saw Swift the writer as a comic-ironist, one who wrote about "privy matters." In the actual text of his "sermon," which is a discussion of Swift's poetry, Clarke directs his remarks to the witty and the scatological.[30]

Clarke's view of Swift is understandable when we recognize the autobiographical elements in the poem. For interspersed throughout the discussion of Swift's character and his writings, a second subject emerges, that of Clarke himself, or, more specifically, the connection between Clarke and Swift. This connection is developed by means of the various asides in the poem, which interrupt Clarke's treatment of Swift and replace it with personal narrative, moments from Clarke's life in which Swift was significant. There is mention of Clarke's discovery as a young man of the ironic humor in *Gulliver's Travels* and in the scatological poems, and of his treatment at Saint Patrick's Hospital for the mentally ill, founded by Swift. There is even a suggestion that Swift may be looking down with approval on Clarke as he is speaking:

> Scarce had I uttered the words,
> "Dear Friends
> Dear Swiftians"
>
> —when from the eastern window
> The pure clear ray, that Swift had known, entered the
> Shady church and touched my brow.
> (*CCP.*, 458)

All of these circumstances, combined with the dramatic event framing the poem—Clarke standing in Swift's pulpit, giving a sermon—fulfill Clarke's intention to show his genuine affinity with the eighteenth-century writer. Having established this kinship, Clarke then found it easy to expand upon his relationship with Swift: "Swift wrote of privy matters/That have to be my text." In calling attention to the ribaldry in Gulliver's adventures with the Brobdingnagian maidens and the indelicate actions of Celia, Corinna, and Chloe, those characters from the well-known scatological poetry, Clarke invites those who know his own works to sense its Swiftian aspects.

Humorous treatment of sexuality occurs in a number of Clarke's later poems, and one in particular compares with

Swift's comic treatment of the "privy matters" of the marriage night in "Strephon and Chloe." "Phallomeda," Clarke's retelling of the misadventures of the Irish god the Dagda, achieves its comic effect by contrasting idealized sexual desire and realistic physical limitation. As in "Strephon and Chloe," the tension in "Phallomeda" becomes humorous through the exaggeration of the physical. The excessive appetite of the Dagda causes him to eat gigantic portions of porridge, swelling his stomach to monstrous size. When he catches sight of the beautiful and alluring goddess Phallomeda, he is eager but incapacitated. The details of the situation are particularly Swiftian.

> His stomach was bulging out with gusto
> Below her bosom, but his lust
> Held him in bonds, he could not burst from.
>   He clasped her, toppled off,
> Rolled over with a double bound
> Impatiently trying to mount himself
> But was unable to rebound:
>   The goddess was on top.
>
> She budded with hope on that mighty paunch
> Pink, white, as he grabbed her by the haunches
> So hard that she was scarcely conscious:
>   Bonnie bush out of reach.
> Then, side by side, they sank. She fumbled
> To fire his godhead while he clumsied,
> Till she could hear the porridge mumble
>   Slapdash as foreign speech.
>
>   (CCP., 454)

Although Swiftian humor surfaces regularly in Clarke's later poems, the obvious link between the two writers occurs in the practice of satire. It was chiefly as a satirist and a critic of society that Clarke was rediscovered in the late 1950s, and commentators have suggested a Swiftian influence on his work.[31] Clarke sensed his own work to be Swiftian in its exposure of hypocrisy, vice, or folly; Swift's combined identities of satirist, wit, poet, Irish patriot, and Dubliner proved irresistible to Clarke.

In his later poems Clarke successfully establishes himself as an original poet, facing up to personal problems and issues of modern life and preferring the ironic to the romantic mode. The clipped syntax, the simple diction, and the sparse imagery in these lines from "Usufruct" are characteristic:

> This house cannot be handed down.
> Before the scriven ink is brown
> Clergy will sell the lease of it.
> I live here, thinking, ready to flit
> From Templeogue, but not at ease.
> I hear the flood unclay the trees.
> Road-stream of traffic.
>
> > (*CCP.*, 207)

The tight-lipped style of this poem shows Yeatsian influence in diction and rhythm combined with a style that had come into its own. The culmination of Clarke's late stylistic development can be seen clearly in the intensely personal "Mnemosyne Lay in Dust," where the language has been boiled down to express the most basic of human experiences, the sense of self, the question of identity:

> Once, getting out of bed, he peeped
> Into the dormitory. Sheet
> And slip were laundry-white. Dazes
> Of electric light came down. Patients
> Stirred fitfully. Their fidgetting marred
> With scrawls the whiteness of the ward,
> Gift of the moon. He wondered who
> He was, but memory had hidden
> All. Someone sat beside him, drew
> > Chair nearer, murmured; "Think!"
> . . . .
> Often he stared into the mirror
> Beside the window, hand-drawn by fear
> He seemed to know that bearded face
> In it, the young man, tired and pale,
> Half smiling. Gold-capped tooth in front
> Vaguely reminded him of someone.
> Who was it? Nothing came to him.

> He saw that smile again. Gold dot
> Still gleamed. The bearded face was drawn
> With sufferings he had forgotten.
>
> (CCP., 330,m 332)

The focus of "Mnemosyne" is on Clarke's own mental break-down and recovery, a subject that took him over forty years to treat in poetry. Such deeply personal and psychological material demanded a poetic style that could reflect the essentials of experience. Clarke opted for a distinct leanness in language which would reflect the struggle of the protagonist, Maurice DeVane, to comprehend reality. In the following excerpt describing Maurice's confinement in a padded cell, the staccato delivery adds to the tension of the narrative:

> Suddenly heart began to beat
> Too quickly, too loudly . . .
> Key turned. Body was picked up, carried
> Beyond the ward, the bedwhite row
> Of faces, into a private darkness.
> Lock turned. He cried out. All was still.
> He stood, limbs shivering in the chill.
>
> (CCP., 335)

The starkness of "Lock turned. He cried out. All was still" and the sense of the impersonal in the loss of the pronoun in "heart" and "body" show Clarke's modern style at its laconic best, thoroughly disciplined and very intense. This stylistic achievement is the result of a deliberate effort in the later poetry to prune any excesses of language, a direction that began with *Night and Morning*, when Clarke moved consciously away from a Yeatsian poetic toward a Joycean realism.

Accommodating the Master

Clarke could not rid himself of Yeats that easily, however; indeed, in a number of the later poems Yeats emerges as the central subject. Some of these, drawing upon Clarke's personal experiences, deal unfavorably with Yeats, focusing on aspects of his personality, on his dominating hold on the Irish literary scene, and on his special coolness to Clarke himself. Occasionally, Clarke yielded to the temptation to show Yeats's ridiculous and pompous side. In one poem Clarke describes himself walking in Gregory's wood as a young literary pilgrim; he spies someone in a bright, sky-blue raincoat, dragging the fierce fishing tackle of a country gentleman. The ironic, urbane description betrays Clarke's sentiments:

> Was it a spirit that eyed me
> Or the great peacock that Yeats made out of pride?
>
> Later in a small house across the road,
> He talked to me of Walter Savage Landor
> And, then, of the Jacobeans. Upright, he rode
> The classical mount, though portly as a landlord,
> Brown shooting-jacket unbuttoned, waved his hand.
> The board was set, the dishes in a row
> And I sat down to lunch. His young wife, George,
> Left us together. Still in that Georgian mansion.
>
> (CCP., 414)

Other poems, however, demonstrate Clarke's genuine admiration for Yeats's enormous achievement.

> Often I thought, only a stone's throw
> From him at Riversdale, of that old man
> Still seeking his perfection, still in the throes
> Of verse, yet every word at his command.
>
> (CCP., 397)

This ambiguity becomes more interesting when we consider that the presence of Yeats goes beyond the poems themselves and can be seen in the very pattern of Clarke's artistry, a pattern that suggests an imitation of Yeats's career. There are the early Celtic poems and Clarke's attempts at a Yeatsian metaphor with the Gaelic medieval materials. Yeats's dramatization of his literary and political friends was undoubtedly the inspiration for

Clarke's treatment of his elders in *The Echo at Coole*. The satirical poetry in *Flight to Africa* with its biting social criticism finds its equivalent in Yeats's *Responsibilities*. In addition, Clarke so admired Yeatsian verse dramas that he wrote more than twenty verse plays in the Yeatsian manner and spent a good portion of his creative energy trying to revive Yeats's theater in Dublin during the 1940s and early 1950s. Finally, something that the publication of *Collected Poems* in 1974 allowed us to see for the first time: the chronology of Clarke's poetic development looks particularly Yeatsian—first the narrative poetry based on Irish materials, then the autobiographical poems, the fascination and the preoccupation as an older writer with the subject of sex, and, finally, the return to Irish materials in the last poems.

It is tempting, given this resemblance, to make more of Thomas Kinsella's phrase that Yeats "always hypnotized him [Clarke], even from the grave," that Clarke's entire career was haunted by a Yeatsian specter. To do so, however, would be to misread Clarke's idiosyncratic voice in the later poetry and to overlook his eventual recognition of Yeats's importance to his own poetry. Clarke's commitment in his later work to humanistic and artistic values that opposed the commercialism and materialism of the middle class resembles Yeats's own position in the 1920s and 1930s. Moreover, Clarke's interest in the continuity of an Irish tradition eventually overcame his anxiety and spite; he accepted Yeats as an essential part of his own literary heritage, one whose contribution he both acknowledged and promoted.

Shortly after Yeats's death, Clarke described the great void in Irish writing which he felt personally, despite his mixed feelings about Yeats: "In these days of our new materialistic Irish state, poetry will have a harder, less picturesque task. But the loss of Yeats and all that boundless activity, in a country where the mind is feared and avoided, leaves a silence which it is painful to contemplate."[32] Clarke's own effort to prevent that silence involved heading a group of verse readers who kept Yeats's ideas of theater alive, a commitment of over ten years which eventually led to a kind of one-sided reconciliation.

The plays of Yeats were re-enacted.
Our Lyric Company, verse-speakers,
Actors, had put them on without
A doit for eleven years. We hired
The theatre, profaned the Sabbath
With magic, speculation: *The Countess
Cathleen, The Only Jealousy
Of Emer, Deirdre,* even *The Herne's Egg,*
Moon-mad as Boyne. *The Death of Cuchullin:*
We borrowed a big drum, clarionet, from
The Transport Workers' Union. Ann Yeats
Found in the *Peacock* cellar masks
Dulac had moulded.
             So I forgot
His enmity.
             My own plays were seen there,
Ambiguous in the glow of battens,
Abbot, monk, sinner, black-out of Ireland.
Finis.

                    (*CCP.*, 249)

In one of the last public poems he wrote, "The Stump" from *A Sermon on Swift* (1968), Clarke, secure in his identity as a poet and perhaps even as an elder literary statesman, pays Yeats the ultimate compliment by defending the Yeatsian world against philistine intrusion. The significance of the situation ought not to be missed, for it illuminates Clarke's commitment to literary tradition and, more important, to a sense of continuity within that tradition. In these final poems, he sets aside his former criticism of Yeats—of the Ascendancy reserve and the indifference toward younger writers—and instead praises the values of a former culture in a characteristically Yeatsian confrontation between the poet and the merchant class:

                    Occult
Voices seemed to be leaving
The Seven Woods sold for a song—
Five hundred pounds—to Malachi
Bourke by the Forestry

Department; with the great key
of Coole. So he pulled down
For copper, lead and slate,
A house still remembered abroad,
Untimbered the estate
With cross-cut saw, chain, pulley.
But true to the prophecy
In an old broadsheet,
He failed to make a profit.
Our city trees were impressed.
Words stood their ground.

(*CCP.*, 479)

Toward the very end of his life, Clarke remained the Irish poet, connecting, extending, in this case repairing the poetic tradition. The final poems, the very last that he wrote before his death in 1974, bring the poet full circle, in "The Healing of Mis" and "The Wooing of Becfola," back to the material of Irish legend and folklore.

The Irish Writer

The final assessment of Clarke's importance as a twentieth-century Irish writer emphasizes, but does not solely depend upon, the achievement of the poetry. For one thing, as his editor Thomas Kinsella has admitted, the work is uneven, some of it disappointing.[33] This unevenness comes in part, no doubt, from Clarke's long period of poetic silence, from 1938 until 1955, when he wrote, directed, and performed in verse theater; part of it is due to his interest in topical poetry, and that he could be obscure or even private in his meaning. Much of the poetry is strong, nonetheless, and interesting, particularly in light of Irish literary history. The significance of Clarke's role in the modern Irish tradition becomes clear when we view the poetry in connection with his other work: the plays, the criticism, the fiction, and the autobiography, all deliberate reflections of an Irish sensibility.

The total output of three novels, more than a dozen plays, two books of memoirs, countless book reviews and articles, and two books of criticism, in addition to the poetry, constitutes a remarkable achievement if for no other reason than the steady labor necessary to produce it.[34] Throughout fifty years of writing, Clarke persisted in defining and establishing continuity within a literary tradition. His memoirs describe the awakening of consciousness and the call to art during the turbulent formation of the Irish Free State and the waning of the Irish Revival. In his two books of criticism, *The Celtic Twilight and the Nineties* (1969) and particularly *Poetry in Modern Ireland* (1951), he attempts to account for the unique antimodernist roots of twentieth-century Irish poetry and to explain the special qualities that set it off from English literature. Both the memoirs and the criticism reflect literary values that would influence the new generation of poets who would publish their first poems in the late 1950s and 1960s. These younger writers recognized in Austin Clarke a transitional figure, whose career spanned the romantic preoccupations of the Revival and the critical realism of contemporary literature. They sensed his importance as someone who in his search for continuity made the identification with the Irish tradition his essential preoccupation.

5

Tradition and Continuity II: Patrick Kavanagh

Austin Clarke's struggle with revivalism was a long-suffering affair, fought for the most part in private and manifested in the poetic process gradually over a period of twenty-five years as he moved from romanticism to a realistic view of modern Irish life. For Patrick Kavanagh, however, reaction to the Revival required very little incubation. Almost concurrently with his arrival upon the Dublin literary scene, Kavanagh became a fervent iconoclast, attacking the Irish Literary Revival for its romantic pretensions and its false view of life. Throughout the 1940s and early 1950s he made antirevivalism the central issue of his ideas on literature and art. Moreover, he waged his struggle openly and as regularly as possible, in his poetry, in literary journals, in newspapers and magazines, and in the public house, the most open of all forums in Dublin, assailing both the Revival and its many practitioners.

Kavanagh's strategy evolved from an acute sense of the need for survival. Rather than confront a single figure or become obsessed with one achievement, as so many of his contemporaries had done with the great Yeats, Kavanagh sought to take on the entire literary establishment. Born in Inniskeen in rural County Monaghan, he smarted from what he called "the English-bred lie": the glorification of the peasant in Ireland and the idealization of rural life. Kavanagh came to Dublin as the authentic number, someone who actually had lived off the land, to do battle with false prophets and to clear his own imaginative space. Almost immediately, he set out to shatter the myths of the Revival, creatively misreading the canon of modern Irish literature to insure his own poetic survival. Virtually every Irish writer of the twentieth century save Joyce felt the lash of Kavanagh's criticism, particularly contemporary rivals who, like Austin Clarke, were seeking their own room in the already crowded Dublin literary world in the late 1930s and 1940s.

Kavanagh's attack on Clarke sheds considerable light on the anxiety of the post-Yeatsian poet and on Kavanagh's own peculiar way of coping with his literary competitors. Building his literary reputation in the early stages of his career, Kavanagh continually stressed Clarke's romanticism, placing him among the fabricators and propagandists of the Revival and conveniently overlooking his important turn to realism in the 1938 book *Night and Morning*. This misreading of Clarke was an essential exercise for Kavanagh; a more straightforward reading would reveal the great similarities between his own work and Clarke's. Both poets as young men read and were inspired by the poetry of the Revival; both grew to sense the limitations of the revivalist formula; both became more critical and satirical; and both were influenced by Joyce and cultivated a Joycean dimension in their works. Clarke identified with Dublin's Joyce, as we have seen, particularly in his subject matter, his interest in language, and his special use of the city as a backdrop. Kavanagh was attracted more to Joycean methodology and adapted Joyce's celebration of the local and of ordinary experience to his own descriptions of life in rural Monaghan. Moreover, as it proved for Clarke, the treatment of Catholicism became an essential theme for Kavanagh, a further indication of the importance of Joyce for both poets.

Kavanagh's self-proclaimed iconoclastic isolationism in Irish literary affairs, then, should be seen as a promotional strategy rather than as a true indication of poetic sensibility and ideology. It is certainly true that for most of his career, Kavanagh remained estranged from the closed-in Dublin literati, but much of this estrangement was the result of the gossipy viciousness of that milieu; it is also true, however, that Kavanagh cultivated and perpetuated the role of outsider so that he might take certain liberties as a "character," a Dublin word for eccentric. Intellectually and artistically, Kavanagh was very much at home among the group of writers after Yeats, the generation of Clarke, Sean O'Faolain, and Frank O'Connor, who recognized the perils of the Revival and attempted to strike out in new directions. These writers shared the transitional moment in modern Irish literature, when a majority of them shifted from romance to realism, recognizing the necessity of a delicate balance and of drawing strength and orientation from a literary tradition without being swamped or absorbed by it.

Despite these connections with his contemporaries, however, Kavanagh sought isolation; moreover, his response to the problem of tradition sets him apart. Of all the writers of his generation, none chose to deal so aggressively and so negatively with the immediate past as he did. Both *The Green Fool* (1938) and *Tarry Flynn* (1947), Kavanagh's autobiographical *Küntsler-romane*, describe the difficulties facing a young man of poetic sensibility who lived among pragmatic farmers in rural Ireland. Kavanagh was persistent, however, educating himself by reading and writing after hours or during breaks from his farm work. By 1929, at the age of twenty-four, he had published his first poems, in AE's *Irish Statesman* and in Seamus O'Sullivan's *Dublin Magazine*.[1] These early pieces are vague, romantic impressions of nature, the kind of poetry we might expect from a dreamy youth with literary aspirations. The lines compound visions and drown in emotional intensity, despite their insistence upon distance.

> Rapt to starriness—not quite
> I go through fields and fens of night,
> The nameless, the void
> Where ghostly poplars whisper to
> A silent countryside.

Not black or blue,
Grey or red or tan
The skies I travel under.
A strange unquiet wonder.
Indian
Vision and Thunder.

Splendours of Greek,
Egypt's cloud-woven glory
Speak not more, speak
Speak no more
A thread-worn story.[2]

Publication, however, encouraged the young bard, as the locals called him, and he continued to read and write and to send out poems to various journals and newspapers.

In the autumn of 1930, Kavanagh set off on his famous three-day walk to Dublin, where he met AE and others, receiving encouragement and the loan of many books.[3] He returned to Monaghan a changed man. By 1939 he had left the farm for good to settle in Dublin, attracted to the city for the publishing opportunities it would provide, the libraries, newspapers, and—most of all—the promise of literary conversation and friendships. Living in the city, however, Kavanagh soon became disillusioned. He was struck by the closeness and the pretension of the literary subculture, especially its inbred ideas and conversation. More striking surely for the young hopeful poet from the country was the sheer number of poets and writers in Dublin, some of them with established reputations, others struggling like himself, but all of them his competitors. Like the young Yeats nearly fifty years before, Kavanagh sensed that success as a writer depended upon making oneself unique, thereby reducing, if not eliminating, one's competition.

Kavanagh's dilemma cannot be underestimated, I think, since it typifies the one faced by many Irish writers of his generation. In part it can be explained by the presence of Yeats, whose death in 1939 ironically worsened the literary climate in Dublin for new writers. For as the critics set to work measuring Yeats's accomplishment, they necessarily neglected the work of younger poets. What little critical attention these young poets did receive centered upon the inevitable comparison with Yeats, which tied them more emphatically to him and slighted their own individual achievement. As Donald Davie has suggested, "for Irish poets . . . Yeats must figure as the great ventriloquist, if they relax their concentration for a second, or become any more familiar than they must with the highly distinctive Yeatsian idiom and cadence, they find themselves sitting on the great ventriloquist's knee, using not their own voice but his."[4]

For Kavanagh, the situation was even more complex. He faced not only the formidable challenge of Yeats but also the closed ranks of the Dublin literary crowd. Most of the established writers resented a new talent, since it meant further competition in already crowded circumstances. Thus, to protect themselves they greeted Kavanagh's arrival on the Dublin scene with characteristic reductive humor, seizing upon his raw-boned physique, his unpolished manner, his poverty, and most of all his country background.[5] He was held up as the genuine article of a Revival fiction, the peasant-poet from the bog, capable of stirring poetic utterances yet simple to the core. The identification as the peasant-poet was calculated to be ironical; those who called attention to Kavanagh's rustic ways did so not to celebrate his talent and genius but rather to place him beyond the pale of Irish letters.

Criticism

Finding himself stifled by this derisive atmosphere, Kavanagh hatched a scheme that would serve both as a counterattack against his detractors and as a strategy to establish his credentials as a serious and original writer. The heart of the scheme involved the rejection of revivalism and the dismissal of the importance of nationality in literature. He denied the essence of the Revival—the idealization of rural Ireland and the celebration of the peasant—and he pronounced modern Irish writing to be imitation rather than invention, produced by traders in clichés. These proclamations were to be at the center of his criticism throughout the 1940s and early 1950s. Again and again he attacked the stagnant quality of the literature produced by his contemporaries. In a letter to his brother, Kavanagh writes, "Of the Irish movement you know plenty . . . they presented an essentially sentimental Ireland. . . . The Yeats-Synge phoney Ireland was eminently suited for export to America and it has falsified the picture of this country."[6] This falseness in literature he identified as the "Irish thing," a contrived pastoralism in much of the poetry and the tedious reworking of the folktales and legends of ancient Ireland.

Kavanagh's main line of attack was to focus on those poets who wished to be called "Irish." Nationalism was too inward-looking, he claimed; it bred cant, jingoism, and propaganda, not art.

> Poetry is not Irish or any other nationality; and when writers such as Messrs. Clarke, Farren and the late F. R. Higgins pursue Irish-ness as a poetic end they are merely exploiting incidental local colour. Strip their writings of this local colour and see what re-mains. . . . A great many Protestants seeking roots in this country have attempted to build the national myth into a spiritual reality—Irish horses, Irish soldiers, Irish dogs, Irish poets. There is no poetic merit in the adjective Irish though mediocrity tries to put itself across on this fortuitous and empty distinction.[7]

Irishness was in poetry and fiction what the stage-Irishman had become in theater: a stereotype, thoroughly predictable. "I object to Nationalism, particularly Irish nationalism in letters," Kavanagh writes in a critical essay, "because of the harm it does, the false values it postulates."[8] The minor writers and secondary talents chose nationalism and Irishness because they lacked conviction about the sustaining powers of their own imaginative visions:

> In the corner of a Dublin pub
> This party opens-blub-a-blub-
> Paddy Whiskey, Rum and Gin
> Paddy Three sheets in the wind;
> Paddy of the Celtic Mist,
> Paddy Connemara West,
> Chestertonian Paddy Frog
> Croaking nightly in the bog.
> All the Paddies having fun
> Since Yeats handed in his gun.
>
> (*KCP.*, 212)

Thus Kavanagh describes these writers, not as genuine creative artists but as by-products of the excitement and energy initiated by Yeats and his generation. "The Irish Literary Revival consisted of a few writers of real quality and a large crowd of hangers-on pretending to be drunk on the fumes of the cask. Then—the warm fog lifted, and people began to wonder what had happened to all the young geniuses."[9]

With this constant criticism of the Revival, Kavanagh hoped to accomplish negatively what Yeats had achieved through the use of Celtic materials: an artistic autonomy through a governing fiction, a chance to set himself apart from other writers and to provide himself with some clear ground. By attacking individual writers and general literary trends in Ireland, Kavanagh created a void demanding to be filled by the new poetry he would write. The strategy allowed him to have it both ways. Taken as a peasant-poet by the Dublin literati, he attacked their provincialism; characterizing their work as the worn-out baggage of the Revival, he justified his own poetry.

While Kavanagh's critical attitudes toward the Irish school of literature are consistent in their disdain and censure, his treatment of W. B. Yeats as part of that school is more ambiguous. Occasionally, he blamed Yeats for his role in perpetrating the Irish movement and for the resulting limitations in his poetry: "Yeats took up Ireland and made it his myth and theme. And you can see him today standing in the centre of that myth, uneasy that he doesn't belong."[10] And elsewhere, carrying on his familiar debunking of the Revival, Kavanagh singles out Yeats's Celtic phase: "the work of Yeats which is deliberately Irish in this way sounds awfully phony. Irishness is a form of anti-art."[11] At other times, paradoxically, he attributed the fundamental weakness in Yeats's poetry to not being Irish enough. Commenting on the importance of the primitive in the Irish imagination, Kavanagh claims that Yeats was too refined and theoretical in his poetry:

> . . . now that he [Yeats] is dead we might ever regret that he did not suffer enough from Irish barbarism. Yeats, protected to some extent by the Nationalistic movement, wrote out of a somewhat protected world and so his work does not touch life deeply.[12]

As much as Kavanagh would have liked to dismiss Yeats's achievement, in the end he could not, despite his penchant for denigrating all other writers whose work could be compared with his own. In fact, as Austin Clarke found himself doing in his own criticism, Kavanagh often acknowledged Yeats's achievement, poetic genius, and, particularly, his prominence in modern poetry. He commends Yeats for the artistry and the vitality in the poems. But Kavanagh could never quite commit himself; even in the recognition of Yeats's greatness, the praise sometimes came begrudgingly and mixed with censure:

> Yeats, until his old age, worked a precious and very narrow vein of ore. It was only towards the end that he saw the potentialities of mass-production. . . . Yeats had the misfortune to come at a bad time; in the wake of Victorianism. His material was a weary parochial thing; Irish nationalism. Yet he has a good deal of the voracious appetite and digestion of a great poet.[13]

Furthermore, recognition and praise are often uttered sotto voce, since the real subject of all Kavanagh criticism is Kavanagh himself, and its aim self-aggrandizement, especially at the expense of rival poets and novelists. It is characteristic, therefore, that the respect shown for Yeats's art comes often during commentary on other poets' failures or shortcomings, which the following jab at Kavanagh's contemporaries makes clear:

> The poems being written are like perfectly laid-out corpses on a slab. They are perfectly shaped and perfectly dead. . . . One of the qualities I most admired about Yeats was his contempt for death. During the lifetime of Yeats that living poem appeared again and again . . . the imitators of Yeats are to be pitied rather than censured, as are all who walk the barren fields where the master reaped.[14]

While this wavering aggravates the reader eager for a genuine critical assessment of one Irish poet by another, it points nonetheless to an interesting tendency on Kavanagh's part to avoid any real consideration of Yeats's poetry and to focus instead on his personality or, even more removed, on the Yeats industry. The ambiguity toward Yeats is understandable from a psychological point of view, considering Kavanagh's alienation from the Dublin literary scene and his desire to become a great poet. His vacillation between censure and praise and his consistent reluctance to examine Yeats's work reflect his uneasiness about writing in the proximity of a major talent. By refusing to lionize Yeats and by demonstrating subjectivity in the criticism, Kavanagh showed the important need to establish a certain sense of personal artistic authority. The fact that this need drove him to pose regularly as a literary crank underscores the urgency of his situation; he desperately wanted to escape poetic influence and, at the same time, to distance himself from the Dublin literary crowd that rejected him.

It is important to recognize that Kavanagh's quarrel with Yeats was confused, inconsistent, and forced. The instinct for survival in a crowded literary world caused Kavanagh to become a revisionist, which in turn led him to a purposeful misreading of Yeats simply because he was connected with the Revival. In some cases, of course, Kavanagh's criticism of revivalism has real merit, as in his censure of F. R. Higgins. With Yeats, however, his critical focus is blurred by conflicting designs.

Kavanagh's revisionism forced him to select, interpret, and eventually define the Yeats against whom he did battle. In doing so he obscured the issue deliberately, neglecting the depth and the variety of Yeats's poetry and ignoring the fact that Yeats himself grew weary of revivalism quite early in his career, especially as the mode began to spawn so many imitators. As he did with Clarke's work, Kavanagh chose to overlook crucial aspects of Yeats's poetic development because they exposed and even contradicted his critical dicta and weakened his own role as an iconoclast.

About Joyce, Kavanagh was less uneasy and more definitive. He admired Joyce as the writer who captured the essence of Irish life while at the same time rejecting nationalism. Joyce's criticism of revivalism even as a young writer and his interest in realism and world literature did much to shape Kavanagh's sensibilities. Kavanagh's hard line against romanticism and his realistic portrayal of rural life were modeled upon Joyce's artistic success in treating the raw, unpleasant, and even sordid side of living in Ireland. Indeed, the famous distinction Kavanagh made between parochialism and provincialism grew out of Joycean practice:

> Parochialism and provincialism are direct opposites. The provincial has no mind of his own; he does not trust what his eyes see until he has heard what the metropolis—toward which his eyes are turned—has to say on any subject. . . . The parochial mentality on the other hand is never in any doubt about the validity of his parish. All great civilisations are based on parochialism—Greek, Israelite, English.[15]

For Kavanagh, Joyce was the parochialist par excellence, the writer who captured every detail of his parish and turned it into universal significance. Moreover, it was Joyce's interest in the ordinary which put him in touch with life, giving his writing a quality that Yeats never achieved. The importance of the familiar, the significance of the common, and the vitality of the local— these are the Joycean slants Kavanagh sought to develop in his own writing. To reflect the simple details of life rather than to aim at abstract, high-minded subjects—this was the meaning of Joyce's legacy.

> The exciting quality about Joyce is that when you read him you are not told of the large public issues that were agitating the minds of politicians and journalists in those days. Joyce is interested in the mind of a man who has put five shillings on a horse. Joyce takes the unimportant private lives of people and shows that in the end these private lives are the only lives that matter.[16]

Kavanagh followed this strategy throughout his poetic career. In one of his last commentaries on his own writing, he reiterates his commitment to the ordinary details of life:

> Stupid poets and artists think that by taking subjects of public importance it will help their work to survive. There is nothing as dead and as damned as an important thing. The things that really matter are casual, insignificant little things.[17]

Kavanagh's clarity and consistency on Joyce appear as rare exceptions in what is otherwise a weather-vane approach to literary criticism. Much of this confusion resulted from a conflict of purpose; Kavanagh's criticism of Yeats, for example, ranges between censure and praise, as we have seen. But the focus on Yeats appears blurred for another reason, which demonstrates Kavanagh's acute awareness of his immediate competition. It was largely Kavanagh's own contemporaries and not Yeats himself whom Kavanagh wished to displace; revivalism, then, rather than Yeats, was the real target. Thus when it suited him, Kavanagh could ally himself with Yeats—the implication was that they were equals—when, for example, he belittled those writers who attempted to climb in under Yeats's umbrella. In a letter to his brother written in December 1950, Kavanagh places himself in august company: "There have been, besides myself, only two or possibly three good writers, Joyce, Yeats, O'Casey."[18] From this vantage point he criticizes his contemporaries for revivalism—a slavish imitation of Irish materials and subject matter—and identifies an inanimate condition in Irish letters, caused by beating to death Yeats's tired circus animals. Once he minimized the achievements of his rivals, it was a simple matter for Kavanagh himself to fill the void with a new kind of poetry, unmistakable in its originality, reflecting a hard-wrung knowledge of the land and depicting rural Ireland realistically, as beautiful but backbreaking.

Poetic Realism

Kavanagh's very early poetry, *Ploughman and Other Poems* (1936), starts tamely enough with nature poems very much in the Irish mode. These celebrate the land's beauty, treat folktales and rural legends, and, as one can infer from the title of the volume, even exploit the concept of the peasant-poet, walking his fields and composing verse:

> I turn the lea-green down
> Gaily now,
> And paint the meadow brown
> With my plough.
>
> I dream with silvery gull
> And brazen crow.
> A thing that is beautiful
> I may know.
>
> (*KCP.*, 1)

The treatment of folk material in these early pieces, both in subject matter and in rhythm and sound, suggests an affinity with revivalist poetry. Moreover, the presence of Yeats is very apparent:

> I shall drink of the white goat's milk,
> The old white goal of Slieve Donard,
> Slieve Donard where the herbs of wisdom grow,
> The herbs of the Secret of Life that the old white
> goat has nibbled,

> And I shall live longer than Methuselah,
> Brother to no man.
>
> (KCP., 5)

In all of these early poems, in fact, we sense the imitation and repetition of the literature of the Revival, the very Irish mode that Kavanagh so bitterly denounces in his essays. It is precisely this, as we know from the criticism, that the poet fears: to write your own poetry only to remind your reader of another poet or, worse, a literary movement. Undoubtedly, Kavanagh saw the inevitable difficulty with these early poems and recognized that they were an artistic dead-end. They were a necessary stage, however, part of the struggle to achieve a poetic integrity and an independence of imagination. It is a tribute to Kavanagh as a poet that he understood the complexities of influence this early in his career. Within three years of the publication of *Ploughman,* he had not only freed himself of the seductive influence of the Revival, but he had sounded a truly unique note in Irish poetry, diverting its course away from the romantic, pastoral tendencies of his contemporaries.

In 1942, with the publication of "The Great Hunger," Kavanagh delivered the deathblow to what he saw as the essence of the Revival's falsity, the idealistic portrayal of those who live close to the soil. Instead of lofty sentiment based on spiritual naturalism, Kavanagh presented the grim details of humble, rural life—the rocky hills, potato pits, piles of dung, hard work, long days, monotonous routine. "The Great Hunger" is a long poem—756 lines—describing the life of Patrick Maguire, who farms an unnamed area in the hills of rural Ireland. It presents with painstaking exactness Maguire's attempts to survive physically, psychologically, and emotionally. The poem opens with direct reference to the land:

> Clay is the word and clay is the flesh
> Where the potato-gatherers like mechanised scarecrows
>   move
> Along the side-fall of the hill—Maguire and his men.

From the outset, however, we are far from revivalist pastoralism, sentimentality, and idealism. We see instead rusty ploughs, broken buckets, ditches, frozen ground, and the slow, steady evaporation of the human life-force:

> Watch him, that man on a hill whose spirit
> Is a wet sack flapping about the knees of time
> He lives that his little fields may stay fertile when
>   his own body
> Is spread in the bottom of a ditch under two coulters
>   in Christ's name.

The force of this poem does not come simply from the realistic description of potato and turnip farming, though the harshness of that life is vividly portrayed. It comes, rather, from the story of Maguire himself, whose great hunger is spiritual, intellectual, and sexual. He cares for his mother, who lives to ninety-one:

> She stayed too long,
> Wife and mother in one
> When she died
> The knuckle-bones were cutting the skin of her
>   son's backside
> And he was sixty-five.

He takes no wife while he has other cares; he always waits for better luck, a good harvest, another year, the right woman. Always there is the routine, the work, the woman he sins with in his mind, his guilt, and, at night before the fire, his dreams. The rigid morality of his church closes around him and guilt-ridden responsibility traps him. In the end Maguire never marries and lives out his old age in loneliness, beaten down by his narrow existence. A farmer whose livelihood depends on things thriving and growing, he nevertheless withers:

> No crash
> No drama
> That was how his life happened.
> No mad hooves galloping in the sky,

> But the weak, washy way of true tragedy—
> A sick horse nosing around the meadow for a clean
>   place to die.
>
> <div align="right">(<i>KCP.</i>, 79–104)</div>

The portrait of rural life in "The Great Hunger" spares no detail in its attempt to counter what Kavanagh saw as the false view of the land fashioned by Yeats and Lady Gregory. In an essay written in 1904, Yeats claims that the greatness of Irish literature came from its peasantry, whose simple and hard lives, unbroken religious faith, and traditional beliefs fostered a lively poetic imagination, a passion, and a profound sense of the spiritual.[19] Years later, in "The Municipal Gallery Revisited," Yeats identifies the importance to his own work of that imaginative strength which emanates from the country:

> John Synge, I and Augusta Gregory, thought
> All that we did, all that we said or sang
> Must come from contact with the soil, from that
> Contact everything Antaeus-like grew strong.[20]

Exploiting the irony that Yeats and others who imitated him were essentially urban writers whose understanding of the land and of country people was sentimental and idealizing, Kavanagh sought to depict a genuine contact with the soil and to demonstrate the hostility of rural life to the poetic imagination. We sense in the consistency and depth of the portrait of Maguire's world—the hard work, the poverty of mind and body, and the suffocating closeness of a village community—a bitterness behind the lines, an angry corrective to those poets who would celebrate the beauty and simplicity of rural Ireland. The bitterness extends beyond the human and sociological levels, although it certainly includes them, to the poetic one, specifically, to the implication in Yeats's lines that the poetic imagination would grow stronger with a closeness to the land. Kavanagh suffered personally from such a view both in the hard work it took to overcome a poor education and in his social life, where he was constantly reminded of his rustic background.

Kavanagh's resentment over the peasant-poet fiction is explicit in "The Great Hunger" when he refers directly to the problem of the imagination. The poem shifts in these instances from the specific to the general, particularly in the characterization of Maguire, who becomes a stereotype rather than an individual. In the midst of giving us specific details about Maguire's day, Kavanagh makes references to the peasant who tried to sing but repeated the same melody, "the dragging step of a ploughman going home," or, elsewhere, the peasant-poet whose poems are pulled weeds, which have "withered in the July sun." In section 13 the subject of the poetic imagination is developed at length, as a subject in its own right:

> The peasant has no worries;
> In his little lyrical fields
> He ploughs and sows; . . .
> His heart is pure,
> His mind is clear, . . .
> The peasant who is only one remove from the beasts he
>   drives.
> The travellers stop their cars to gape over the green
>   bank into his fields.
> There is the pool in which the poet dips. . . .
> The peasant is the unspoiled child of Prophecy,
> The peasant is all virtues—let us salute him without
>   irony
> The peasant ploughman who is half a vegetable—
> Who can react to sun and rain and sometimes even
> Regret that the Maker of Light had not touched him more
>   intensely.
>
> (*KCP.*, 100)

With these lines the harsh realities presented in the poem go beyond tragic narrative; in the context of modern Irish poetry, they criticize "the Irish thing" dreamed up by a previous generation of writers and mimicked by the present. The balance here, however, is precarious, with the bitterness and preachiness threatening to overturn the poem. Yet, in light of the entire work, they do not. It is a credit to Kavanagh's poetic control that the focus remains essentially fixed on its true subject. The powerful depiction of rural life, chiefly through the characterization of the protagonist, Paddy Maguire, balances those rare moments when Kavanagh as critic enters the poem.

In his antipathy for revivalism and Yeatsian romanticism, Kavanagh turned instinctively toward a Joycean perspective, particularly the numerous depictions of spiritual and mental torpor in *Dubliners*. These stories of bourgeois urban life, which stress the complexity of emotional and intellectual emptiness, provided an alternative to the romantic poetic tradition dominated by Yeats. This alternative aesthetic emerges forcefully in "The Great Hunger," where Paddy Maguire can be seen from a Joycean perspective as a rural counterpart of the characters in *Dubliners*.[21] Maguire's failure is one of imagination, and Kavanagh uses an allusion to Joyce to emphasize the poverty of rural life. Celebrating a successful harvest, Maguire believes that he has slipped the nets holding other men back.

> . . . he laughed over pints of porter
> Of how he came free from every net spread
> In the gaps of experience.

But because of his complacency and lack of vision, he succumbs to forces that create a Joycean paralysis: a domineering mother, a dulling routine, and a life-draining church. Maguire's fall becomes more emphatic with Kavanagh's echo of the moment in *A Portrait* when Steven denounces the nets that hold people back.[22] Unlike Dedalus, Maguire cannot fly past the nets, despite his claims of freedom; he is snared emotionally, spiritually, and psychologically.

Kavanagh remained true to his Joycean heritage in stressing the special pressures the Church applies to Irish men and women. In "Lough Derg," a long poem written as a sequel to "The Great Hunger," he describes the narrow piety of individuals who twist God's purpose—"Their hands push closed the doors that God holds open"—and their pettiness, which distorts their religious visions:

> Solicitors praying for cushy jobs
> To be County Registrar or Coroner,
> Shopkeepers threatened with sharper rivals
> Than any hook-nosed foreigner.
> Mothers whose daughters are Final Medicals
> Too heavy-hipped for thinking,
> Wives whose husbands have angina pectoris
> Wives whose husbands have taken to drinking.

Their prayers eventually become extensions of selfish and banal desires, which Kavanagh sets down in a lame parody of intercession:

> That my son Joseph may pass the Intermediate
> We beseech Thee to hear us. . . .
> That her aunt may remember us in her will
> We beseech Thee to hear us. . . .
> That my indigestion may be cured
> We beseech Thee to hear us.
> (KCP., 105, 119)

Kavanagh spares religion itself in most of "Lough Derg" to concentrate primarily on the hypocrisy of people. In "The Great Hunger," however, the criticism of religion is clear, particularly its power to restrain Maguire's sexuality with a fear of sin and his curiosity intellectually with a sour kind of humility.

> . . . he saw Sin
> Written in letters larger than John Bunyan dreamt of.
> For the strangled impulse there is no redemption.
> . . . .
> Religion, the fields and the fear of the Lord
> And Ignorance giving him the coward's blow,
> He dare not rise to pluck the fantasies
> From the fruited Tree of Life.
> (KCP., 85–86)

Like Joyce and Austin Clarke, Kavanagh emphasizes here the repressive side of Irish Catholicism. Maguire, unlike his urban and educated prototype Stephen Dedalus, quietly, almost passively, follows the Church's strict teaching.[23] As a result, his chances for human joy gradually and inevitably pass by unrealized, until it is too late; "He will hardly remember that life happened to him."

Another important Joycean element in Kavanagh's poetic strategy derived from *Ulysses*, a book he admired greatly and reread often. Joyce's plan to treat the local as the universal, to record countless details of the familiar, to present the life of a place, so painstakingly carried out in *Ulysses*, inspired and encouraged Kavanagh to concentrate on the details of the twisted furrows and black hills of his parish. The celebrated sonnet "Inniskeen Road: July Evening" presents the local and the familiar in a refreshing, realistic manner.[24]

> The bicycles go by in two and threes—
> There's a dance in Billy Brennan's barn to-night,
> And there's the half-talk code of mysteries
> And the wink-and-elbow language of delight.
> Half-past eight and there is not a spot
> Upon a mile of road, no shadow thrown
> That might turn out a man or woman, not
> A footfall tapping secrecies of stone.
>
> I have what every poet hates in spite
> Of all the solemn talk of contemplation.
> Oh, Alexander Selkirk knew the plight
> Of being king and government and nation.
> A road, a mile of kingdom, I am king
> Of banks and stones and every blooming thing.
>
> (KCP., 18–19)

The rural details in the octet supply the material that paints the scene, the "half-talk code of mysteries" and the "wink-and-elbow" subterfuge of rural courtship. The poem's meaning shifts in the sestet from a composition of mood and place to the subject of poetry itself, especially the poetic strategy shaping the details. The poet's voice admits to the narrowness of his world and identifies with Alexander Selkirk, Defoe's source for *Robinson Crusoe*, who was confined to an island kingdom; but the reference to

Selkirk and, by implication, to Defoe confirms the power of the imagination to transform the details of a small world into a wonder of experience. Kavanagh holds dominion over this world and, with the rich pun "blooming" in the final lines, allows us to see the depth of that dominion. As we shall see, he went on to emphasize the local and everyday details of life even more completely in his later work. But the purity of expression, the admission of realistic detail for its own sake, and the digression on the theoretical aspects of his poetic vision were never more clearly stated than in "Inniskeen Road: July Evening."

As Kavanagh began to mature poetically, he drew increasingly upon familiar and well-understood material but strove to separate himself artistically from his subject matter, a strategy he recognized in Joyce's work. The self-conscious poetic voice entering the sestet in "Inniskeen Road: July Evening" is an early example of this tendency and represents Kavanagh at his best, when he wrote easily and naturally, offering rich details about things he knew at firsthand. When he becomes too self-conscious about his own role as poet, or when he dons the mask of public poet—as he does in his satirical poetry on literary Dublin—he loses his authenticity. Public poetry summons the ghost of Yeats, however, and any Irish poet who attempts this mode invites comparison with the master. Kavanagh understood this very well and, as a consequence, pushed himself in his satirical poems to be different, often to his disadvantage. Too often his public voice is shrill and cantankerous; at other times, in a poem like "A Wreath for Tom Moore's Statue," the voice simply complains out of self-pity:

> They put a wreath upon the dead
> For the dead will wear the cap of any racket,
> The corpse will not put his elbows through his jacket
> Or contradict the words some liar has said.
>
> (KCP., 148)

Lines that purport to consider the importance of poetry in Ireland by reflecting upon a monument to a popular writer revert instead to a personal anger at the lack of reward for Kavanagh's own work. The rancor that lies behind much of his satire effectively reduces any sense of public consciousness in these poems by personalizing the issues. The few satirical or public poems that succeed do so only when Kavanagh distances himself either through form or conscious literary echoes. "The Paddiad," an attack on Kavanagh's rivals, owes much in spirit to Pope's attacks on the Grub Street hacks; in "Candida," a poem for John Betjeman's daughter, whatever poetic merit Kavanagh manages is cribbed from Swift.[25]

> Candida is one and I
> Wish her lots and lots of joy.
> She the nursling of September
> Like a war she won't remember.
> Candida is one to-day
> And there's nothing more to say.
>
> (*KCP.*, 140)

The poetic voice we hear in Kavanagh's descriptive poetry about Ulster, however, shows a remarkable, even an astonishing sincerity free from any restraint.

> We borrowed the loan of Kerr's big ass
> To go to Dundalk with butter,
> Brought him home the evening before the market
> An exile that night in Mucker.
>
> We heeled up the cart before the door,
> We took the harness inside—
> The straw-stuffed straddle, the broken breeching
> With bits of bull-wire tied;
>
> The winkers that had no choke-band,
> The collar and the reins . . .
> In Ealing Broadway, London Town
> I name their several names
>
> Until a world comes to life—
> Morning, the silent bog,

> And the God of imagination waking,
> In a Mucker fog.
>
> (*KCP.*, 254)

The loose way of country speech—"we borrowed the loan"—coupled with the treatment of the act of poetic invention in the final lines—"I name their several names"—show the poet at ease, yet at full strength, secure in both the range and the tone of expression.

The authenticity of Kavanagh's poetic voice comes from this interesting use of the local and the familiar to raise questions or make statements about the poetic act itself. In these moments of clear equilibrium, art and criticism combine as the poem implies that the poet can be vital only when writing about his own familiar world.

> I have lived in important places, times
> When great events were decided, who owned
> That half a rood of rock, a no-man's land
> Surrounded by our pitchfork-armed claims.
> I heard the Duffys shouting "Damn your soul"
> And old McCabe stripped to waist, seen
> Step the plot defying blue cast-steel—
> "Here is the march along these iron stones"
> That was the year of the Munich bother. Which
> Was more important? I inclined
> To lose my faith in Ballyrush and Gortin
> Till Homer's ghost came whispering to my mind
> He said: I made the Iliad from such
> A local row. Gods make their own importance.
>
> (*KCP.*, 238)

The remaking of trivial, common details, "a local row" between Duffy and McCabe or the daily routine of rural labor, takes precedent over great events of history such as the "Munich bother" because by being familiar they require no real invention; they are part of the poet's sensibility. The real challenge facing the poet resides in the shaping of that material into art, transforming the ordinary and the common. Again and again Kavanagh insists upon the integrity and depth of his parish:

> My hills hoard the bright shillings of March
> While the sun searches in every pocket.
> They are my Alps and I have climbed the Matterhorn
> With a sheaf of hay for three perishing calves
> In the field under the Big Forth of Rocksavage.
>
> (*KCP.*, 13)

The depiction of rural life, even of the small details of farming, does not in itself distinguish Kavanagh's poetry. Many dislocated urbanites have written of their memories of life on the land; Yeats's famous "Lake Isle of Innisfree," for example, grew out of disenchantment with London life. The difference with Kavanagh's poetry, however, is its general lack of nostalgia; the treatment of the country remains essentially nonsentimental. The memories of the land are those about the hard days of labor, the struggle with the soil, or the race with the weather over a meager crop, the unglamorous task of carting dung, and the firm hold the land has over those who live close to it:

> O stony grey soil of Monaghan
> The laugh from my love you thieved . . .
> You flung a ditch on my vision
> Of beauty and love and truth.
>
> (*KCP.*, 73)

This insistence upon genuine rural experience along with the intrusion of artistic personality on the subject matter set Kavanagh's poetry off from all other treatments of country life in Irish poetry.

Joycean realism, then, made perfect artistic sense for Kavanagh, providing an orientation and strategy without the accompanying burden of the formal aspects of poetic style and imagery. The simple fact that Joyce accomplished what he did in fiction allowed Kavanagh an opportunity in another genre; thus a Joycean direction in poetry was liberating rather than restricting. Furthermore, what Joyce did with the Irish city, Kavanagh felt he might do with the Irish countryside. Scrutinizing the Catholic experience and depicting the rural Irish scene realistically and exactly allowed him to exploit the benefits of a literary model without becoming stifled; he could be innovative if not original.

Rebirth and the Later Poetry

After Kavanagh's very dangerous illness in 1955, which resulted in the removal of a cancerous lung, a noticeable shift took place in his poetry. The illness itself was looked upon by Kavanagh as a turning point at which he felt he was born as an artist. In "Lines written on a seat on the Grand Canal, Dublin, 'Erected to the memory of Mrs. Dermot O'Brien,'" written during recuperation, new life is announced in baptismal imagery:

> O commemorate me where there is water,
> Canal water preferable, so stilly
> Greeny at the heart of summer. Brother
> Commemorate me thus beautifully.
> Where by a lock Niagariously roars
> The falls for those who sit in the tremendous silence
> Of mid-July.
>
> $\qquad\qquad\qquad\qquad$ (*KCP.*, 295)

The poem abounds with confidence, with skillful ease in such phrases as "stilly/Greeny" and in the bold auditory imagery "Niagariously roars." More than skill and confidence, however, the poetry written from this period until Kavanagh's death in 1967 is characterized by a rejection of satire, particularly of the steady attack upon his contemporaries which had occupied his attention in the late 1940s and early 1950s. The new mood is best expressed in the four-line poem appropriately entitled "Freedom":

> Take me to the top of the high hill
> Mount Olympus laughter-roaring unsolemn
> Where no one is angry and satired
> About a mortal creature on a tall column.
>
> $\qquad\qquad\qquad\qquad$ (*KCP.*, 288)

The turn from satire toward love—"my intention is not satire but humaneness"—becomes in these last poems a theme in itself as well as an attitude. The realistic treatment of rural life continues to be important, but there is a noticeable change both in the voice and in the scope of the treatment. The bitterness of the narrative voice, obvious in "The Great Hunter," gives way to a quiet acceptance and a comic vision:

> A humble scene in a backward place
> . . . .
> A primrose, a violet,
> A violent wild iris—but mostly anonymous performers
> Yet an important occasion as the Muse at her toilet
> Prepared to inform the local farmers
> That beautiful, beautiful, beautiful God
> Was breathing His love by a cutaway bog.
>
> (*KCP.*, 292)

The difference here is that the emphasis falls upon the contemplation, rather than simply the representation, of life. The act of the imagination, or what Kavanagh calls in a number of poems "naming," takes precedence over the realistic world that is being seen:

> This is what love does to things: the Rialto Bridge,
> The main gate that was bent by a heavy lorry
> The seat at the back of the shed that was a suntrap.
> Naming these things is the love-act and the pledge.
>
> (*KCP.*, 280)

With contemplation and imagination emerging here as subject matter, the later poetry expands its perspective to contain the poet himself as subject, sometimes as a youth, or in middle age struggling with materials and themes that form the basis of art; more often, however, the poet appears as the established writer, reflecting on the art of poetry. References to writing and rewriting, to the source of his poetry, and to the loss of inspiration, when "Old Cunning Silence might not be a better bet than poetry," are frequent in these last poems; in some, such as "Come Dance with Kitty Stobling," or in the following lines from "Intimate Parnassus," the poet as hero is the subject of the poem:

> . . . mere men
> Are climbing out on dangerous branches
> Of banking, insurance, and shops;
> Poet, you have reason to be sympathetic—
> Count them the beautiful unbroken
> And then forget them
> As things aside from the main purpose.
>
> (KCP., 257)

Occasionally in these pieces, we are reminded of the tendencies in the later Yeats to focus on the subject of poetry and the making of poems. With Kavanagh's later work, however, questions emerge about poetic inspiration or the problem of composition so often that the poetry is overcome by a discussion of poetic process. Moreover, an important part of that discussion in these last poems focuses on the loss of creative power, the lack of inspiration, and even the failure of the imagination:

> I have nothing to announce
> On any subject yet one
> I was full of bounce
>
> (KCP., 307)

and

> I am here in my own acres again
> Looking around me, thinking
> Thoughts that have no life
> Though it is mid-summer I've
> No wish to rhapsodize,
> Thus a poet dies.
>
> (KCP., 335)

John Nemo, in his study of Kavanagh's writing, suggests that the bitter disappointment over his outsider status among the Dublin literati, his loneliness, his loss of a lawsuit, and his nagging poverty eventually overcame him, particularly when his health was poor toward the end of his life.[26] Undoubtedly, these factors contributed to Kavanagh's disinterest in writing during his last seven years. What the final poems reflect, however, is an imprecision due to a lack of technique, as if the poet could manage to face his subject matter only once. The weakness appears in Kavanagh's tedious obsession with rhyme:

> The theme here invented
> And by me pa-tented
> Psychology bended
>
> Is about a poor hero
> Who gambled on Zero
> There's no rhyme but Nero.
>
> > (KCP., 308)

It also appears in his inability to sustain the importance of the local scene, so essential to his earlier poetry. "Literary Adventures" begins with a control of material reminiscent of the early Kavanagh, characterized by an ease of expression, the sense of the familiar, and the promise of development.

> I am here in a garage in Monaghan.
> It is June and the weather is warm,
> Just a little bit cloudy. There's the sun again
> Lifting to importance my sixteen acre farm.

But the imagination cannot hold nor develop the details, and the poem drifts off into personal musings and quips.

> Spread this news, tell all if you love me,
> You who knew that when sick I was never dying
> (Nae gone, nae gone, nae free us torn
> But taking a rest like John Jordan).
>
> > (KCP., 320)

Many of these final poems give the impression of slapdash composition, impatience, and carelessness, as if the poet would not, or could not, return to them to shape them more precisely.

Poetics and Aesthetics

Despite the failure of many of the final poems, this last stage of Kavanagh's writing is not without interest or significance, particularly when read alongside Yeats's last poems, many of which also focus upon poetic strategy. Yeats reflected deeply and often in his later years on the difficulty of writing, taking the loss of imagination as his principal subject. But as painful and disturbing as this subject was for Yeats in old age, he still managed to treat it with sufficient energy to create great poetry. The inner strength he discovers and celebrates in "The Circus Animals' Desertation" as the source of poetic inspiration, "where all ladders start," sustained him in the end. As a result most of his last poems reverberate with power, authority, and a rich complexity.

Kavanagh, however, could not discover such strength, nor could he feel such conviction. His deliberations on the difficulties of writing poetry reveal an inability to sustain any artistic struggle. The poetic vitality he creates in these last works comes only in short bursts within poems, as we noted in "Literary Adventures," or in isolated instances when he seems to have been provoked. A clear example of the latter can be seen in Kavanagh's response to Yeatsian poetics, especially Yeats's preoccupation with hard-riding country gentlemen and lords and ladies gay. Kavanagh replaced this version of the Ascendancy tradition with one that stressed decadence and corruption.

> I came to a great house on the edge of the park
> Thinking of Yeats' dream Great House where all
> Nobility was protected by ritual
> Though all lay drunk on the floor and in the dark
> Tough louts and menial minds in the shrubberies lurk
> And negative eunuchs hate in an outer hall.
>
> (*KCP.*, 333)

The criticism here fits with Kavanagh's previous attacks upon the fabricated, sentimental version of nationalistic literature, but unlike the earlier practice, ridicule and reproof are not the essence of the poetic strategy. Instead, Kavanagh shifts from a denial of Yeats's continued interest in seeking higher realities through myth, history, and visionary schemes—

> No system, no Plan
> Yeatsian Invention
> No all-over
> Organisational prover

to an affirmation of the simple and the ordinary couched in his own advice to younger poets.

> Name for the future
> The everydays of nature
> And without being analytic
> Create a great epic.
> Girls in red blouses,
> Steps up to houses,
> Sunlight round gables,
> Gossip's young fables,
> The life of a street.
>
> (*KCP.*, 287)

Although the language verges on doggerel here, Kavanagh remains consistent in poetic strategy: he continues to stress the importance of the local, the habitual, and the ordinary. It is only in the treatment of these that the poet can achieve sincerity and authenticity.

Kavanagh's struggle for authenticity necessarily involved the inevitable conflict with Yeats, the chief architect of the Literary Revival and the greatest poet of the early twentieth century. For Kavanagh the conflict was inescapable: Yeats was the rootless force creating its own base and context, conceiving a literary nationalism that sought its validation in a rural fiction, "from contact with the soil," while remaining essentially urban. Kavanagh, in contrast, represented rooted experience, which knew too well the realities of rural life. The fact that Yeats was the dominant presence in Irish poetry made Kavanagh's difficulty more pronounced. He had to walk the thin line between admiration and recognition of genius on the one side, and imitation and assimilation on the other. To achieve this balance, he followed a Joycean direction in his poetry which allowed him ease in expression. But a Joycean direction alone was not enough, apparently; Kavanagh also needed to resort to extreme posturing, living as a Dublin character, speaking outrageously about his own abilities, misreading and misjudging many writers including Yeats. Nonetheless, he also wrote five or six great poems and a number of other very memorable ones; moreover, in his insistence upon the local and the familiar, Kavanagh provided an important new strategy for modern Irish poetry which stirred the imagination of yet another generation of poets.

6

Poetry at Mid-century I: Thomas Kinsella

Despite the spadework of Austin Clarke and Patrick Kavanagh which cleared the ground under the giant upas tree, problems of tradition and continuity were by no means solved for the next generation of Irish poets. Yeats, it was true, no longer loomed menacingly, distanced as he was by Clarke's and Kavanagh's more immediate struggle with him. Joyce's example liberated the Catholic bourgeois consciousness and promoted realism, evident again in Clarke's and Kavanagh's practice. Other problems carried over, however. Nationalism both beckoned and repelled, an ebb and flow of cultural and psychological rhythms which promised poetic independence but could also stifle individual expression. Nationalism also necessarily implied the matter of Ireland, which continued to offer mythical and historical meaning for the modern age. Modernism itself, apparent in the work of Joyce and T. S. Eliot and that of American poets such as Ezra Pound, Wallace Stevens, and William Carlos Williams, finally reached Irish shores in the 1950s, offering a widening prospect of style, image, and technique. Along with the innovations in style and form, however, modernism brought with it an emphasis upon discontinuity which for Irish poets touched a tender nerve and threatened the precarious and tenuous position of the poet within an inherited literary tradition.

It is not surprising, then, to see in the work of Thomas

Kinsella and John Montague, two poets born within a year of one another who began their literary careers in the late 1950s, the same wrestling with the problems of continuity and tradition that occupied their elders. While the struggle for Kinsella and Montague has not involved the usual grappling with a predecessor, it has been a formidable struggle nonetheless, demanding both the understanding of an expanding poetic inheritance and the questioning of the efficacy of the tradition. Montague has suggested that the difficulty resembles a balancing act, writing poetry that is "indisputably Irish" but at the same time "modern," reflecting a sense of the world.[1] For Kinsella this has meant facing up to the modern condition "that every writer . . . is the inheritor of a gapped, discontinuous, polyglot tradition," which in an Irish context means the loss of one part of the national culture.[2]

The difficulty, then, for Irish poets at mid-century came in the search for continuity, finding something that would suffice to provide cultural identity and also to admit the modern world. Montague has described his generation's moment as "the extraordinary hour of calm/And the day of limitation," when even poetic reaction is out of fashion, since Clarke and Kavanagh had already burst the revivalist bubble. As a result, Montague has seen a greater task for the contemporary poet, "the struggle with casual/Graceless unheroic things," making poems out of the essentially unpoetic details of modern life. We note in Montague's phrase a Joycean tenor that establishes a direction but also implies special difficulties: the acceptance of fragmentation and the "task" of making poetry out of common, everyday experience. Both Kinsella and Montague continue to define that task within an Irish context and to seek out a tradition that will inform their expression. But they are modernist enough to understand that their poetical inheritance involves not only Irish but also other literature, especially English and American.[3] They understand the importance of both Pound and Eliot, whose major poetry underscores the predominance of fragmentation and dissociation in modern culture, the inevitable result of an internationalist aesthetic. Kinsella's and Montague's poetry reflects this understanding; there is a tendency in both their work to reconcile the past with a modern context, to allow the authentic voice its utterance, which, if it is to be authentic, must admit its fractured as well as its integral relation to the past; it must admit as part of its historical sense the pastness of the past as well as its presence. Much of Kinsella's and Montague's poetry attempts to order this essentially confused historical consciousness.

It is tempting to link Kinsella and Montague more closely than one should, perhaps, to infer from their works common expressions of similar problems because they began their careers as writers together, publishing their first poems almost contemporaneously and collaborating as editors on an anthology of new Irish writing. Both writers caution against such a connection, however. In the foreword to the *Dolmen Miscellany of Irish Writing* (1962), in what might pass as the ineluctable manifesto of a new generation,[4] Montague and Kinsella point to a change in sensitivity in contemporary literature, one that acknowledges the modern world and a new role for Irish writers, but they deny the existence of a new school or movement. The foreword announces their intention to avoid conventional Irishisms in their work, but stops short of any collective poetic blueprint. Indeed, their only declaration in that text is one of poetic independence: establishing the freedom to cultivate the individual talent.[5] We can safely add to their quiet manifesto the acknowledgment of a fractured Irish tradition and the willingness to discover a continuity that would inform, if not correct, that fracture. The means by which each poet identifies that continuity, however, insists upon individual expression.

Poetic Identity

In his influential essay on the Irish tradition, Kinsella expresses some ambivalence about the importance of the literary past:

Is there then any virtue for literature, for poetry, in the simple continuity of a tradition? I believe there is not. A relatively steady tradition, like English or French, accumulates a distinctive quality and tends to impose this on each new member. Does this give him a deeper feeling for the experience gathered up in the tradition, or a better understanding of it? I doubt it . . . for the present it seems that every writer has to make the imaginative grasp at identity for himself, and if he can find no means in his inheritance to suit him, he will have to start from scratch.[6]

Strong words, even astonishing words, when we listen to Kinsella a few years later, explaining his decision to translate the great Irish epic, *The Tain:*

It's an act of responsibility. It's ours, Irish, and it deserved a new currency; I'm also translating some from the Middle Irish. . . . It's a commitment to tradition; and understanding of them, as part of our past, is an understanding of our totality.[7]

The apparent discrepancy between these two views reveals a tension that runs throughout Kinsella's poetry, growing out of the poet's knowledge of the past and his sense that as a writer he is separated from it. Much of this tension stems from his deeply self-conscious sense of isolation, the awareness of what he calls a "gapped, discontinuous, polyglot tradition." In fact, this is a problem for all twentieth-century writers who recognize that they cannot possibly apprehend—Kinsella's word is "possess"—all of the world's great literature. The problem is worse for the modern Irish writer, Kinsella believes, because he faces not only the enormous achievement of world literature but also his own lost native Irish tradition.

. . . for my own part I simply recognize that I stand on one side of a great rift, and can feel the discontinuity in myself. It is a matter of people and place as well as writing—of coming, so to speak, from a broken and uprooted family, of being drawn to those who share my origins and finding that we cannot share our lives.[8]

This is not idle thinking served up for the literary column; Kinsella carefully worked through these ideas, weighing his thoughts against his own poetry, producing at least four different versions of the argument, each one shifting slightly to coincide with his own poetic development. The passage quoted above appeared in 1970 and reflects Kinsella's struggle with identity in his own poetry up to and including *Nightwalker and Other Poems*, published in 1967.[9] In a 1972 version, Kinsella changes the emphasis once again to stress the modern poet's acceptance of discontinuity as a necessary condition to writing. This shift in thinking is evident in the new work, beginning with *Notes from the Land of the Dead and Other Poems* (1973), which shows the poet more absorbed in an inner journey, making sense of his alienated consciousness.

Kinsella's early poems manifest a confusion about a poetic identity which eventually culminates in the self-questioning and psychological poetry in *Nightwalker*. The earliest poems in *Another September* (1958) reflect the young poet's sense of the burden of a tradition, especially the task of moving against a slackening tide. The great deeds and characters of Irish myth, "the heroic agenda" as Kinsella calls it, cannot suffice for a poet living in the modern world, which requires "Things to kill or love or level down." Moreover, the pastoralism and the delicate spiritualism of the Celtic Twilight have also run their course and seem especially unappealing to someone like Kinsella, who grew up during World War II and who lives in the new Ireland committed to material and economic growth.

Kinsella's commitment to modernism began with a purgation of revivalism, especially its reliance upon "the heroic agenda" of historical and legendary material. In his first poems, Kinsella confronts romantic Ireland head-on and declares it inappropriate for modern poetry. Heroes from mythology and legend, figures from folklore, tragic characters from history—all of these serve only to remind the poet of the impossibility of romantic idealism in his own age: "For reply I find I am left/With an unanswerable dawn upon my hands." In the face of the modern condition, the heroic tradition appears symbolically as a crumbling ruin, which once "held speechless under its cold a whole province of Meath"; now the broken casements and fallen walls remind the poet only of lost power, a decayed and collapsed civilization.

> Life, a vestigial chill, sighs along the tunnels
> Through the stone face. The great collapsed rooms,
>   the mind
> Of the huge head, are dead. Views open inward
> On empty silence.[10]

Despite Kinsella's refutation of heroic and romantic Ireland, a curious reversal occurs in these early poems, which undercuts the demythologizing of the Irish past. Amid the metaphorical structure that links historical Ireland with decay and death, a vital sense of beauty emerges in many of these poems, suggesting that the past still fascinates and attracts the poet. The poignant lines from "Death of a Queen," for example, which question the efficacy of an older heroism in the face of a new reality, are remarkable nonetheless for their clarity and beauty:

> Reality, nagging like the tide,
> Undermined her voice
> Until its mass almost vanished.
> Only a shell of speech,
> Covered with wild flowers,
> Clung to the necessary bones in her mouth.
>
> They sent counsellors and music
> Out across the promontory of her grief;
> And anger, after a while,
> Was released, shouldering like a ball;
> But startle or sweeten to life
> Her eyes, streaming with memory, could not.[11]

There is a good deal of Yeats in Kinsella's first poems, as one might expect from a young writer conscious of his own national heritage in literature and its greatest twentieth-century poet. Yeats's presence is most noticeable in the form, the rhythm, and in some places even in the borrowing of conspicuous inventions such as circus animals.

Soft, to your places, animals
Your legendary duty call.
  It is, to be
Lucky for my love and me.
  And yet we have seen that all's
  A fiction that is heard of love's difficulty.

(*P.*, 16)

Echoes of Yeats resound elsewhere in the general vehicle of the
love lyrics, in the elegiac tone of the heroic poems, and sometimes in the use of characteristically Yeatsian devices such as
birds—"transcendental birds that soar," "all manner of birds,"
"the shore-bird's psychotic shriek"—or the rose, in a line that
betrays an uneasy personal anxiety toward the Yeatsian achievement: "To one sick of the rose the flash is barren."

Other voices echo here, as well. The clipped diction of
Auden is evident—"Readier than flags rippling in the sun/To
turn tragic in elegiac weathers"—as is the imaginative verbal
pairing of Dylan Thomas: "apple-tasted darkness," "ticking
stairs." For some critics these ghostly presences in Kinsella's
early poems expose too much youthful uncertainty and stiffness.
Edna Longley believes that the mixture of influences unsettles
the poetry, producing an imbalance between Yeatsian abstractions and Audenesque language.[12] Calvin Bedient sees the exaggeration of technique and literary effect as stifling the poet's
personality.[13]

In one remarkable early poem, however, Kinsella manages
to control influence and balance style, qualifying, if not disprov-
ing, the critics' views. "Baggot Street Deserta," a poem which
might be regarded as an early manifesto, declares Kinsella's
intention to probe his own identity as an artist with a highly
personal, psychological poetry of introspection. Maurice Harmon has called the poetry in *Another September* proof of the
"meditative poet in the making,"[14] and nowhere is this more
evident than in "Baggot Street Deserta." But the poem does
more than announce theme and method; it also illuminates the

path Kinsella eventually chose to expand the territory of the modern Irish tradition.

"Baggot Street Deserta" depicts the artist in his attic study gazing through the window at the city stretched out below. As his mind unravels, he reflects upon the role of the writer in society, revealing much about the poetic strategy that will be at the heart of his work. The poet accepts his "call of exile" and, isolated, will both inflict and endure the mental sting involved in "obsessed honesty" with the "business of the border-marches/ Of the Real." The essential condition of this real world for Kinsella is its mysterious, alienating chaos, which the artist must attempt to contact and order.

> The slow implosion of my pulse
> In a wrist with poet's cramp, a tight
> Beat tapping out endless calls
> Into the dark.
>
> (P., 30)

The obsession with honesty, the interest in the real, the acknowledgment of the modern world, the heroic stance of the artist, and the effort, stated in poetic terms, to order recollections and thoughts all suggest a Joycean tenor in the poetry, an urban sensibility that is also a weltanschauung.

Joyce's importance to Kinsella's work can hardly be overlooked. One of his first publications, a short story entitled "Seamus Hero," written when he was a student at University College, Dublin, portrays the isolation of an artistic, intellectual boy at odds with his environment.[15] The conscious allusion in the title and the deliberate choice of subject matter and tone are decidedly Joycean. Even in Kinsella's critical work Joyce is the dominant presence, "the true father" of modern Irish writing. Yeats remains an important ancestor, but in Kinsella's version of the family tree, he is a distant uncle with no heirs: "Yeats stands for the Irish tradition as broken; Joyce stands for it as continuous, or healed—or healing—from its mutilation."[16]

This startling remark has intrigued many of Kinsella's readers, and its implications have worked their way into the commentary on his poetry without the benefit of a full hearing.[17] The judgment upon Yeats seems clear from a number of perspectives. As part of a psychologically comforting pruning to allow himself some sunlight, Kinsella sees Yeats as an Ascendancy poet, a branch of the Irish tradition, but not its trunk. Furthermore, Yeats's poetic criteria were essentially connected to romanticism, an orientation that has clearly been rejected by contemporary Irish writers. And, of course, Yeats did not understand Catholic Ireland, its sociology, its theology, and, as Hugh Kenner has so aptly put it, its "night sweats," which Joyce knew and Kinsella knows at first hand.[18]

The image of Joyce as healer, however, seems incongruous and suggests a role in Irish letters that he was never willing to play. His contempt for the national movement and for the Revival is evident, among other places, in his essay "Day of the Rabblement" and in the final chapter of *A Portrait*. Yet Kinsella sees Joyce not only as the father of contemporary Irish writers but also as the heir of seventeenth- and eighteenth-century Gaelic poets whose works express the sense of dispossession and alienation associated by Kinsella with the modern mind.[19] Kinsella links Joyce with the seventeenth-century Gaelic poets because of their common treatment of the material of "daily human consequences" and the problem of isolation within a dominant foreign culture; Joyce's depiction of the new urban proletariat as displaced country people resembles the Gaelic poets' treatment of the dispossessed native population of eighteenth-century Ireland. Thus as Kinsella reads him, Joyce becomes the significant twentieth-century connection with the tail end of the Gaelic poetic tradition and, once connected, offers continuity to the modern Irish writer.

"Old father, old artificer"

Evidence of Joyce's paternity emerges in three or four different aspects of Kinsella's poetry: in the general urban presence in many of the poems, in the artistic personality behind the poetic voice, in the announced tendency toward ordering experience, and in the use of modernist techniques. Joyce is present also through allusion in key poetic texts and in the echoing of certain passages. The essential Joycean quality of Kinsella's poetry, however, appears in the ethos or voice that stands behind the poems as an ubiquitous sensibility, which emphatically accepts the modern world. It is this ethos, rather than any deliberate emulation of Joycean practice, that informs Kinsella's poetry; the obsession with honesty and the "tugging scruple" announced in "Baggot Street Deserta" create that pervasive influence which Stephen Spender has called "the felt presence of one poet in the sensibilities and attitudes of other poets."[20]

The essential poem that reflects most clearly Kinsella's modernist sensibilities is "Nightwalker," a rambling, shuffling walk after dark through the streets of a Dublin suburb. The controlling posture of isolation and alienation emerges early on, as the poet as nightwalker rejects the naive and ideal notions that meaning can be found in traditional external structures: "I only know things seem and are not good." Repeatedly throughout the poem, in night-thoughts about education, government, religious sentiment, and history, he admits the disappointing gulf between appearance and reality. The commitment to order remains, but as the poem reveals the incoherence of traditional forms of meaning, the solitary nightwalker falls back upon subjective meaning, upon the self and the imagination. The familiar Kinsella trope of the journey takes shape as an internal quest, an adaptation of the Joycean presentation of psychological realities occasioned by time and space.[21]

The poem begins ominously, with the speaker alienated even from his body—"A brain in the dark, and bones, out exercising/Shadowy flesh; fitness for the soft belly"—and moves from the physical present—"The smell of gardens . . . /Clipped privet, a wall blotted with shadows"—into memory and hallucinatory reflection. The moon above becomes "a fat skull," "a mask of grey dismay sagging open," and "the Mark of Cain," evoking memories of innocent play of Irish children, ignorant of the torture and the destruction in other parts of Europe during World War II.

> Not far from here it passed through
> —remorseless cratered face
> Swift as the wind: a bludgeon tears free
> From the world's bones, spikes breaking off
> —Millions of little sharp limbs, jets of blood
> Petrified in terror, jetted streams—
> . . . .
> It meant little to me then.
>
> (*P.*, 102)

It is a significant measure of the nightwalker's sense of history that he now sees his childhood as only the shadowy appearance of innocence in the face of a more brutal reality. This pattern of alternating representations of time and space continues throughout the poem, triggered by the nightwalker's consciousness, sometimes reflecting physical reality and sometimes drifting off by association into dream.

In the poem's opening section, the nightwalker depicts his environment in a manner suggesting the mean streets and the half-life of Joyce's *Dubliners*. People slump in front of television sets, "sick spirits," citizens of Necropolis, with whom the nightwalker himself is tethered, a victim of the same deadly paralyzing routine.

> I must lie down with them all soon and sleep
> And rise with them again when the new dawn
> Has touched our pillows and our wet pallor
> And roused us. We'll come scratching in our waistcoats
> Down to the kitchen for a cup of tea;
> Then with our briefcases, through wind or rain,
> Past our neighbours' gardens—Melrose, Bloomfield—
> To wait at the station, fluttering our papers,
> Palping the cool wind, discussing and murmuring.
>
> (*P.*, 104)

Reflection on this monotonous life leads into a consideration of society at large and of the nightwalker's dissatisfaction with modern Ireland. In a satirical fantasy the image of Kathleen Ni Houlihan transforms into a grotesque parody of the Statue of Liberty, welcoming foreign investors and signifying Ireland's willingness to be exploited for profit in an elaborately developed satire on violence and betrayal in the early years of the Irish Free State. Political violence and shortsighted economic policies resulting from selfish expediency bring only one end, weakness, which "turns upon itself." More sinister, however, is the daily routine, which reflects new materialism, a life "without principle, based on fixed ideas." The exemplar of this routine is modern urban bureaucracy, whose effects the former civil servant Kinsella knows at first hand.

> All about and above me
> The officials on the corridors or in the rooms,
> Work, or overwork, with mixed motives
> Or none. We dwell together in urgency;
> Dominate, entering middle age; subserve,
> Aborting vague tendencies with buttery smiles.
> Among us, behind locked doors, the ministers
> Are working. . . .
> . . . .
> Dragon old men, upright and stately and blind,
> Or shuffling in the corridor finding a key.
>
> (*P.*, 105)

From the old ministers whose politics consist only of memory and grudges—"their youth cannot die in them"—the nightwalker's thoughts move to present political leaders, whose rise to power involves complicated maneuverings, duplicity, and betrayal. Part 1 of "Nightwalker" closes with a meditation on the heavens, as the protagonist imagines his thoughts played out in the stars, the tragic tale of contemporary politics immortalized in a new Irish constellation, "The Wedding Group."[22]

Part 2 opens back on the streets again, this time near Martello Tower, stirring the nightwalker to evoke Joyce's spirit:

> Watcher in the tower, be with me now
> At your parapet, above the glare of the lamps.
> Turn your milky spectacles on the sea
> Unblinking; cock your ear.

The invocation appeals directly to a Joycean intelligence to gather all that surrounds the nightwalker and to aid in the shaping and ordering of impressions and memories. It also proclaims the ubiquitous presence of Joyce in this section, from the allusions to *Finnegans Wake* and *Ulysses*[23] to the well-known Joycean techniques such as the use of newspaper headlines to comment ironically upon action and the constant intrusion of the consciousness upon the narrative chronicle. Joycean shifts in voice and style also occur in this section, first in the punning mock-heroic—

> The sonhusband
> Coming in his power: mounting to glory
> On his big white harse!

and then in the clipped rhetoric, which mimics a bureaucratic memo:

> . . . subjects will find
> The going hard but rewarding. You may give offence
> But this should pass. Marry the Boss's daughter.

Contrasting styles work effectively to advance the satire, as the blunt and cynical advice "Marry the Boss's daughter," explodes the preceding advice about hard work. The poems shifts to the nightwalker's memory of his school days with the Christian Brothers, further evidence of Joycean echoes. Schoolboys listen to Brother Burke's exhortations to work hard in language that echoes the rhetorical sermons in *A Portrait.*

> And you will be called
> In your different ways—to work for the native language,
> To show your love by working for your country.

Today there are Christian Brothers' boys
Everywhere in the Goverment—the present Taoiseach
Sat where one of you is sitting now.

(*P.*, 108–110)

Joycean irony allows Kinsella to demonstrate the discrepancy between the brother's idealistic words and the reality of political deeds in Ireland. Since the government officials have been indicted in early parts of the poem, the speaker's polished advice to study hard to achieve takes on an ironic cast.

The vision that closes part 2 confirms this. A seamew flies overhead crying out, lamenting the loss of tradition in modern Ireland—"Eire, Eire, is there none / To hear? Is all lost?"—a question of personal interest to Kinsella himself.[24] In the face of the selfishness, materialism, and brutality of contemporary life, the nightwalker senses the hollowness of the idealism he was taught as a schoolboy. The education he was given fails to nourish and serves only to remind him that he is lost and cut off: "Bread of certainty; scalding soup of memories,/For my drowsy famine." At this point Joyce's importance to Kinsella's poetic strategy becomes quite clear; the "Father of Authors" has led the way by showing that poetry can be created out of such isolation and alienation; for the modern writer, corruption and disappointment can serve art extremely well. As Kinsella declares in part 1, we construct our monuments out of the base and common: "Clean bricks/Are made of mud; we need them for our tower."

With the first and second sections of "Nightwalker" questioning the possibility of meaning in external structures, the third and final section shows the complete isolation of the artist as he turns to a subjective, internal landscape of memories and hallucinations. An invocation to the lunar goddess prompts the nightwalker to begin an imaginary voyage to the extreme depths of the self, embodied in the poem's final image of the lunar landscape, in which the poet must explore and discover order:

I arrive, enveloped in blinding silence.
No wind stirs

> On the dust floor. Far as the eye can see
> Rock needles stand up from the plain; the horizon
> A ring of sharp mountains like broken spikes.
>
> (*P.*, 113)

The hostile environment, despite its strangeness, seems oddly familiar, and the nightwalker struggles to identify it:

> In the mind darkness tosses;
> The light deceives. A vivid ghost sea
> Quivers and dazzles for miles.
>
> (*P.*, 114)

The nightwalker, though oppressed, begins the process of poetically shaping this new landscape, giving a human quality to its craggy and dusty surface, naming it the Sea of Disappointment, and framing it with the earth in blue splendor hanging in the background. The closing lines of the poem reveal the artist's true courage, emphasized elsewhere in this final section by the general notion that understanding depends upon the persistence against adversity. Thus though isolation is not overcome in "Nightwalker," it is accepted as the essential part of the artistic process which must be endured and which will provide the context for the modern struggle of ordering and shaping.

Isolation and Response

We have discussed "Nightwalker" in detail because its central importance to the development of the Kinsella canon cannot be overemphasized. It presents a crucial anxiety that runs throughout the poetry—artistic isolation and cultural alienation—and it offers the characteristic responses to that condition, an inward searching for markings to aid in the struggle to establish identity and order. The anxiety of "Nightwalker" reverberates throughout other poems, but with varying degrees of intensity. The early poems tend to establish and describe the conditions that caused the poet to be isolated, while the later poems, beginning with *Notes From the Land of the Dead and Other Poems*, emphasize the acceptance and attempted reparation of the anxiety.

Such an assessment is possible in Kinsella's case because of the preponderance of journey poems throughout the various stages of his oeuvre. Sometimes, as in "Nightwalker," the journey is nothing more than an evening walk; at other times it appears as river travel or a sea voyage; but regardless of its form the external journey always involves an inner, psychological journey as well. The early journey poems such as "A Country Walk" and "Downstream" concentrate on the discontent with outward appearances and conditions and only hint at the psychological. The later poems, especially "Phoenix Park," the sequence in *Notes*, "The Route of the Tain," and one or two others, treat the inner journey as the primary material and the real focus of the poem.

"A Country Walk" from *Downstream* (1962) demonstrates the extent to which landscape and external phenomena dominate the poet-walker. The opening sections of the poem portray scenes, landscape, ruins, a town, with Wordsworthian exactness.

> . . . with a lighter step
> I turned an ivied corner to confront
> The littered fields where summer broke and fled.
> Below me, right and left, the valley floor
> Tilted in a silence full of storms;
> A ruined aqueduct in delicate rigor
> Clenched cat-backed, rooted to one horizon
>
> (P., 53)

As the path meets the river, the walker meditates upon the flow of history, on the famous battle between Cuchulain and Ferdia, fought at a ford in a river, and on the many battles in Irish history from the Norman period to the 1798 rebellions. The sense of the past overcomes the walker; he sees its presence everywhere. And as he turns from the river "through the greasy lusk, uphill/Into the final turn," that sense of the past measures the present and finds it wanting. Heroics have faded, crushed by crass materialism; the poem raises in a deliberate parody of Yeats the question of the possibility of heroism in the modern age. Men now have forgotten the sacrifice,

> . . . have exchanged
> A trenchcoat playground for a gombeen jungle.
>
> Around the corner, in an open square,
> I came upon the sombre monuments
> That bear their names: MacDonagh & McBride
> Merchants; Connolly's Commercial Arms.
>
> (P., 56)

The poem shifts here to a more personal reflection, the scenes an extension of the narrator's feelings of separation from the present. The orientation of the poem shifts as well with a cumulative effect—"Down the sloping square," "A car plunged . . . /Pitching downward"—representing the sinking from tradition which the narrator-walker senses in modern Ireland. But by now the narrator's consciousness has become the real subject—"I too descended"—and his disaffection and isolation demand our attention. The scenes with which we are presented in the final section of the poem—"other-worldly gloom," "a urinal," "the silent handball alley," "endless debris"—represent the stuff of modern living as seen by the numbed narrator, indications of his sense of loss and degradation. The final image of the river pouring below him reflects the dilemma of the modern artist: to sense in the surface flow of the continuous current the deeper pattern and structure.

The same difficulty dominates "Downstream," the other journey poem from the same volume. Again, the surface narrative—this time a river journey in a small boat—becomes the vehicle for the gradual revelation of the narrator's thoughts and attitudes. Here, as in "A Country Walk," the external environment involves the inner mind, which then gradually displaces it. The final section, when the small boat passes through a dark and dangerous part of the river, is an example of the poetic imagination transforming nature.

> The river bed
>
> Called to our flesh. Across the watery skin,
>   Breathless, our shell trembled. The abyss . . .
>   We shipped our oars in dread. Now, deeper in,
>
> Something shifted in sleep, a quiet hiss.
>
> (*P.*, 60)

As in "A Country Walk" and "Nightwalker," the persistence of the imagination overcomes the sinister moment. The unity becomes apparent, however momentarily, as the poet-narrator senses some order or understanding. In a Wordsworthian moment, a giant rock appears to offer the possibility of a distant landing place:

> A barrier of rock that turned and bared
>   A varied barrenness as toward its base
>   We glided—blotting heaven as it towered—
>
> Searching the darkness for a landing place.
>
> (*P.*, 61)

The trope of searching the darkness powerfully stated in these early journey poems and fully developed in "Nightwalker" defines the central theme of Kinsella's work. Although the imagery used to depict a landing place varies considerably in the poetry—sometimes it is a clearing, a fixed point among the stars, a smooth current in the river—the pattern of the imagery remains consistent: the promise of meaning, even if vague, provides sufficient reason to continue the search. This artistic pattern is part of a much larger problem, however, one that is only implied in these journey poems, but that is developed fully in the later works. The traveler-narrator-poet probes his history, his literary tradition, and his own past, not only for poetic

framework but also for the deeper sense of culture that deter-
mines nothing less than personal identity.

In the two final poems of *Nightwalker*, the quest for the
cultural and psychological identity turns inward. "Ritual of Departure" attempts to identify personal patterns in recent Irish
history when so many Irish (Kinsella's family among them)
were driven off the land by famine and came to Dublin, only
"to vanish in the city lanes." The notion that Dublin is filled
with the dispossessed exacerbates the poet's sense of alienation;
his beginnings are elsewhere: "I scoop at the earth, and sense
famine a first/Sourness in the clay. The roots tear softly," an
indication of the subtle ease of social rupture in Irish life.

In "Phoenix Park," the torn roots are those of love, which
the alienated, contemplative poet-speaker uncovers not only for
the subject itself—the shared life of the lovers—but also for the
life of the imagination. It is through his careful tracing of the
depths of love that he intuits a coherence and an order to shape
his thoughts.

> . . . structure
> Without substance, all about us, in the air,
> Among the trees, before us at the crossroads,
> On the stone bridge, insinuating itself
> Into being.
>
> (P., 122)

As the poet-speaker struggles to give this feeling a voice, he
discovers the markings, parables, and emblems that convey
poetic expression. Love becomes the reference and the source
of meaning in a fragmented world, the poet leading to understand and clarify his thoughts and emotions. The now-familiar
strategy unfolds: the external world calls forth the inner world,
a psychic mixture of memory and desire for his loved one,
whose "thoughtless delicate completeness" gives him strength.
In the act of composing the parables for his lover, that she might
understand the importance of her love for him, the poet discovers a deep significance:

> Laws of order I find I have discovered
> Mainly at your hands . . . of failure and increase,
> The stagger and recovery of spirit:
> That life is hunger, hunger is for order,
> And hunger satisfied brings on new hunger.
>
> (*P.*, 120)

The significance comes also in the understanding of the continual struggle for order, which, once achieved, will demand new
order made possible by the process of love: "the unmoving /
Stare of full desire. Given undying love."

The darkness of the poet's thoughts without love, "Before/
You came," are recalled in echo of the early poem "Baggot Street
Deserta": "One midnight at the starlit sill I let them/Draw near."
In this early poem the poet-narrator attempts to seek order in
the darkness but senses only a sinister, abstract light at midnight
harbours human darkness," and whose daily routine prevents
understanding or communication: "the umpteenth city of confusion. . . . And there dead men,/Half hindered by dead men,
tear down dead beauty." In "Phoenix Park", however, ten years
after "Baggot Street Deserta," the poet seemed ready to abandon
any attempt at discovering meaning in external reality and,
instead, to allow the quest its own direction inward, toward the
self. The final lines of "Phoenix Park" show a pattern beginning
to emerge which looks forward to the poetry ahead, to *Notes
From the Land of the Dead*. In a nightmarish image, vague shapes
close and begin to sharpen:

> A few ancient faces
> Detach and begin to circle. Deeper still,
> Delicate distinct tissue begins to form.
>
> (*P.*, 126)

That Kinsella was inviting the reader to connect the end of
"Phoenix Park" with the poetry that followed in *Notes* is clear
from a simple change in punctuation. The version of "Phoenix
Park" in *Nightwalker and Other Poems* ends the final line with a

period to signify that end of the poem and the volume. But in subsequent publications, including *Poems, 1956–1973*, the poem ends with a comma, suggesting that more is to come. In the 1973 publication of *Notes*, Kinsella purposefully alludes to the earlier poem by quoting the last four lines of "Phoenix Park," with the new punctuation, as a prologue to the new poem, which begins in mid-sentence with "hesitate, cease to exist." The last lines of "Phoenix Park," then, announce the beginning of new poetic directions, which take further shape in *Notes*.[25]

In the search of these deeper patterns, which would provide a sense of order, Kinsella continued to explore the inner-life in a manner first seen in "Nightwalker," moving from the conscious to the subconscious, from the outside world to an internal world of memory, emotion, and thought. The difference in the poems in *Notes* lies in the greater emphasis given to the inner world in the hopes of discovering an essential identity. The opening poem proclaims the difficulty of such a quest from the perspective of one who has completed his journey and now looks back.

> Dear God, if I had known how far and deep,
> how long and cruel, I think my being
> would have balanced: appalled.
>
> (*P.*, 129)

The other poems in *Notes* attempt to substantiate that claim by recalling the quest and probing the memory,

> searching in its own tissue
> for the structure
> in which it may wake.

The need for structure remains essential in these later poems, connecting them with the early pieces, which consistently search for landing places. But the direction of poetic strategy changed radically in the poetry after 1973. In *Notes, One* (1974), and *A Technical Supplement* (1976), the poet allows the quest its own momentum and direction, even if it means probing deep within the psyche. The result is a greater insistence in these later poems upon both the autobiographical and the psychological. Many of them explore family events, particularly the feelings and memories of the aging process and death. Others treat the artist himself in the process of making his art.

> I am simply trying to understand something
> —States of peace nursed out of wreckage.
>
> . . . .
>
> I tinker with the things that dominate me
> as they describe their random
> persistent coherences.
>
> (P., 179)

This treatment of the inner life underscores the importance of poetic identity in Kinsella's overall schema and stresses its complex mixture of psychological, cultural, and literary elements. By shifting to the subconscious and to psychological identity in these works, Kinsella hoped to discover in some deep memory bank the clues to a cultural continuity, the loss of which he has expressed throughout his poetry and criticism. The search for identity originates in the poet's personal history, as the voice of memory reveals small details that connect the self with the past.

> Your family, Thomas, met with and helped
> many of the Croppies in hiding from the Yeos
> or on their way home after the defeat
> in south Wexford.[26]

The new strategy offers Kinsella the possibility of continuity in what was formerly poisoned fruit, the old myth and legends of ancient Ireland. In "Finistere," the poet personalizes and internalizes material from The Book of Invasions, exploring the need to search for new lands from a psychological perspective. The poem treats the invasion of Ireland by the Sons of Mils, whose leader Amhairgin sings of the desire to create a new civilization.

As a younger poet, Kinsella dared not use Celtic materials without risking poetic oblivion. Now, however, with a more secure sense of poetic voice and more defined artistic focus, he could use ancient materials and make them reflect his own modern consciousness. Note the emphasis upon Amhairgin's questioning and his concern for cultural meaning:

> A maggot of the possible
> wriggled out of the spine
> into the brain.
>
> We hesitated before that wider sea
> but our heads sang with purpose
> and predatory peace.
>
> And whose excited blood was that
> fumbling our movements? Whose ghostly hunger
> tunneling our thoughts full of passages
> smelling of death and clay and faint metals
> and great stones in the darkness?
>
> (PP., 56)

As Kinsella read it, the Milseans' voyage replicated his own poetic quest to seek new meaning through an imagination that could sense order. The voyagers' dream of this new land, Ireland, reflects the cultural values of their old civilization. The creation of the new order comes only after a predatory action and involves risking the long passage through darkness and toward death. Amhairgin, the leader-narrator, struggling to describe the moment of landing on the shore, becomes the archetypal poet seeking a coherence that will contain the past and the present:

> I stood
> searching a moment for the right words.
> . . . I chose the old words once more
> and stepped out. At the solid shock
> a dreamy power loosened at the base of my spine
> and uncoiled and slid up through the marrow.
> A flow of seawater over the rock fell back

> with a she-hiss, plucking at my heel.
> My tongue stumbled.
>
> (*PP.*, 59)

The same concerns that have haunted Kinsella about the efficacy of his own poetry are reflected in Amhairgin's example. The searching for a landing place becomes intimately connected with the complex poetic act: the anxiety over the authenticity of expression, the awareness of the past, and the relationship of the poetic voice or personality to the experience. All of this is made more difficult because the search for meaning takes place amid the fragmentation of modern life.[27]

The difficulty became more grave for Kinsella because of his wide knowledge of Irish literature and his love of the Irish language. His awareness of this rich legacy aggravates his sense of discontinuity in the modern world. As he has put it,

> I recognize simultaneously a great inheritance and a great loss. The inheritance is mine, but only at two enormous removes—across a century's silence, and through an exchange of worlds——I stand on one side of a great rift, and can feel the discontinuity in myself.[28]

The recognition of the discontinuity has proved to be the central insight in Kinsella's poetic career, dictating the various directions we have noted in the journey poems and emphasizing the probing of the alienated consciousness in "Nightwalker," "Phoenix Park," and the more psychological poetry of the 1970s. At the same time, this recognition has caused Kinsella to become more interested in the translation of ancient Irish literature. Translation, which he has described as "an act of responsibility," serves to connect him directly with his literary tradition, the imaginative bedrock of his culture. The translations themselves are important contributions to twentieth-century literature and reconstruct for non-Irish readers the rich tradition of one part of Irish culture.[29] At the same time, as Kinsella has admitted, they can only be an inferior version or copy of the original expression.

The importance of these translations to Kinsella's assumptions about culture, particularly his deep concern for continuity, becomes clear in a remarkable poem, "The Route of The Tain," which describes a walk through the Irish countryside in an attempt to trace the ancient route of Queen Medb's army during her cattle raid on Ulster.[30] The poem opens with confusion as Kinsella and his friends are bogged down, lost in modern maps and books, disorganized, "Scattering in irritation . . . wandering off, ill-sorted,/like any beast of the field." Only when they observe a natural sign—a red fox running across a hillside vanishes into "a savage sharpness/out of the earth"—do they see the pass they have been seeking. The moment becomes symbolic for Kinsella, a sudden flash of coherence in which he senses the past in the present:

> We should have known it, by now:
> the process, the whole tedious
> enabling ritual! Flux brought to fullness
> —saturated—the clouding over—dissatisfaction
> spreading slowly like an ache: something
> reduced shivering suddenly into meaning
> along new boundaries.
>
> (P., 177)

Moments of discovery such as this, though not rare in Kinsella's poetry, often are qualified or reduced by the preponderance of the actual searching or probing. But in "The Route of The Tain," we are close to an unqualified moment of clarity. For despite its troublesome, shadowy line "dissatisfaction/spreading slowly like an ache," the poem ends in a discovery of meaning—and its contextual appearance has great significance for Kinsella's work. A poet who has written often about finding the way and searching for a clearing has given us a poem that treats the discovery by modern travelers of an important ancient route, none other than that of the central Irish tale. The significance of this for Kinsella's poetics ought not to be missed. The imaginative link with the past gives the poet a sense of congruity and continuity in a fractured world. Although the modern poet faces the inevitable difficulties of representing his world and expressing his thoughts, with the example of "The Route of The Tain" he might identify with others who have struggled before him, and in this identification he may find significance.

> . . . before us
> the route of the Táin, over men's dust,
> toward these hills that seemed to grow
> darker as we drove nearer.
>
> (*P.*, 177)

The preoccupation with continuity has determined Kinsella's view of his cultural heritage, his reading of both Yeats and Joyce, and his sense of isolation, as we have seen. His response has resulted primarily from a recognition of the loss of continuity and has tended to emphasize a resignation to dissociation. Occasionally, however, in a scattering of poems, the matter of continuity is treated differently, almost as if the poet was altering his stance of isolation. These poems, though few in number, aggressively force the issue of continuity, in a sense create it, by taking as their subject matter the connection with previous writers. We have seen this done in poems like "The Route of the Tain," which makes the discovery of an ancient route an emblem for understanding the past, with particular reference to the writing of poetry. We have noted as well the allusions to Joyce and the deliberate use of Joycean materials and techniques in "Nightwalker." Kinsella also has explored the concept of continuity by direct references to other Irish poets, particularly his contemporaries, who themselves were struggling within the Irish poetic tradition.

One such example occurs in Kinsella's treatment of Austin Clarke, whose career exemplifies the painful transition from revivalism to modernism. Kinsella initially wrote of Clarke in 1956, in a review of *Ancient Lights*, Clarke's first book of poems in almost twenty years. The review criticizes the narrow range of the book and labels the satires against Irish society ineffective, the product of an angry mind that ranted and raved, only to "beat the wall."[31] The concern over bitter alienation undoubtedly troubled a young Kinsella and surfaced in an early poem, "Thinking of Mr. D," about a poet at odds with his society: "A barren Dante leaving us for hell," filled with rage and "wrecking humour." The tone of the poem repeats the censure, voiced in the review of Clarke's poetry, that bitterness and anger can blunt poetic purpose. It is not surprising that the young Kinsella seemed concerned about this tendency in poetry. His own alienation from modern Ireland mirrored Clarke's, causing the younger poet to see in his elder's angry responses the possibility of his own.

An older, more secure Kinsella shows considerably less nervousness and anxiety in "Magnanimity," a poem written for Clarke's seventieth birthday in 1966. It responds to Clarke's desire that Ireland might formally recognize the achievements of her poets.

> I am sure that there are no places for poets,
> Only changing habitations for verse to outlast.
> Your own house, isolated by a stream, exists.
>
> For your use while you live—like your body and your world.
> Helpless commonness encroaches, chews the soil,
> Squats ignobly. Within, consciousness intensifies:
>
> Sharp small evils magnify into Evil,
> Pity and mockery suggest some idea of Good,
> Fright stands up stiffly under pain of death.
>
> (P., 95)

The mild criticism in these lines echoes the meaning behind "Thinking of Mr. D.," that the poet in his private crusade or his tirade against society risks losing perspective, allowing small evils to grow into large ones, and takes his ideas of good only from personal views. This same figure reappears in poem 21 of *A Technical Supplement* as one whose words are self-serving and therefore ineffective. Again, what Kinsella stresses in his characterization is the bitter anger that blinds one,

> . . . energy wasted
> grimacing facetiously inward. And yet
> a vivid and lasting image: the racked outcast.
>
> (*PP.*, 93)

Similar concerns over bitterness and anger surface in Kinsella's commentary on Clarke's works. "The narrowness of reference . . . the courting of obscurity . . . the virtually private nature of the poems,"[32] the struggle with the Irish literary tradition—these phrases appear repeatedly in references to Clarke's poetry. This view of Clarke as a private poet nursing a personal grudge has been noted by critics and reviewers, so Kinsella broke no ground here. What is interesting, however, is the tenacity with which Kinsella has pushed these observations throughout his work, from early reviews to late poems. The negative fascination Clarke holds for Kinsella is interesting also for what it tells us about Kinsella's attitudes toward his own poetic practice. Those qualities he has observed in Clarke—the insularity of the anger, the obscurity, the narrowness of satire—could emerge in many of his own poems. The criticism of Clarke, then, might be seen as self-criticism, a reminder of the special pressures upon the Irish poet who wishes to write publicly on behalf of some sense of community, yet who recognizes the fragmentation of modern life.

Curiously, Clarke seems to be a more imposing and threatening figure for Kinsella than the great Yeats. Kinsella's treatment of the latter is less intense and personal, as if Yeats's stature and reputation provided a comfortable distance. "Death in Ilium" (subtitled "In Yeats's Centenary Year") identifies Yeats with Hector as one who died gloriously for a lost cause, but whose genius rendered him impervious to those who would destroy his body. Instead, "He grows whole and remote." For a gloss on this poem we can recall Kinsella's commentary on Yeats as one who isolated himself from modern Ireland and fought a rear-guard action for the Protestant Ascendancy.[33] His unity and wholeness came from his dramatization and absorption of his separation, chiefly through the power and force of his personality. Thus Yeats created and offered tradition, but could provide no continuity for the modern Irish poet. Because Kinsella believes these to be limitations to Yeats's poetics, he can admire Yeats's greatness without fear of any significant influence. Kinsella's reading of the immediately post-Yeatsian generation—Higgins, Clarke, Fallon, and Kavanagh—suggests that these poets were not as fortunate as he:

> The tireless shadow-eaters
> close in with tough nose
> and pale fang to expose
> Fibre, weak flesh, speech organs.
>
> They eat, but cannot eat.
> Dog-faces in his bowels,
> Bitches at his face,
> He grows whole and remote.
>
> (P., 98)

Their examples not only saved Kinsella from a dangerous wrestling with the dead but spared him a negative and destructive effort in his poetry. He could grant Yeats his proper respect and appreciation and accommodate him at a safe distance as an example of tradition.[34]

One final word on Kinsella's interest in continuity. As we have seen in the poetry since *Nightwalker*, Kinsella has integrated Irish history and legend into his work in an attempt to blend the traditional with the autobiographical. "Finistere" draws heavily from *The Book of the Invasions*, particularly the songs of Amhairgin, which end the poem. The *Invasions* material also forms part of a number of other poems, including "Nuchal," "Survivor," and "The Oldest Place." In these works the *Invasion* sagas combine with personal and psychological details to support the internal quest that dominates the newer poems. But even in the autobiographical poems such as "Finistere," Kinsella allows the old stories center stage, to be heard for their own sake as well as for contemporary meaning. The archetypal character of the search in "Finistere," or the establishment of community in "The Oldest Place," provide meaning for a contemporary Irish situation and, at the same time, demonstrate poetic continuity, the idea that ancient literature can be useful to the modern writer.[35]

The Search as Meaning

We have read Kinsella in a context of continuity largely because inside and outside his poetry he has invited us to do so. The essay "The Irish Writer" establishes the primary and essential inheritance of the modern writer as no inheritance, the realization that he is isolated and cut off from the past, the recipient of a gapped and discontinuous tradition. This realization is the starting point for all of Kinsella's poetics. From this general assumption, he established an Irish context to his modernism, looking to Joyce rather than to Yeats for guidance and inspiration.

Kinsella's Joycean practice, while intentional and important to his overall poetic strategy, needs to be seen as a tendency that informs the poetry rather than dominates it. Particularly in the later work, Joycean directions frame the poems rather than determine central meaning. The internal probing of these later verses begins from a perspective that recognizes the achievement of other writers and, almost in spite of that recognition, remains persistent.

> Yes, I suppose I am appalled
> at the massiveness of others' work.
> But not deterred; I have leaned my shed
> against a solid wall.
>
> (P., 180)

The inward direction of the latest poems moves the anxiety of continuity and tradition from the solid wall of external reality to the more fragile window to the private self. In "Good Night," the final poem in Notes, the noises in the house, including voices from another room, eventually blend together as an incongruous mix, bringing the poet to his overwhelming question: "Would you agree, then, we won't/find truths, or any certainties." The question, which assumes agreement, actually must be answered negatively, since it comes from one who has searched consistently throughout the making of poems for an ordering principle, a philosophical or psychological focus. The search itself, then, rather than the objects it turns up, becomes the certainty in Kinsella's poetry. As he says of love in "Phoenix Park," it "continues till we fail"; the structure falls away when we "refuse the cup."

It is in the process of searching that Kinsella broke from those restrictive aspects of his inherited literary tradition to establish his own integrity and individuality. The act of the imagination which was so essential in "Nightwalker," "Ritual of Departure," "Downstream," and "Phoenix Park" continues to be the essential feature of the later poetry, which probes a different essential psychological landscape. Kinsella has chosen to search for his own identity, and we read this search in the poems as primarily psychological, but inextricably connected with poetic and literary identity. In making the search for meaning an essential problem in his work, Kinsella has extended the Irish poetic tradition and given it a distinct cast, shaped by Joycean modernism.

7
Poetry at Mid-century II: John Montague

Like his contemporary Thomas Kinsella, John Montague was determined as a young poet in the 1950s to avoid the sins of the fathers in matters of poetic practice. Montague also shared Kinsella's sense of literary heritage, including, of course, Yeats and Joyce, but also recent writers such as Clarke, Kavanagh, Frank O'Connor, and Sean O'Faolain. And like most young writers with more promise than publications, Montague had a strong sense of the necessity of both imaginative space and freshness, if not originality, of expression. Thus, in an early essay entitled "The Irish Writer," he participates in the predictable scourging of his elders, only this time the generation under attack is not Yeats's, but the more immediate and the more competitive one of Clarke and Kavanagh. Carefully preparing the case for a "contemporary literature" in Ireland, Montague argues that recent writers had bogged down in a conscious attempt to create a specifically Irish literature and, as a result, had separated themselves from contemporary European literature with its expanding audience.[1] Even writers like O'Faolain and Kavanagh, who attempted to break away from revivalism, were consumed by it; the problem, Montague contends, was that their rejections and denials eventually evolved into polemical writing and exaggerated argumentation. The quarrel with their ancestors had distorted O'Faolain's and Kavanagh's vision. Montague goes on to say that the young writer should avoid any efforts at reviving a past tradition and should "move on to fresh and original work . . . [and] avoid wrangling with his elders," a statement that shows how the desire to be innovative can blind writers to tendencies in their own work, even in their criticism. A good deal of Montague's argument is devoted to the very wrangling with elders against which he cautions others.

What Montague specifically calls for in his essay is a new focus that demands criticism and satire; the new Ireland needs a Catholic Swift "to clear this apathy from the air," to address society's ills and its sense of tiredness, aimlessness, and disgust.[2] The modern writer should also examine both the strength and weaknesses of Catholicism as a living force in Irish life. Realism and criticism should displace any sentimental treatment of Irish society. The freshness of Montague's position lay not in his call for realism, however, since Joyce, and then Clarke, Kavanagh, O'Faolain, and O'Connor, had already moved in this direction; it came rather in his demand for satire and criticism. And even in this he was not original; he merely demonstrated how deeply the Irish writer at mid-century felt an estrangement from his own society.

That Montague's own poetry does not venture very far in this critical direction is due, no doubt, to the appearance of Clarke's satires between 1955 and 1963 and to the publication of Kinsella's *Another September*, which showed the promise of a satirical mind. With the usual sensitivity over imaginative space which Irish writers possess, Montague may have felt that his opportunities as a satirist were limited. Nonetheless, his essay is interesting on two counts: it predicts the satirical direction in Clarke's and Kinsella's poetry in the 1960s, and it also reveals the importance of social criticism for the writers of Montague's generation.

The urgency of this situation led to Montague's exile, first to America in the early 1950s and then to Paris in the 1960s. As he explains in his introduction to *Poisoned Lands* (1961), the literary atmosphere in post-war Dublin was fouled with "acrimony and insult," so that his "leaving to America became partly a flight." Only later, buoyed by his meeting with the American writers W. D. Snodgrass, Robert Bly, and Gary Snyder, could he feel "strong enough to return to Ireland,"[3] and then only for a short time. He became the Paris correspondent for the *Irish Times* in the early 1960s.

Montague's sensitivity to the Dublin scene can partly be explained, I believe, by his unusual background, which produced a very singular attitude toward Ireland. Born in Brooklyn to Irish parents who had been forced to emigrate because of political activities in Ulster, Montague was sent back to Ireland at the age of four to live with his aunt on the family farm in County Tyrone. In some respects, his boyhood was like that of many other Northern Irish children: he inherited a strong religious tradition and a sense of tribal community; he attended the local Catholic school and eventually went on to the National University in Dublin.[4] The one striking and significant difference in Montague's case was his awareness of his exiled family—in Brooklyn—which caused him to wonder about his own sense of place:

> I had moved from one of the most advanced areas of the twentieth century, New York, back to one of the more . . . shall we say, nineteenth century ways of life. . . . These contrasts were unconsciously implanted in me. . . . When I came down south I moved to the Irish Free State, which again, was a different world.[5]

This confusion about place, extended by his university education in Dublin, has caused Montague throughout his poetry to explore the already nagging question of Irish identity. The characteristic manifestation of this exploration appears as a drive toward reconciliation, a balancing of opposites, a desire for restoration piqued by an awareness of separation. The concern for reconciliation manifests itself not only in subject matter, where it can be discerned in the treatment of love, family loyalty, and politics, but also in his poetics, in a style that seeks experimental forms and in a method that accommodates two different views:

. . . on the one hand continually . . . dig deeper in your own garden patch, in whatever garden patches you have been given or you have claimed, and on the other hand, to try to discover anything across the world which can become accessible to you.[6]

Digging in his garden allowed Montague to discover his historic and personal roots, which he would trace fully in his well-known long poem *The Rough Field* (1972). Sampling the poetic harvests beyond Ireland by discovering the technique and practice of American, French, and English poetic traditions provided him with a wider perspective. In the process he himself has extended the Irish poetic tradition, tapping its fundamental strength of particularity and nudging it forward into a modernist and internationalist stage. The pattern of a modernist reconciliation which unfolds in Montague's poetry appears as a smaller version of what he regards as the essential rift in the modern Irish poetic tradition: the accommodation of both Yeatsian and Joycean directions. Montague's gradual movement from a Joycean sense of exile and isolation toward what resembles a Yeatsian dramatization of history and family has been a conscious attempt on his part to creatively merge two orientations in his literary past.

The Poetics of Ambivalence

The early posture of Montague's art is reflected in the title of his first book, *Forms of Exile* (1958), and in the themes of many of his early poems collected in *Poisoned Lands*. This posture was struck partly out of fascination with Ireland but also out of regret and rejection, the "odi atque amo" of Louis MacNeice's portrait of Ireland in *Autumn Journal*. This stance assumes a Joycean detachment not only toward society but also toward the artistic process of creation. Montague's attitude toward society surfaces in the criticism of Irish life he calls for in his early essay, particularly criticism of the Church for its inward, Jansenist teaching and of the general oppressiveness throughout Ireland, described in "Irish Street Scene, With Lovers": "skies washed and grey;/A tiredness as though the day/Swayed toward sleep." His aesthetic detachment is evident in the treatment of subject matter, particularly those poems which deal with Irish material.

These early poems are remarkable because of their ambivalent attitude toward the idea of an Irish tradition. They appear to reject outright the superficial use of Irishisms condemned in the introduction to the *Dolmen Miscellany;* at the same time, however, they seem to be obsessed with the very subject they would reject. In "The Sean Bhean Bhocht," for example, Montague chooses to emphasize the traditional personification of Ireland as the poor old woman rather than the inspiring Kathleen ni Houlihan, since, from the point of view of the young poet, Ireland is the old sow who will eat her farrow. Parallels to Joyce run throughout the poem, calling to mind Stephen's fear of the old hermit of the west, whose red-rimmed, horny eyes and Gaelic ways threaten to overwhelm the young artist.[7] Montague reflects the spirit of Stephen's rejection of the native tradition with an allusion to the Joycean fascination with eyes and with aged decrepitude:

> Eyes rheumy with racial memory;
> Fragments of bread soaked in brown tea
> And eased between sunken gums.
> Her clothes stank like summer flax;
> Watched all day as she swayed
> Towards death between memories and prayers
> By a farmer's child in a rough play-box.[8]

The same sense of rejection carries over into "Old Mythologies," which on the surface seems to condemn the heroic agenda that Clarke and Kinsella, among others, had declared obsolete. As the poem develops, however, a romantic attachment to the old material briefly asserts itself in the final lines:

Mouths dust-stopped, dark they embrace
Suitably disposed, as urns, underground. . . .
This valley cradles their archaic madness
As once, on an impossibly epic morning,
It upheld their savage stride:
To bagpiped battle marching,
Wolfhounds, lean as models,
At their urgent heels.

(*SP.*, 28)

The striking power of these lines, especially in their rhythm, and the beautiful image at the close of the poem qualify the purported denunciation of heroic Ireland.

This ambivalence occurs again in another early poem, "Like Dolmens Round My Childhood, The Old People," where the criticism of traditional Ireland begins emphatically in the opening of the final stanza—

Ancient Ireland indeed! I was reared by her bedside.
The rune and the chant, evil eye and averted head,
Fomorian fierceness of family and local feud,

only to be softened, dramatically, by a sudden realization of a larger, more coherent pattern of history:

Gaunt figures of fear and friendliness,
For years they trespassed on my dreams,
Until once, in a standing circle of stones,
I felt their shadows pass

Into that dark permanence of ancient forms.

(*SP.*, 27)

These early poems show us a tentative poet, distanced from his material and wary of the tradition he has inherited. They also reveal the increasing tendency among Montague's and Kinsella's generation to use the making of poems as subject matter for poetry. In "Portrait of the Artist as a Model Farmer" Montague again outlines the dichotomy of Irish poetry, those two extreme positions that deny each other, the provincial and the cosmopolitan. The provincial poet-narrator claims that real art "springs only from the native part" and that he should shun foreign influence. But, as the poem's irony leads us to understand, the poet-narrator knows that by shielding his art from "foreign beetles and exotic weeds," he may grow a truly local species but will gain only "fierce anonymity." Eventually, in his later poetry, Montague overcomes this mistrust of the native tradition, but the general mood of the early poems is ambivalent. Like the exile in "Murphy in Manchester," with "half-stirred memories and regrets," the poet views both the old country and the new world as a stranger, removed from each, yet a part of both.[9]

The tentative posture revealed in *Poisoned Lands* resulted in part from Montague's exiled psyche; a stranger in his own land, he has remained distanced from his own traditions and roots. This psychic distance is especially evident in his collection of short stories, *Death of a Chieftain* (1964). The majority of the stories are set in rural Ulster and feature an isolated character whose spiritual separation from his community allows him to probe below its surface. Montague adopted the Joycean technique used so effectively in *Dubliners*, combining intimate understanding with fierce aesthetic detachment to depict the closeness and narrow-mindedness of his Irish characters. In one story, Françoise, a young Frenchwoman married to an Irishman, finds a preoccupation with sin to be rampant in the minds of everyone she meets, even her husband, whose only safeguard is that he is married to her; in another, Bernard Corunna Coote, an exile in Panama, reconstructs his Ulster homeland in hazy, heroic dreams. "The City," the most relevant of these stories to Montague's poetic strategy, focuses upon Peter Douglas, an educated journalist living and working in London, who comes home to a small Ulster town to visit his parents. After being awakened by a cry of a man being attacked in the streets, Peter sets out to investigate what happened to him, only to discover that he was a Catholic, savagely beaten by the Protestant police

as a result of the old tribal hostilities. As he gathers his informa-
tion to expose this bigotry, Peter discovers that no one on either
side wishes to pursue the matter; all are content to let it die
down. His mother discourages him from writing the article:
"Oh, it's easy for you. You don't live here all the year round,"
and the victim's father condones the action: "If he'd stayed at
home with his mother the way a dacent-rared boy should, not
a hate would have happened to him."

The feeling of separation cuts both ways in "The Cry." It
allows Peter his detached, almost objective censure of the fear-
ridden, close-minded tribal consciousness; it also underscores
the alienation of the exile and emphasizes the mistrust and lack
of acceptance on the part of the community toward the outside.
In the final scene in the story, Peter, ruminating over his type-
writer, looks out his window to see the town idiot on the street
below trying to get his attention. As their eyes meet the idiot
smiles and triumphantly holds up a crude sign: "Nosy Parker
Go home."

The delicacy of Peter Douglas' situation in "The Cry" reflects
the direction of Montague's poetic development in the early
poetry. Drawing his poetic identity from an established literary
tradition, Montague nevertheless could not fully accept it, just
as he could not feel completely at home in Ireland, knowing that
he belonged to other places as well. Poised between two worlds,
he inherited the traditionalism of Ireland and aspired to the
experimentalism of international culture, as embodied in American and French literature. The metaphorical representation of
this tension is caught nicely in "The Water Carrier," the opening
poem in *Poisoned Lands*. The crucial image of precarious balance
opens the poem:

> Twice daily I carried water from the spring,
> Morning before leaving for school, and evening;
> Balanced as a fulcrum between two buckets.
>
> A bramble rough path ran to the river
> Where one stepped carefully across slime-topped stones,
> With corners abraded as bleakly white as bones.

The artistic implications here are easy to see. The spring, a source of poetic inspiration, runs pure and cold and gives off the sense of life around it.

> One stood until the bucket brimmed
> Inhaling the musty smell of unpicked berries,
> That heavy greenness fostered by water.

Connected inseparably in the poet's mind with boyhood memories of rural Ulster, the spring becomes in the final stanzas a symbol of restoration for the poet. The imagery of the filling of the buckets becomes "stylized" in memory as the imagined portrait of an Egyptian water-carrier:

> Recovering the scene, I had hoped to stylize it,
> Like the portrait of an Egyptian water-carrier:
> Yet halt, entranced by slight but memoried life.
>
> I sometimes come to take the water there,
> Not as return or refuge, but some pure thing,
> Some living source, half-imagined and half-real
>
> Pulses in the fictive water that I feel.
>
> (*SP.*, 21)

In this early poem the poet senses the limitation of the spring; its cold water "fell/Like manacles of ice on the wrists"; tradition can restrict as well as inform. But these restrictions are Blake's "mind-forged manacles," as Montague's final lines make clear. The poet must apply his imagination to plumb the depths of the spring; mere representation will not do. The poet recognizes the precarious balance, "half-imagined and half-real," and can create only once he has accepted the vitality of the world around him. The precariousness of the task must be emphasized—"one stepped carefully across slime-topped stones"—particularly in the Irish context where, beginning with Yeats, poets announced their intentions to transform their pasts.

As we have noted, Montague has not consistently displayed the imaginative control over his material necessary for such a transformation. The ambivalence toward his roots which has surfaced in a choice of two poetic strategies has caused some critics to read his work as a constant endeavor to marry the local and the cosmopolitan.[10] Yet his understanding of poetic difficulty, again made more poignant with Montague's expressed awareness of the development of the Irish poetic tradition by Yeats and later by the revivalists, has shown a growing poetic maturity:

> Who today asks for more
> —Smoke of battle blown aside—
> Than the struggle with casual
> Graceless unheroic things,
> The greater task of swimming
> Against a slackening tide?
>
>   (*SP.*, 11)

Montague's Joycean posture, evident in these lines in the recognition of the unheroic, has shaped his sensibilities, particularly toward his Irish origins. Moreover, if we read correctly the scattered evidence in *Poisoned Lands* and in the short stories from *Death of a Chieftain,* then we can discern the posture of the wary exile easing into an accommodation of the tribal memory. From the young poet's ebb and flow over the matter of Ireland, we infer those concerns that eventually culminate in a poetic blend of traditionalism and modernism, particularly in Montague's impressive *The Rough Field.*

The Exile as Poet

The Joycean direction in Montague's poetry and in his overall poetic strategy came easily to the young poet. It implied distance, criticism, cosmopolitanism, and the emphasized heroic stature and hauteur of the artist. As an exiled writer living in Paris, Montague saw the Joycean dimensions in his own experiences. Unlike Joyce, however, Montague decided against permanent exile. Ever aware of polemics, he chose to return to his rural beginnings and familiar locales in order to try the other half of his poetic method. Although Joyce provided the initial example, Montague began to see that example elsewhere as well, particularly in the work of Yeats and Patrick Kavanagh. Aided by a developing perspective and a confidence in his own talent, he could regard the modern Irish poetic tradition and the work of specific poets as informing rather than as threatening his own work.

Kavanagh's importance to recent Irish poetry has been recognized in criticism and literary commentary over the last ten years. Both Seamus Heaney and Seamus Deane, among others, have explored Kavanagh's enormous influence over recent Irish poets.[11] The unique qualities of his parochial realism—the iconoclastic treatment of revivalism, the resistance to Yeatsian abstraction, the insistence upon a fidelity to the local, the commitment to a trusting of ordinary experience—all these extended the concept of the Irish poetic tradition by granting greater authority to a poetry that attempted to probe what was intimately known. Moreover, Kavanagh's Ulster heritage is of no small significance to contemporary poets in Ireland, many of whom—like Heaney, Montague, and Deane—are from Northern Ireland. Kavanagh's treatment of Monaghan's landscape with its twisted furrows has encouraged others to treat their own familiar locales.

As Montague turned more to the treatment of his Ulster heritage, his poetic development moved gradually toward the acceptance of the implications of Kavanagh's poetic strategy. Throughout the 1960s, Montague drew upon the memories of the time he had spent growing up on the family farm, Gavaghey, in County Tyrone, Northern Ireland. The results appeared as *The Rough Field* and reflect more than a decade of rethinking, rewriting, and rearranging. Throughout this process Montague drew constantly on his sense of place and attempted to create a structure that would explain the complex questions of identity and origins.

It is important to stress the deliberate creative process of *The*

Rough Field, especially the conscious rethinking and rearranging, because the book, or more properly the poetic sequence, collects poetry written over a ten-year period and represents the culmination of an important phase in Montague's work. As he explains in the preface,

> This poem begins in the early 'sixties. . . . I had a kind of vision, in the medieval sense, of my home area, the unhappiness of its historical destiny. . . . I managed to draft the opening and the close, but soon realized that I did not have the technique for so varied a task. At intervals during the decade I returned to it, when the signs seemed right.[12]

While waiting for the right signs, Montague published two books of verse, *A Chosen Light* (1967) and *Tides* (1971), both of which provided proving grounds for theme and technique. In each, the poetry treats the posture of exile, gradually injecting it with a homing instinct and a sense of community.

A Chosen Light explores the emotional limits of exile by setting many poems in Paris and the French countryside, emphasizing a distanced and obscured vision: "Through the poplars we spy the broken/Shape of the *chateau*." The French locale does not in itself provide sufficient value in these poems; rather, it functions primarily to trigger boyhood memories of Ireland.

> On the first Thursday of every month
> The sirens sound through Paris
> A warning exercise. It begins
> With the sobbing call of the Alert
> Which, against my will, seems
> A nostalgic, almost homely sound
> Recalling nights in Armagh school.[13]

The self-conscious phrase "against my will" marks a psychological shift in the poetic strategy. It implies a certain inevitability that the poet will be drawn back to Ireland, to excavate the rough field of his Ulster beginnings; that the cosmopolitan orientation of Paris may offer perspective, but not sustenance. The drive toward identity proved too much in the end even for Montague's internationalist inclinations.

Tides confirms this notion. The instinctual action of love in the titular poem,

> in obedience to
> the pull & tug
> of your great tides.
>
> *(SP., 71)*

applies to the overall tendency behind the book: the passivity of the poetic imagination as it is urged along by powerful forces. In general, this tendency advances by means of the metaphorical unity suggested by the book's title, with constant references to the sea and to the pull of gravity. Sometimes, the metaphor explains the force of love upon the poet; occasionally, however, the sea is portrayed in more personal and individual terms, revealing something of the poet's concern for identity:

> the coastal waters recede,
> transparent passages of light
> green expanding to the long
>
> periodic rhythms of the open sea
> upon which we balance and slide,
> hoping for pattern.[14]

The pattern of identity originates in childhood, which exerts its own gravitational pull as the poet begins to focus on his boyhood in rural Ulster: "I go to say goodbye to the Cailleach/that terrible figure who haunted my childhood." In the probing of childhood, the sea functions metaphorically, first as memory—the deep storehouse and "tangle of our minds"—and then, in the force of the tide, as a poetic guest moving the poet into deeper waters, where he accepts and understands the importance of

> the wine dark
> sea of history

on which we all turn
turn and thresh and disappear.

(*SP.*, 97)

A Chosen Light and *Tides* both demonstrate Montague's increasing willingness to follow Kavanagh's advice never to doubt the validity of one's own parish. The direction of the poetry written in the mid-1960s shows a growing conviction about the integrity of the locale, however small and remote, as a source of both personal and universal meaning. At the same time, however, undoubtedly anticipating the design of *The Rough Field*, Montague saw the need to expand Kavanagh's poetics to account for a historical perspective; for this Montague adopted a Yeatsian technique as well.

The Rough Field

Yeats's interest in esoteric schemes of history and his well-known practice of mythologizing his friends and family provided Montague with successful poetic strategies that assigned universal significance to the personal events of his life. Also, Yeats's special use of Georgian Ireland and his symbolic treatment of Parnell's fall have had particular relevance for Montague. In designing *The Rough Field*, he chose to apply Elizabethan historical background to modern Ulster and to focus on the fall of the Clan O'Neill, each strategy deriving much from Yeatsian practice. Moreover, the use of history which runs throughout *The Rough Field* implies a sense of loss, both Montague's own and his community's. His consciousness of his own role as the voice of a community expressing its loss resembles the later Yeats, whose celebration of the Protestant Ascendancy stressed the loss of its power and influence in Irish life.

The blending of various poetic postures adds complexity to a poem that ostensibly sets out to explore the formation of the self. Technique, style, and voice allow Montague to deal with autobiographical material and the implications of its universal meaning. Poetic assertions of this kind require authority or conviction to carry them off, and the poet-narrator of *The Rough Field* establishes both. Through the application of history, the blending of style, and the choice of subject matter, Montague shows a remarkable maturity in this poem, which allows him to accommodate antithetical aspects of his poetic tradition, particularly Joycean and Yeatsian elements. Montague's control over his material is never more evident than in *The Rough Field*, a sequence which gathers shorter, individual poems into a single work; the successful manipulation of form and style demonstrates great poetic maturity, evidence of "a poet coming to terms with his own artistic past, discerning pattern and significance within it."[15]

In the opening section of *The Rough Field*, "Home Again," the poet-narrator describes the psychological quest behind the complete poem.

> . . . I assume old ways of walk and work
> So easily, yet feel the sadness of return
> To what seems still, though changing. . . .
> Harsh landscape that haunts me
> Well and stone, in the bleak moors of dream.
> With all my circling a failure to return.
>
> (*RF.*, 13)

The task throughout the poem is to return imaginatively to the old farm and countryside in order to recover a sense of identity and cultural meaning. Montague's method combines his Irish poetic heritage with his interest in modernist technique. He comments on his methodology in an essay that appeared during the writing of *The Rough Field*:

> Sooner or later, if one continues to write poetry, the desire grows to write a long poem or sequence, something more expansive than the lyric to which anthologies have reduced English poetry, something which is co-terminous with at least one whole aspect of one's experience. It is this latter aspect of modern poetry which is particularly irritating; that while novelists have ransacked the details of

twentieth-century life (it is to *Ulysses,* not "The Waste Land," or even *Paterson,* we must go for a contemporary equivalent of the "felt life" in *The Canterbury Tales*), poets have limited themselves, like the castrati of the Papal choir, to certain complex, and asocial tones.[16]

The length and the form of the poem gave Montague the opportunity to allow the "felt life" to emerge gradually, refracted from many angles so that it might be seen completely. The poet's own family history collided with Irish history to create a complete and complex sense of cultural identity and personality. The sequential design complements the strategy, moving from the poet's own feelings about the present to his feelings about the past, to a meditation on Ulster history, and, finally, to reflections on the present Ulster crisis and its impact upon contemporary Irish society. The sequence coheres by associational or psychological threads rather than by chronology. This type of organization permitted Montague to establish the mythic qualities of history and landscape which he sees as shaping the Ulster consciousness.

Much of the critical commentary on *The Rough Field* emphasizes Montague's attempts to reconcile his understanding of a local, rural sense with his professed commitments to internationalism and cosmopolitanism. There is some debate over Montague's success in balancing this tension, but virtually all commentators agree on the essential nature of his poetic task.[17] In the process of granting Montague a poetic success or charging him with a failure, these critics have concentrated upon what Terence Brown has identified as the poem's central problem: the clash between contemporary, worldly, urban values and timeless, parochial, rural ones.[18]

Certainly, *The Rough Field* exhibits such a tension. The specific details that embody the felt life of Garvaghey and its environs are carefully and completely recalled so as to recreate a lost world. Ruminating upon deserted cabins and thatched cottages with their roofs slumped in—ruins of a former community—the poet remembers the simplicity and purity of childhood.

> Old Danaghy raging
> With his stick, to keep our
> Cows from a well, that now
> Is boarded up, like himself.
> Here his son and I robbed a
> Bee's nest, kicking the combs
> Free; our boots smelt sweetly
> For days afterwards. . . .
> . . . Remembering,
> I seem to smell wild honey
> On my face.
>
> (*RF.*, 52–53)

The "small backward place" in section 6, "The Good Night," recalled through memory, idealized and romanticized for its particularity—"Each grassblade bends with/Translucent beads of moisture"—becomes in section 9, "A New Siege," an emblem of general significance:

> the rough field
> of the universe
> growing, changing
> a net of energies
> crossing patterns
> weaving towards
> a new order
> a new anarchy
> always different
> always the same.
>
> (*RF.*, 75)

The dramatic conversion of the "small backward place" into the universal field evolves gradually so as to lessen its apparent inconsistency. Section 4, "A Severed Head," introduces the theme of the loss of cultural heritage, first with the flight of the Irish earls in 1607 and later with the death of the Irish language in the nineteenth century. Without a culture the Ulster Irish have lost a part of themselves; as a result they lack the ability to encounter or recover the past and meaning.

> All around, shards of a lost tradition . . .
> The whole landscape a manuscript
> We had lost the skill to read,
> A part of our past disinherited.
>
> (*RF.*, 34–35)

Echoing Kinsella's concerns in "Nightwalker" about a society ignorant of its own cultural heritage, Montague here measures cultural loss against present values. Without a sense of tradition, contemporary Ireland looks only to the short-term future; people become profit-driven and materialistic, cut off from any sense of communal understanding. Even the transformation of physical reality reflects this loss. The older appreciation of beauty, implicit in the design of farms and fields, is displaced by functionalism:

> Row after row of council cottages
> Ride the hill, curving up to the church
> Or down to the docks
> Where a crane tilts into emptiness.
>
> Here nothing has been planned—
> Assembled, yes, casual
> And coarse as detritus
> Affronting eye and mind
>
> Only a drift of smoke
> And the antlike activity of cars
> Indicate life; with the wild flap
> Of laundry in a thousand backyards.
>
> (*RF.*, 67)

The final transformation of the small place, Garvaghey, into the universal grows out of a recognition of the futility and emptiness of the modern condition not only in the social unrest in Northern Ireland but also in the world at large:

> Lines of protest
>   lines of change

                    a drum beating
                            across Berkeley
                    all that Spring . . .
                    running voices
                            streets of Berlin
                    Paris, Chicago
                            seismic waves
                    zigzagging through
                            a faulty world

                                                    (*RF.*, 74)

The attempt to equate Northern Ireland's political turmoil
with a worldwide movement is only part of Montague's reconciliation of tribal Ulster with urban worldliness. In section 10, "The
Wild Dog Rose," he adapts a Joycean strategy that rejects narrowness, superstition, ignorance, and hatred in favor of understanding and love. The poet-narrator describes a visit to an old
woman near the family farm and recalls the childhood memories
of an old hag,

                    . . . the great hooked nose, the cheeks
            dewlapped with dirt, the staring blue
            of the sunken eyes, the mottled claws
            clutching a stick.

                                                    (*RF.*, 78)

But as an adult the poet-narrator understands the reality behind
the appearance: that the woman has lived a lonely life, enduring
the taunts of children. Moreover, she suffered from a violent
crime one night when a drunkard attempted to rape her. Yet
despite her mistreatment, she is able to forgive, if not forget,
and to find solace in religion or nature. She reads a lesson of a
simple but profound beauty in the wild rosebush at her door,
"the only rose without thorns":

                    Whenever I see it, . . . I remember
                    the Holy Mother of God and
                    all she suffered.

                                                    (*RF.*, 80)

The magnanimity of her response stands as an emblem of love, understanding, and forgiveness for the poet and his own struggle with past and present injustices.

For some of Montague's readers, however, these attempts at connecting the tribal with the universal fall short; the planned reconciliation is not realized. Douglas Dunn has sensed an imbalance in the urban and rural tensions which inclines toward an idealization of the rural.[19] Terence Brown believes that Montague's romanticism undermined his sense of history, causing the poem to end with a "touchingly naive example of historical faith."[20] Edna Longley, wishing to have it both ways, has criticized *The Rough Field* for lacking cultural resolution, but has praised it as an ambitious attempt.[21] The logical outcome of Longley's assessment, although her argument does not go this far, would be to make Montague a distant heir of Keats, whose failed poetic quests are read as great expressions of romantic searches for unity.

The connection with romanticism has proven to be important to *The Rough Field*, one that Montague himself insists upon in a revealing denial: "No Wordsworthian dream enchants me here/With glint of glacial corry, totemic mountain." Montague protests too much here, of course, and in the process not only irradiates the Wordsworthian context of the poem but also introduces another subject, the struggle of the poetic imagination as the source of art. This second subject is crucial to Montague's meaning. It is in the treatment of the imagination and of the power of the poetic act to transform surroundings that the poet truly defines identity. The subject of poetry, especially the poetic imagination, rather than the political and cultural materials identified by most of Montague's readers, leads us to a proper understanding of the poet's insistence upon reconciliation.

References to a Wordsworthian preoccupation with memory, with childhood experiences, and with the role of the imagination are sprinkled throughout various sections of *The Rough Field*. The opening denial cited above occurs in the very first poem, gaining our attention from the outset. In section 6, the debt to Wordsworth is apparent in the emotional experiences of boyhood walks—"every crevice held/A secret sweetness"—and in the description of attempts to catch the monster trout, which the poet mythologizes in an allusion to Finn's salmon of wisdom:

> Was that
> The ancient trout of wisdom
> I meant to catch? As I plod
> Through the paling darkness
> Details emerge, and memory
> Warms.
>
> (*RF.*, 52)

The Wordsworthian parallels are so strong as to echo language;

> . . . a thread
> Of water still leading me on
> Past stale bog-cuttings
>
> (*RF.*, 52)

resembles the young Wordsworth in *The Prelude* "being led" by the force of nature.

The importance of memory and imagination to the entire poem becomes clearer a few lines later:

> . . . but I am
> In the possession of their past
> (The pattern history weaves
> From one small backward place)
> Marching through memory magnified.
>
> (*RF.*, 53)

Montague describes no less than the poetic act itself here, declaring its importance to the strategy behind *The Rough Field*. Reentry to the "small backward place" must be accomplished through the imagination, or "memory magnified," since, as we know from section 4, "The Severed Head," the poet must reconstruct a lost world.

> Like shards
> Of a lost culture, the slopes
> Are strewn with cabins, deserted

In my lifetime.
. . . .
All around, shards of a lost tradition:
From the Rough Field I went to school
In the Glens of the Hazels.

(*RF.*, 34)

The real "task," a word Montague equates with the making
of poems, is not only to reenter and reclaim Garvaghey but also
to remake it. Thus, the idea of tradition becomes essential to the
poem's purpose. To read the landscape and recall its Irish names
is to attempt to bridge what Thomas Kinsella has called the
"gapped, discontinuous" condition of Irish culture. History and
culture have been absorbed by the landscape, preserved there
by the old language, which signifies location; the poet's task is
to reflect the greater depth of that absorption. To illustrate that
depth, Montague utilizes the image of the grafted tongue, the
alien English language that the Irish were forced to learn:

An Irish
child weeps at school
repeating its English.
After each mistake

The master
gouges another mark
on the tally stick
hung about its neck.

(*RF.*, 39)

But in Montague's version, the older language retains its persistence, shaping the grafted tongue with the effects of the older
culture.

Yet even English in these parts
Took a lawless turn, as who
Would not stroll by Bloody Brae
To Black Lough, or guddle trout
In a stream called the Routing Burn?
. . . .
And what of stone-age Sess Kill Green
Tullycorker and Tullyglush?

> Names twining braid Scots and Irish,
> Like Fall Brae, springing native
> As a whitethorn bush?
>
> (*RF.*, 40)

The poet, who in section 1, "Home Again," discovered the gift of poetry and the power of making music with language, must divine the cultural meaning behind the old words that describe places:

> A high, stony place—bogstreams,
> Not milk and honey—but our own:
> From the Glen of the Hazels
> To the Golden Stone may be
> The longest journey
>   I have ever gone.
>
> (*RF.*, 40)

The task is made more difficult because modern life in its materialism and commercialism seems indifferent, if not hostile, to past culture. Irish as a language is useless in the modern European marketplace. In such a world, even the past achievement of poetic tradition seems in jeopardy of being forgotten.

> The visitor to Coole Park
> in search of a tradition
> finds
>   a tangled alley-way
> a hint of foundation wall
> (the kitchen floor)
>   high wire
> to protect the famous beech-tree
> from raw initials
>   and a lake
> bereft of swans.
>
> (*RF.*, 67)

Left to itself, tradition cannot serve; it becomes only a monument, another relic of the past, merely a ruin of a foundation for what was once a big house.

The poetic challenge for Montague, then, shifted to the problem of continuity, restoring or reclaiming the efficacy of poetic values. The intrusion of this modern world in its various forms—"a hint of foundation"; the raw, unfinished, concrete dance hall in the middle of the country (poem 5, section 6); or the new Omagh road, which has chewed up the landscape and the wildlife—underscores the importance of memory and imagination to recall the traditional world, which has almost vanished. Thus the poet's confrontation with the Cailleach, the old woman of his childhood, becomes an important link with the past as well as the promise of a reconciliation.

> Memories have wrought reconciliation
> between us, we talk in ease at last,
> like old friends, lovers almost,
> sharing secrets.
>
> (*RF.*, 78)

In the epilogue, the poet has accepted the inevitability of a lost world, claiming that "only a sentimentalist" would want to live the difficult life of the past. At the same time, however, he acknowledges that "something mourns" and that while modernization promises much, it also takes much away:

> . . . part
> of a world where action had been wrung
> through painstaking years to ritual.
>
> Acknowledged when the priest blessed
> the green tipped corn, or Protestant
> lugged pale turnip, swollen marrow
> to robe the kirk for Thanksgiving.,
>
> (*RF.*, 82)

Recollection and memory blend the past and present into a significance that becomes personal as well as cultural. In the search for the self, Montague has not only found tradition but also, through its extension and use, the possibility of continuity.

Garvaghey, Montague's rough field, may be the victim of twentieth-century progress, but through poetic effort it has achieved a symbolic significance impervious to change.

Poetic Style and Form

With its emphasis upon the universal within the particular, *The Rough Field* was the culmination of one stage of Montague's poetic career. The amalgamation of poetic strategies and postures, the creative and selective ordering of the Irish poetic tradition, the decision to explore and reclaim the local and the familiar—all these characteristics resolve in some manner the tension between the native and the cosmopolitan impulses in his writing. The resolution takes place not through the choice of specific subject matter but primarily through the discovery and development of an innovative poetic style, which Montague brought chiefly from American poetry to augment and expand conservative and inward-looking Irish practices.

The very design of *The Rough Field* shows how style and form gradually emerged to provide the blend of domestic and foreign stock which Montague sought. The earliest parts of the poem, some written as early as 1962, tend to rely upon traditional forms such as the sonnet and the quatrain and on consciously poetic language that leans toward an Irish exuberance: "gaunt farmhouse . . . plaintive moorland," "with glint of glacial corry," "oozy blackness of bog-banks," "slabbery gaps of winter." Parts of the poem written later are dramatically more innovative, combining different styles within a new form of alternating dimeter lines. Stark and emphatic contemporary language contrasts with the archaic rhetoric of seventeenth-century Derry, blending past and present.

> SMALL SHOT HATH
> POURED LIKE HAIL
> THE GREAT GUNS
> SHAKEN OUR WALLS
> . . . .

> GOD HAS MADE US
> AN IRON PILLAR
>   AND BRAZEN WALLS
> AGAINST THIS LAND.
>
> Lines of suffering
>   lines of defeat
> under the walls
>   ghetto terraces
>
> . . . .
>
> love's alleyway
>   message scrawled
> Popehead: Tague
>   my own name
> hatred's synonym

$$(RF., 74)$$

The changing form and style owe much to William Carlos Williams, whom Montague admires and remembers as a father-figure.[22] Williams' influence is certainly apparent in the various short-line stanzaic patterns in section 9, "A New Siege"; the alternating three-line pattern in *Paterson* provided Montague with his model. Williams' presence also figures elsewhere in the poem, in the clean rhythm and ordinary language of section 2, "The Leaping Fire"—

> Your white hair
> on thin rack
> of your shoulders

$$(RF., 22)$$

—and in the echo in section 4, "A Severed Head," of Williams' famous imagist poem "The Red Wheelbarrow":

> Only the shed remains
> In use for calves, although fuschia
> Bleeds by the wall, and someone has
> Propped a yellow cartwheel
> Against the door.

$$(RF., 34)$$

While Montague was affected particularly by Williams' innovations, he was impressed also with the openness and experimental quality of American poetry in general.[23] English poetry, on the other hand, seemed to him to be rigid and conservative. As Montague began to develop the special use of marginal material in *The Rough Field*, he rejected English conservatism in favor of American inventiveness:

> . . . there is an inhibiting traditionalism in contemporary English poetry on this side i.e., the British side of the Atlantic which saps inventiveness. It is only a habit of the mind which makes us expect a poem to march as docile as a herd of sheep between the fence of white margins. And what about all that waste paper, not reserved for silences but left fallow at the poem's edge? No farmer would allow such poor ploughing.[24]

The agrarian references explain Montague's purpose in using quotations, descriptions, and phrases in the marginal notes and prose passages between verses; he wishes to sow exotic American seeds of experimentation in the native ground of Irish experience in order to produce a truly modern Irish poem. Innovation in style and form would allow traditional historical and political subject matter to be seen in a different light.

Montague's use of collage is especially effective in developing both social and autobiographical meaning in *The Rough Field*. Historical material, religious ideas, and descriptions of Ulster landscape are presented by means of experimental techniques and inventive forms, allowing the poet to see his own roots with a distancing perspective. In section 3, "The Bread God," the poet scatters genuine religious messages from pamphlets, letters, and newspaper advertisements throughout the poetry to create a clash of ideas.[25] First we are presented with a reverential description of Catholic worship—

> The crowds for communion, heavy coat and black shawl,
> Surge in thick waves, cattle thronged in a fair,
> To the oblong of altar rails, and there
> Where red berried holly shines against gold
> In the door of the tabernacle, wait patient

And prayerful and crowded, for each moment
Of silence, eyes closed, mouth raised
For the advent of the flesh-graced Word.

—and then a hostile Protestant extremist reaction:

DEAR BROTHER!
ECUMENISM *is* THE NAME *of the* WHORE OF BABYLON!
SHE *who* SHITS *on the* SEVEN HILLS
ONE CHURCH, ONE STATE
WITH THE POPE THE HEAD OF THE STATE: BY RE-UNION
ROME MEANS ABSORPTION
UNIFORMITY MEANS TYRANNY
APISTS = PAPISTS
But GOD DELIGHTS IN VARIETY
NO *two leaves are* EXACTLY *alike*!

(*RF.*, 28)

In section 7, "Hymn to the New Omagh Road," factual statements in the form of lists are mixed in with fragments of romantic and sentimental poetry. The collage technique presents a
series of separate voices, each of which offers a particular image
or message; often, these images contradict or clash with those
which precede or follow them. In the search for meaning, the
reader must complete the poem, connecting the voices and
drawing upon inference about their collective significance. The
sense of Ulster reality comes finally in the recognition of
pluralism, a recognition made possible chiefly through poetic
form. Montague thereby escapes the necessity for editorializing,
while at the same time, by his selection of materials and his
formal presentation, he urges a particular interpretation upon
the reader.

Continuity Discovered

The balance Montague achieved in *The Rough Field* between
modernist techniques and native subject matter lessened his
anxieties and the ambivalence regarding his use of the Irish

poetic tradition. With the possibilities provided by American and French literature clear in his mind, he softened his views about the limitations and restrictions of tradition, which he had subsequently described as lifeless conventions and predictable subject matter. In an essay written for the 1974 *Faber Book of Irish Verse*, he admits the possibility of continuity within the tradition, as long as Irish writers recognize and capitalize upon their diverse cultural backgrounds:

> An Irish poet seems to me in a richly ambiguous position, with the pressure of an incompletely discovered past behind him, and the whole modern world around. . . . A tradition, however, should not be an anachronistic defense against experience, and through our change of languages we have access to the English-speaking world . . . the Irish writer, at his best, is a natural cosmopolitan.[26]

All of the concerns of Montague's early poetry are here—the fear of inbred Irishism, the deadness of tradition, the promise of modernism and internationalism—but they are rearranged and emphasized to show that the poet has placed himself within the tradition, draws his identity from it, and, through his own contributions, has declared the tradition continuous. We can sense a blend of Yeatsian and Joycean perspectives here, used to turn both an incompletely discovered personal past and a lost language and culture into positive strengths.

This conviction lies at the center of some of Montague's more recent poems, particularly the 1975 book *A Slow Dance*. The opening poem reveals the strategy and the preoccupation of the book, a slow dance back to the earth, to its myths, and to its landscapes, which contain the memory of a culture.

> Darkness, cave
> drip, earth womb
>
> We move slowly
> back to our origins.[27]

The emphasis here is not on the complacent acceptance of a sentimentalized view of Irish myth and culture; Montague does not imply that there is any place for stasis in the poet's world. Rather, the tradition offers the context and the subject matter with which the poet must remake his world. The very awareness of his lost culture provides the prospect of renewal.

> I still affirm
> That nothing dies, that even from
> Such bitter failure memory grows.
>
> (*SD.*, 19)

The emphasis on continuity, "that nothing dies," frames the final poem in the book, "O'Riada's Farewell," a tribute to Sean O'Riada, the Irish composer and musician who died in 1971. Like his contemporary Thomas Kinsella, Montague sees O'Riada as an important connection with the Irish past and with traditional Gaelic culture. For Montague, O'Riada's passing was both a personal and a cultural loss, since his music bridged the gap between modern and ancient Ireland. It is as a fellow artist that Montague addresses O'Riada's shade, imploring his old friend to "leave us your skills," so that other artists might carry on.

That O'Riada's achievement has great significance for the Irish poetic tradition and for Montague's own poetry is made clear from the poem's opening scene, in which the poet and his old friend discuss a common problem, the preservation of traditional culture: "two natives warming ourselves/at the revived fire." The echo of "revival" in "revived" indicates the importance of continuity in tradition, that a fire unattended will soon grow cold. The fire *is* revived chiefly through the artist's efforts to recapture the past,

> the music leaping
> like a long candle flame
> to light ancestral faces.
>
> (*SD.*, 57)

This has been Montague's concern, of course, particularly in *The Rough Field*, where ancestral faces give the poet an understanding of his own past and identity. He reminds O'Riada of their common cause, of the struggle to light the way; both musician and poet resemble their Gaelic predecessors, the harpist Carolan and the poet Raftery, blind and wandering from house to house.

> chill of winter
> a slowly failing fire
> faltering desire
>
> Darkness of Darkness
> We meet on our way
> in loneliness
>
> Blind Carolan
> Blind Raftery
>
> (*SD.*, 60)

The final section of the poem shifts to a consideration of an expanded view of death, so that the "failing fire" suggests both O'Riada's life forces and the vitality of the Irish tradition. Dying so young, O'Riada's name was "extinguished," never to be connected with the other greats of music with whom he deserved to be considered: Mozart, Mahler, and Bowley. Montague grieves for the loss of an authentic Irish voice, but is compelled by O'Riada's example to grow another tongue, to create terrible beauty and thereby extend the tradition.

> a voice
> like an animal howling
> to itself on a hillside
> in the empty church of the world
>
> a lament so total
> it mourns no one
> but the globe itself.
>
> (*SD.*, 63)

In his final tribute to O'Riada, Montague shapes the poem's epigraph by quoting Ezra Pound: O'Riada has "gathered from air a live tradition."

The global concerns expressed in this poem's closing lines reiterate Montague's drive for universals in his poetry; yet that far-reaching perspective originated in the local, the traditional, and the familiar. These have been coinsistent tensions in his poetry, and they reveal a steady commitment to solving a particular artistic problem. They also demonstrate a determined effort on Montague's part to identify himself with an Irish poetic tradition that would expand rather than restrict his art. As the poetry of *The Rough Field* and *A Slow Dance* shows, the continuity of that tradition has been a major concern, so much so that it has emerged as poetic subject matter in its own right. Montague's great task of sensing the poetic in the ordinary and even the unheroic has revealed the deeper and more basic struggle for a sense of cultural identity.

8

The Poetry of Commitment:
Seamus Heaney

With the example of the previous generations before him, Seamus Heaney would appear to inhabit a pacified poetic territory. Clarke and Fallon had done battle with the great Yeats; Kavanagh used Joycean technique to uncover and celebrate the ordinary; Kinsella and Montague have applied international practice to Irish subjects. The Irish poetic tradition has been thoroughly explored and mapped, offering the promise of continuity and marking clearly for the new generation the false trails of those who have gone before.

On the surface, Heaney's work, particularly his early poetry, seems to reflect and corroborate this view. The descriptions of rural life in Derry and the treatment of nature in *Death of a Naturalist* (1966) and *Door into the Dark* (1969) demonstrate the fluency and ease with the local and the familiar which produces what Kavanagh would call authenticity or truthfulness in poetry. Moreover, Heaney seems to have accommodated the presence of Yeatsian influence, the litmus test for poetic survival; his occasional romantic treatment of nature and his capacity for mythmaking and the manipulation of history in *North* (1975) demonstrate the confidence and ease with which he moves within his tradition.

But despite his early success and the favorable and serious reception that has greeted Heaney's work, powerful and serious self-doubts and uncertainty about his place in the Irish poetic tradition have emerged in his recent poetry. Some of this anxiety is the natural result of maturity and growth, as Heaney's poetic horizons have expanded from a regional view of rural life in Derry to a more universal consideration of human nature. The widening of poetic focus has led Heaney inevitably to deep, disturbing questions about the conflict between self-expression and the public voice, a conflict that has produced, in Derek Mahon's words, "a voice which, whilst remaining true to the ancient intonations, had something to say beyond the shores of Ireland."[1]

Mahon's phrase aims at the general direction of Ulster poetry, but applies particularly to the central tension in Heaney's work. "Remaining true to ancient intonations" means fidelity to roots and familiar places, an obvious characteristic of Heaney's early poetry and something he has woven into the fabric of recent poems. It provides the essence of his integrity as an artist and allows him a coherence and a clarity in shaping images and thoughts. The other half of Mahon's phrase aptly describes Heaney's inclination, and the inclination of most post-Yeatsian poetry, to become more universal, to transcend the limitations of the local and to appeal to a wide reading public. The tension in Heaney's writing occurs in the effort to expand poetic range without losing the authenticity of the voice shaped by those ancient intonations. The struggle has been exacerbated by the Ulster crisis, the recent events of which have coincided with Heaney's development as a poet. His attempts to respond to that crisis, to allow his poetry to find a suitable metaphor that could express his feelings about events in Northern Ireland, have placed a special demand on his work, both from within himself, as a self-conscious artist, and from without, from a reading public that demands political poetry that is clear in its commitment.

The results of these pressures can be seen clearly in Heaney's recent books *North* and *Field Work* (1979), both of which, in different ways, measure the public and the private voices of the poet. Critical reactions to these books, particularly to *North*, have centered primarily on the political aspects of the poems, dividing those who see the work as an imaginative triumph over terror from those who regret its timidity and unwillingness to face up to commitment.[2] That the critical responses emphasize the political is not surprising when we consider the extent to which the Northern Ireland crisis has been made a literary subject, in drama, in poetry, in criticism and in literary journalism.[3]

Heaney himself has been a part of the latter development, drawing readers' attention to the political side of his works in numerous recent interviews and essays.[4] We learn a good deal from these pieces about the background of the poetry and, particularly, the poet's understanding of his own writing, "poetry as divination, poetry as revelation of the self to the self, as restoration of the culture to itself; poems as elements of continuity."[5] These views from an Ulster poet do not surprise us. Revealing the self and restoring a culture seem natural consequences of living in a bifurcated society, a half-culture that exists as a result of the clash of British and Irish traditions in Northern Ireland. The attempt at revelation through poetry makes Heaney's task more complicated, since as an Ulsterman he has inherited a literary tradition that, as he says, is two-humped.

> I speak and write in English, but do not altogether share the preoccupations and perspectives of an Englishman. I teach English literature, I publish in London, but the English tradition is not ultimately home. I live off another hump as well. . . . At school I studied the Gaelic literature of Ireland as well as the literature of England, and since then I have maintained a notion of myself as Irish in a province that insists that it is British.[6]

The problem in Heaney's poetry becomes one of commitment which extends beyond the obvious dilemma of Ulster politics. It extends as well to a broad cultural context marked by the clash between Irish and British traditions in literature as well as in politics and religion. It has become the essential act for the modern Irish writer, from Yeats and Joyce to the present, to define that particular context. Under the strain of restoring a culture to itself, literary expression seeks to find some means of clarifying issues while maintaining a constant vigilance against insincerity. The struggle takes place between the poet's public and private voices and between an identification with a literary tradition and the instinct of individuality. Any reading of Heaney's poetry which restricts the notion of commitment only to politics, ignoring the question of poetics, misses the deeper, more complicated tension in the work. The powerful appeal of *North* and *Field Work* resides both in the treatment of politics and in the depiction of the labor that shapes it, especially the necessary tentativeness and humility involved in writing and in wrestling with a complex Irish poetic tradition.

North

The critical reaction to *North*, particularly its discussion of the treatment of political terror and contemporary violence in Northern Ireland, has claimed for the book a supreme control over material through the creation of a powerful poetic myth. The critics have pointed to the dazzling use of material from P. V. Glob's *The Bog People*, which builds upon the idea of the bog as a preserver of history, a notion Heaney has been working into his poems since "Bogland," from *Door into the Dark:*

> Our pioneers keep striking
> Inwards and downwards
>
> Every layer they strip
> Seems camped on before . . .
> The wet centre is bottomless.[7]

Other readings of *North* have stressed the continued predominance of the essential trope in Heaney's early poetry, the breaking of the surface, the pushing down, the delving toward the bottom, implying that the bog poetry in *North* represents the flowering of a thematic development begun in "Digging," the first poem in Heaney's first book, *Death of a Naturalist.*

> . . . heaving sodes
> Over his shoulder, going down and down
> For the good turf. Digging.
> . . . .
> But I've no spade to follow men like them.
>
> Between my finger and my thumb
> The squat pen rests.
> I'll dig with it.[8]

On the whole, the accumulation of critical commentary has resulted in an illumination of some of the dark layers of Heaney's excavations, particularly the practice of delving into old languages to capture cultural meaning and the implicit comparison between Celtic ritual sacrifice in Jutland and twentieth-century political killings in Ireland.[9] As helpful as these interpretations are, however, they also tend, ironically, to obscure an important direction in *North*. In their emphasis upon the analogy of the bog myth, they divert readers from a second, but equally powerful, subject, one that focuses upon the poetic act itself, particularly the poet's uneasiness over the Shelleyan role of the unacknowledged legislator whose art attempts to define and interpret political and social subjects. The uneasiness manifests itself in the form of a conflict between the public voice and the private self and produces an intense self-scrutiny, which grows more and more disturbing throughout the book, undercutting the mythmaking and eventually culminating in the poet's isolation in the volume's final poem, "Exposure." This conflict emerges gradually in the poems, producing a pattern of vacillation in which the poet agonizes over the inefficacy of the poetic act in its attempts to restore society.

While there are hints of such vacillation in earlier poems such as "Viking Dublin: Trial Pieces" and "Punishment," it appears as a fully developed theme in "Kinship," a poem that occupies the middle of *North*, summing up the bog material and looking forward to the personal reflections in part 2 of that volume. Here, for the first and only time in the book, the mythmaking and the self-questioning are presented side by side, in the form of a contest in which the poet creates and then withdraws from his imaginative structure. The poem relies heavily upon Glob's narrative of ritual sacrifice, which describes the male victim riding in a symbolically decorated wagon. He is on his way to be killed and offered to the bog, which is presented a fertility goddess hungry for sacrifice:

> Insatiable bride . . .
> sump and seedbed,
> a bag of waters
>
> and a melting grave.[10]

This is also a very personal poem about the effectiveness of the bog myth as an explanation of contemporary violence in Ulster. "Kinned by hieroglyphic peat," the poet confesses that he has become absorbed by his creation, that the bog has become "the outback of my mind." And, in a moment crucial not only for "Kinship" but for the entire volume, the poet dramatizes his own role as digger and discoverer in such consciously sexual terms that he becomes, by implication, at once bridegroom and victim:

> I found a turf-spade
> hidden under bracken,
> laid flat, and overgrown
> with a green fog.
>
> As I raised it
> the soft lips of the growth
> muttered and split,
> a tawnny rut
>
> opening at my feet
> like a shed skin,

> the shaft wettish
> as I sank it upright
>
> and beginning to
> steam in the sun. . . .
>
> I stand at the edge of centuries
> facing a goddess.
>
> (N., 42)

The poet enters the bog with all recent history on his hands, both political and poetic, and in the process transforms Glob's narrative into a myth for his own time.

For Heaney, the goddess is certainly Kathleen ni Houlihan—"Our mother ground/is sour with the blood/of her faithful"—who demands great sacrifice from Irish males. Yet, it is as a poet facing the goddess that Heaney feels truly victimized as one who must remake in metaphor the political violence and report the tribal terror, the layers of sectarian hatred which have built up for over three hundred years in Ulster.

The tension between Heaney's private understanding of the Ulster crisis and his poetic treatment of the subject surfaces throughout the second half of *North* as the poet becomes increasingly aware of his own role as an interpreter of history. Simultaneously with this awareness, a note of reticence and of uncertainty sounds in the poetry, as the poet begins to question his own ability to write publicly, with a wide sense of community. In the final lines of "Kinship," he seeks guidance from Tacitus, the Roman historian of Iron-Age Jutland:

> Come back to this
> "island of the ocean"
> where nothing will suffice.
> Read the inhumed faces
>
> of casualty and victim;
> report us fairly,
> how we slaughter
> for the common good

and shave the heads
of the notorious,
how the goddess swallows
our love and terror.

(N., 45)

These lines not only make explicit the horrible and disheartening contemporary meaning behind the bog poems; they also indict the poet himself as interpreter and reporter of action. The reference to Tacitus is crucial and telling, since it introduces a countermovement in the poetry which rounds upon the poet as mythmaker. Here Heaney implores Tacitus to come to his aid to "report us fairly," since as poet Heaney might be too close to his subject to truly understand it. This is a crucial issue for a poet who has struggled to be faithful to his known and given life, but who also understands the lessons of history; Heaney is doubting his very strength as an interpreter of his times.

The extent of the poet's self-doubt is revealed in a negative allusion to Wallace Stevens' well-known poetic axiom "The poem is the act of the mind/Finding something that will suffice"; Heaney echoes Stevens' lines to contrast his own poetic failure "where nothing will suffice." The questioning of the poetic response is further developed with references to poems as "trial pieces"; in descriptions of the poet standing dumb, or sinking like Onan; and in a telling identification with Hamlet, whose self-doubts evolved from speculations upon the inability to respond to crises.

I am Hamlet the Dane,
skull-handler, parablist,
smeller of rot

in the state, infused
with its poisons,
pinioned by ghosts
and affections,

murders and pieties
coming to consciousness

> by jumping in graves
> dithering, blathering.
>
> (*N.*, 23)

No less than the very basic of the skull-handling parablist's blathering comes under scrutiny in "Hercules and Antaeus," the final poem of part 1 of *North*. Hercules, "sky born" and associated with light, lifts Antaeus high above the ground and holds him there, away from the earth, the source of his power,

> into a dream of loss
>
> and origins—the cradling dark,
> the river-veins, the secret gullies
> of his strength,
> the hatching grounds
>
> of cave and souterrain.
>
> (*N.*, 52–53)

The personal implications of these lines are immediately apparent. Heaney's poetic strength, not only in the bog poems but elsewhere, has come from contact with the soil. Yet the poet now feels the need for a new perspective and allies himself with heavenly Hercules, "a spur of light," to challenge the basic gravity and dark instinct of Antaeus.

Heaney has placed a great deal of importance on the theoretical implications of "Hercules and Antaeus," especially for *North*. Calling the poem "dangerous to have written," Heaney suggests that it epitomizes the dilemma of the Ulster writer who looks toward the rational to control illiterate fidelities; in so doing he risks separation from the local and the familiar, the very source that shapes and nurtures his writing.[11] The conflict between Hercules and Antaeus reveals what Heaney calls an advance-retire situation, in which the poetry moves toward the rational and then seeks to avoid it, thus striking a precarious balance. The essential ingredients of Heaney's own poetic struggle shape the poem: the rational intelligence, which tends toward heavenly abstractions, on the one hand, and the emotional instinct attracted to the natural world, on the other.[12]

The importance of this polemic became clear to Heaney as he sought to consider questions of personal and cultural identity in his poetry. Forced to a kind of moral crisis during the summer of 1969 when political violence broke out in Northern Ireland, he recognized the need to rethink his poetic strategy.

> From that moment the problems of poetry moved from being simply a matter of achieving the satisfactory verbal icon to being a search for images and symbols adequate to our predicament. . . . I mean that I felt it imperative to discover a field of force in which, without abandoning fidelity to the processes and experience of poetry as I have outlined them, it would be possible to encompass the perspectives of a humane reason and at the same time to grant the religious intensity of the violence its deplorable authenticity and complexity.[13]
>
> (*Pre.*, pp. 56–57)

It is this attention to the authentic—both in finding the adequate symbol or image for the Ulster predicament and in maintaining the integrity necessary to write poetry that reveals the self to the self—that causes Heaney to waver. The search for an exact posture induces, ironically, a hesitation and a cautious scrutiny that measures and dissects the poetry. Antaeus' sense of place is countered by Hercules' stark intelligence; the mythical perspective in part 1 of *North* is undercut by the direct and explicit poetry in part 2, the exploration of Ulster as a ministry of fear,

> The famous
> Northern reticence, the tight gag of place
> And times. . . .
>
> . . . .
> Where tongues lie coiled, as under flames lie wicks,
> Where half of us, as in a wooden horse
> Were cabin'd and confined like wily Greeks,
> Besieged within the siege, whispering morse.
>
> (*N.*, 59–60)

This poetry depicts the frustrations of the poet attempting "to lure the tribal shoals to epigram/and order."

Poetic Dualism

Part of the meaning of "Hercules and Antaeus," however, lies outside the political arena, in the mesh of the Irish poetic tradition which continually catches the post-Yeatsian poet. The polemic implied in "Hercules and Antaeus" carries over into part 2 of *North* to reveal a deep rift in Heaney's overall poetic schema, what can be recognized as a vacillation between two parts of a powerful poetic dichotomy. Heaney has explained some of this vacillation as the Ulster condition, the psychology of a bifurcated society. A more precise identification would be Heaney's own poetic heritage, which, for him as for all Irish poets writing in the latter half of the twentieth century, has presented two distinct directions, the Yeatsian and the Joycean.

As we have seen these two directions offer a difficult choice. The poet must be faithful to experience to give his poetry authority and authenticity, but he must also be careful to allow some subjectivity in order to provide a personal and unique shaping of material. Heaney has explained this dichotomy as "the need for a structure and a sustaining landscape and at the same time the need to be liberated and distanced from it, the need to be open, unpredictably susceptible, lyrically opportunistic."[14] For him, and for other contemporary Ulster poets, this means placing poetry at a great risk. Expressing the sense of place demands a communal—or what Heaney has called a "tribal"—perspective; being too true to tribal matters, however, inevitably causes a loss of perspective and a lapsing into quarrels with others.

The extent to which dualism affects Heaney's ideas about poetry can be seen clearly in his essay "Fire in the Flint: Reflections on the Poetry of Gerard Manley Hopkins." Heaney reads Hopkins's poetry as a succession of struggles between two poetic voices, which reflect masculine and feminine modes. In

Hopkins's early poetry the tendency was toward the feminine, producing a passive artistic posture which surrendered to experience. As Hopkins matured, he moved toward a masculine mode characterized by an intellectual mastery over his material. According to Heaney, these two distinct tendencies form the extreme edges of Hopkins's poetic response.

> In the masculine mode, the language functions as a form of address, of assertion or command, and the poetic effort has to do with conscious quelling and control of the materials, a labour of shaping; words are not music before they are anything else, nor are they drowsy from their slumber in the unconscious, but athletic, capable, displaying the muscle of sense. Whereas in the feminine mode the language functions more as location than as address, and the poetic effort is not so much a labour of design as it is an act of divination and revelation; words in the feminine mode behave with the lover's come-hither instead of the athlete's display, they constitute a poetry that is delicious as texture before it is recognized as architectonic.[15]

As critical theory, these remarks break down somewhat in their application to Hopkins's poetry. In fact, the crucial and interesting aspect of Heaney's ideas about Hopkins is that they grow out of a misreading of the poetry. Quoting the oft-discussed "The Wreck of the Deutschland," Heaney suggests that Hopkins's poetry demonstrates a masculine forging and an imaginative shaping, a conclusion reached only by overlooking crucial elements of the poem. Despite the masculine sound of Hopkins's opening stanza, for example, the sense of the lines is feminine and passive,

> Thou mastering me
> God! . . .
> Thou has bound bones and veins in me, fastened me flesh,
> . . . and dost thou touch me afresh?
> Over again I feel thy finger and find thee

In the poem's fourth stanza, the feminine qualities occur in both sound and sense.

> I am soft sift
> In an hourglass—at the wall
> Fast, but mined with a motion, a drift,
> And it crowds and it combs to the fall.[16]

As Heaney reads the poem, Hopkins's general tendency both as a poet and a priest to surrender to God's grandeur seems less important than the impressive artistry of that surrender, particularly the powerful rhythmic and inventive use of language, which is labeled masculine. The point here, however, is less to quarrel with a particular reading of Hopkins than to notice what one poet chooses to see in another. In an extremely revealing and interesting sentence in the essay, Heaney comments on Hopkins's view of Keats: "as is so often the case when a poet is diagnosing the condition of another poet, Hopkins is here offering us something of a self-portrait." Turning Heaney's words back upon himself, his criticism of Hopkins reveals much about the sensibility behind *North* and *Field Work*. Quoting Hopkins's sonnet "To R.B."—

> . . . the strong
> Spur, live and lancing like the blowpipe flame,
> breathes once, and quenched faster than it came,
> Leaves the mind a mother of immortal song.
> . . . .
> Sweet fire the sire the muse, my soul needs this;
> I want the one rapture of an inspiration.[17]

Heaney points to a union of the two modes, the masculine spur firing the flint, which releases the feminine potential, the exquisite flame inherent in the soul. When this blending occurs and combines with an apprehension of the natural world, as it does, for example, in "The Windhover," Hopkins, as Heaney reads him, achieves the full realization of his poetic gift. The union of disparate poetic tendencies in Hopkins's poetry inspired Heaney to recognize artistic control and growth, whose implications for his own work we cannot fail to see. Heaney's own dualism, the tribal and the universal aspects in his poetry or—as he describes it elsewhere—the instinctive and the rational, mirrors the tension in Hopkins's work.

Poetic growth through the union of two opposed tendencies appeals to a poet who feels the strain of vacillation between two voices. In terms of craft alone, it offers a marvelous technical solution to the problem of direction, allowing two voices to have their say. Yet in Heaney's case, the idea of blending opposites goes beyond the merely technical; it touches his own sense of literary identity, which is pulled in two directions by Yeats and Joyce. One part of his sensibility, Antaeus-like, inclines naturally toward Joyce and his admirer Patrick Kavanagh, who drew from the simple details of everyday life, believing that real poetic strength came from a trust in the local and the familiar. Heaney alludes to this tendency in a recent interview: "whatever poetic success I've had has come from staying within the realm of my own imaginative country and my own voice."[18] At the same time, another part of him recognizes the need for detachment in favor of the cultivation of a poetic persona and the creation of intellectual poetry, both of which were characteristic of Yeats.

As an Ulster poet, Heaney sees Kavanagh's Joycean practice as an important and liberating phase in Irish poetry. Kavanagh's insistence upon the importance of the parochial and his celebration of life in Monaghan in a sense justify the treatment of Northern Irish subject matter in Heaney's early work. Furthermore, Heaney reads Kavanagh's poetry as more than regional naturalism. As his criticism makes clear, he sees Kavanagh as an important theorist whose poems discuss the process of poetic composition.

> What we have in these poems are matter-of-fact landscapes, literally presented, but contemplated from such a point of view and with such an intensity that they become "a prospect of the mind" . . . their concern is, indeed, the growth of a poet's mind.[19]

Despite his assimilation of Kavanagh's poetics, however, Heaney does not dismiss nor eschew Yeatsian practice. On the contrary, with the examples of Kavanagh's and Austin Clarke's opposition to Yeatsian influence as part of his literary heritage, Heaney has been spared the necessary confrontation with a predecessor; instead he has accepted Yeats's silhouette on the poetic horizon, as Clarke and Kavanagh could not, without the threat of domination. Indeed, Heaney finds much to admire in Yeats's example.

> . . . he bothers you with the suggestion that if you have managed to do one kind of a poem in your own way, you should cast off that way and face into another area of your experience until you have learned a new voice to say that area properly . . . above all he reminds you that art is intended, that it is part of the creative push of civilization itself.[20]

In addition, Yeats provides Heaney with both substantial and theoretical directions for his poetry. The Yeatsian distinction between poetry and rhetoric, essential for any writer who treats social themes, has become part of Heaney's conceptual framework.[21] The success behind his public poetry lies in the quarrel with himself—what Yeats calls poetry—rather than the quarrel with others which produces only rhetoric. Furthermore, Yeats, not Joyce and Kavanagh, is the real presence behind *North*. The book's metaphorical structure, particularly in part 1, offers a degree of objectivity which allows the poet to avoid directly the rhetorical quarrel with others. Even the self-doubt and the dramatization of the poetic voice questioning itself appear as a version of the Yeatsian dialogue in which the mind turns in upon itself and, in the process of a quarrel, produces art.

Yet for all of its dialogue between self and soul, *North* produces no balance, no union. Indeed, it demonstrates the opposite. The extent to which the poetry depends upon the rational, masculine, Yeatsian posture creates an imbalance, which unsettles the poet in the latter half of the book, as we have noted.[22] The mythmaking structure, which expedites the treatment of contemporary events in Ulster, eventually calls attention to itself and raises questions about the nature of the poetic response.

The critical realization occurs in an emblematic moment in "Hercules and Antaeus." Held aloft by sky-bound intelligence and cut off from his strength, Antaeus mirrors Heaney's plight as a poet concerned over the source of his art and the authenticity of his personal voice.

This concern lies behind "Exposure," the final poem in *North.* In such a deliberately thematic book, one would expect Heaney to look back through the poetry with a sense of satisfaction, perhaps even triumph. Instead, he speaks only of being lost in a wet, cold forest in the south of Ireland, far off from his own imaginative north, trying to salvage something from a dying light. A sense of failure dominates the poem, as Heaney berates himself for missed opportunities and for his unsuccessful attempts at unraveling his "responsible *tristia.*" He even questions the price he has paid by moving from strife-torn Northern Ireland to peaceful Wicklow:

> I am neither internee nor informer;
> An inner emigre, grown long-haired
> And thoughtful; a wood-kerne
>
> Escaped from the massacre,
> Taking protective colouring
> From bole and bark, feeling
> Every wind that blows;
>
> Who, blowing up these sparks
> For their meagre heat, have missed
> The once-in-a-lifetime portent,
> The comet's pulsing rose.
>
> (*N.*, 73)

Although this admission suggests a political meaning through such terms as "internee" and "informer," there is also present in these lines a poetical regret that the pressures and, more important, the strategy for dealing with social unrest have led Heaney astray, that "blowing up these sparks/For their meagre heat" has caused a disorientation in poetic sensibility and vision.

And yet, despite its insistence upon loss, indeed because of it, the poem gives evidence of a sense of growth. The dissatisfaction apparent in the final moments of *North* comes only after a consideration of poetic identity and direction, the necessary step that allows the poet to look forward with a renewed commitment to the familiar, trusting "the feel of what . . . /your hands have known."

Field Work

The idea of poetic commitment in *Field Work* does not emanate from a drastic change in subject matter, nor does it appear in the self-doubting voice we have become accustomed to since "Kinship." Both Ulster's unrest and the poet's agonizing self-questioning are present in this later book, linking it deliberately to the development of *North*. A number of the poems deal directly with the grim details and results of violence; indeed, the specter of life in Ulster hangs over the entire book. In "Triptych," for example, a sibyl, when asked what will become of Ireland, speaks clearly about the agony of sectarian violence:

> Unless foregiveness finds its nerve and voice,
> Unless the helmeted and bleeding tree
> Can green and open buds like infants' fists. . . .
>
> The ground we kept our ear to for so long
> Is flayed or calloused, and its entrails
> Tented by an impious augury.
> Our island is full of comfortless noises.[23]

Other poems reflect upon victims of the violence, the friend whose "candid forehead stopped/A point blank teatime bullet," a cousin whom the poet finds "on your knees/with blood and roadside musk in your hair and eyes," or the friend blown up in a pub because he refused to obey the IRA curfew. We catch that familiar deliberation about the poetic process, when the poet seems uneasy, even insecure about his experience and his choice: "Did we come to the wilderness for this? . . . /What is my apology for poetry?"

Despite these echoes from *North*, however, there is evidence of change in *Field Work*, in a subtle shift in poetic strategy and a variation in tone, both of which announce the movement from tentativeness to commitment. The shift occurs in the poet's treatment of violence, which becomes a willfully personal description of an intense human feeling and an act of the imagination:

> I dab you clean with moss
> Fine as the drizzle out of a low cloud . . .
> With rushes that shoot green again, I plait
> Green scapulars to wear over your shroud.
>
> (*FW.*, 18)

The ordering of the experience appears in the process of composition and makes the poet's own feelings as much the focus of the poem as the eulogized subject, as is clear in what the poet chooses to remember about an old friend gunned down in Belfast:

> Fifteen years ago, come this October,
> Crowded on your floor,
> I got my arm round Marie's shoulder
> For the first time.
> "Oh, Sir Jasper, do not touch me!"
> You roared across at me,
> Chorus-leading, splashing out the wine.
>
> (*FW.*, 32)

The reflections on his own feelings about lost friends lead him to considerations of other deaths—not related to Belfast violence, but losses still—of musician Sean O'Riada and, in the lines from "Elegy," of poet Robert Lowell:

> You were our night ferry
> thudding in a big sea,

> the whole craft ringing
> with an armourer's music
> the course set wilfully across
> the ungovernable and dangerous.
>
> (FW., 32)

The tribute to Lowell is especially revealing, not only in its admiration of a life's work but also in its identification with Lowell's ambition. Heaney, too, wishes to chart rough waters, and his interest in public and private poetry resembles Lowell's practice in *Life Studies* and *For the Union Dead*.

The tone of these elegies and poems about Ulster violence produces a public posture that is Yeatsian, based upon rational conviction and revealing a clear sense of communal values. The public posture, however, is tempered by deep personal emotion that somehow blunts it and renders it humane, without lessening its moral effect.

> There they were, as if our memory hatched them,
> As if the unquiet founders walked again:
> Two young men with rifles on the hill,
> Profane and bracing as their instruments.
>
> Who's sorry for our trouble?
> Who dreamt that we might dwell among ourselves
> In rain and scoured light and wind-dried stones?
> Basalt, blood, water, headstones, leeches.
>
> In that neuter original loneliness
> From Brandon to Dunseverick
> I think of small-eyed survivor flowers,
> The pined-for, unmolested orchid.
>
> (FW., 12)

This unique blend of public and private sensibilities highlights the achievement of *Field Work*; the poetry demonstrates both the resolution to sound the communal chord with a distinctive public voice and the conviction to remain faithful to the personal and the familiar. The public voice presents the tense scene and attempts to derive some universal response, "that we might dwell among ourselves/In rain and scoured light and wind-dried stones"; the private voice sketches the personal healing and hope in the indomitable natural surrounding, "the original loneliness . . . small-eyed survivor flowers . . . unmolested orchid."

The subtle manner of tone in these public poems testifies to genuine poetic growth—a voice constrained by a sense of personal grief and loss, so that the private self intrudes. Self-questioning and doubt still haunt the voice, but the questions are more essential and more complex. In the poem "The Badgers," the animals who prowl the countryside mysteriously signify aspects of the poet's public conscience.

> The murdered dead,
> You thought.
> But could it not have been
> some violent shattered boy
> nosing out what got mislaid
> between the cradle and the explosion.

Posing this question, itself a mixture of social and personal concerns, the lines press more closely to the poet himself.

> At a second house I listened
> For duntings under the laurels
> and heard intimations whispered
> about being vaguely honoured.
>
> (FW., 25)

These dense lines embody the difficulties of public poetry, both in the poet's attempts to understand the "duntings" in his country and in society's muted appreciation of his efforts, hinted at in the "intimations, whispered/about being vaguely honoured." The lines also lead us obliquely toward a resolution. The poet who connects the audacious and notorious badgers with Ulster night-fighters first fears them and then grows to understand them. The badger's scratching, rooting, and nosing about become at the end something very close to Heaney's familiar trope of digging below the surface; in this case, however, the emphasis shifts from discovery to the acceptance of what is uncovered: "How perilous is it to choose/not to love the life we're shown?" The implications of this simple question, posed so offhandedly near the close of "The Badgers," set the tone for the remainder of *Field Work*. The poet's grappling with his role as the unacknowledged legislator ceases, and he turns instead to the exploration of a more personal and individual meaning. This proves to be a crucial turn, not only for the remainder of *Field Work* but for Heaney's general poetic sensibilities as well.

In a poem published recently in honor of the James Joyce centenary, Heaney reveals the importance of the cultivation of the personal.[24] The ghost of Joyce speaks to him about the Irish tradition, offering important advice to the younger poet:

> What I did on my own
> was done for others but not done with them—and this
> you have failed to learn. Your obligation
>
> is not discharged by pious exercise.
>   . . . I was at nobody's service
> the way you are at theirs.

What Joyce's ghost says touches the dilemma in *North* and, to some degree, in the political poetry in *Field Work*. Heaney's response to Ulster violence is constrained by his awareness of the public voice in Irish poetry, particularly the powerful example of Yeats. By allowing Joyce to have his say, Heaney relieved himself of the Yeatsian burden of tradition, which involves the shaping of the public conscience through the force of the poetic personality. Joyce advises the younger poet to liberate himself from the responsibility of public poetry so he might concentrate on the familiar world.

> Get back in harness. The main thing is to write
> for your own joy in it. . . .

                    . . . don't be so earnest,

        let others wear the sackcloth and ashes.
        Let go, let fly, forget.
        . . . .
                                        . . . swim

        out on your own and fill the element
        with signatures on your own frequency,
        echo soundings, searches, probes allurements.

Heaney's imaginary meeting with Joyce tells us much about the
notion of commitment in *Field Work*. In a Dantesque moment,
the younger writer meets the shade of the master, who tells him
to make his own way, to use tradition only to inform his work,
being careful not to be bound by it, to feel no obligation. Joyce's
own practice, Heaney feels, gives abundant life to younger writers, enables them to sound the depth of their own experiences.

    The encounter with Joyce and the poetic strategy that
Heaney has identified as Joycean provide a footnote to the second half of *Field Work*, especially the Glanmore sonnets. Heaney
not only sheds the sackcloth and ashes, but he seems to draw
strength from the searching and probing of his own experiences.

        Now the good life could be to cross a field
        And art a paradigm of earth new from the lathe
        Of ploughs. My lea is deeply tilled.
        Old ploughsocks gorge the subsoil of each sense
        And I am quickened with a redolence.
                                        (*FW.*, 33)

Here, and elsewhere, the strategy is responsiveness and openness, a keen observation and a celebration of the everyday details of nature and the ordinary. The implications of this faithfulness to ordinary things and to the simple moments of rural
observation appear, clearly stated, in the second of the Glanmore Sonnets, where the poet sets forth a manifesto:

        Then I landed in the hedge-school of Glanmore
        And from the backs of ditches hoped to raise

> A voice caught back off slug-horn and slow chanter
> That might continue, hold, dispel, appease:
> Vowels ploughed into other, opened ground,
> Each verse returning like the plough turned round.
>
> (*FW.*, 34)

The direction here resembles the familiar poetic trope of digging down, pushing past the surface—ploughing, tilling, gorging the subsoil—but the meaning differs from the mythmaking of *North*. The imagination in *Field Work* shifts itself to a reflective, almost passive posture, so that the opening of the ground allows the fragrance of the earth to reach the receiving poet: "I am quickened with a redolence." Fieldwork in "the hedge-school of Glanmore" will provide the raw material for the poetic act, material that will be teased out from hiding places, "Words entering almost the sense of touch/Ferreting themselves out of their dark hutch." On familiar ground again, refreshed by the prospect of the natural surrounding, the poet allows the mystery of the place to reveal itself, like

> . . . stone
> That connived with the chisel, as if the grain
> Remembered what the mallet tapped to know.
>
> (*FW.*, 34)

The strategy here follows Kavanagh's dictum of faithfulness to the local and celebration of the ordinary yet essential moments of life, transforming them into art, but with an important added difference. In describing the sonnets as "the centre of the book," Heaney has stated that they are "about choice and commitment," and that he had learned "something of how to speak in the first person out of the self." The commitment we sense in these poems does not come simply from an insistence upon reporting the local or the familiar; rather, it comes as both an acceptance of one's place and as a willingness to indulge and develop the thoughts behind that acceptance. It is precisely the conviction called for by Joyce's shade in the centenary poem. The strength the poet feels comes not primarily from the immediate apprehension with nature but rather from a trusting of personal feelings through memory. The method in sonnet 5 is characteristic; in it a direct apprehension of nature leads backward into the self:

> Soft corrugations in the boortree's trunk,
> Its green young shoots, its rods like freckled solder:
> It was our bower as children, a greenish, dank
> And snapping memory as I get older. . . .
> I love its blooms like saucers brimmed with meal,
> Its berries a swart caviar of shot,
> A buoyant spawn, a light bruised out of purple.
>   . . . bower tree where I played "touching tongues"
> And felt another's texture quick on mine.
>
>   (FW., 37)

Nature in these sonnets is the seedbed for memory; the "fuchsia in the drizzling noon" recalls "that winter/of nineteen forty-seven" when a story "quickened us, a wild white goose/Heard after dark above the drifted house." It is in the context of the remembered self that Heaney's remark about choice and commitment becomes clear.

The Glanmore Sonnets postulate a poetic credo as much as they etch a rural scene and push Heaney's art as far as he has yet gone in reliance on one kind of poem. The result is slightly surprising. Rather than completely adopt Kavanagh's notions of the parochial and the importance of place, Heaney presents the local scene as a means to an end. The real action of the Glanmore Sonnets is contemplative, drawing from the present a recollected scene from the past. And memory here is restorative, reminding us of Wordsworth's "Tintern Abbey" as much as of Kavanagh's "Inniskeen Road: July Evening." A Wordsworthian trust in the natural world, first in its attention to rural detail—"The head/Of a horse swirled back from a gate," "small buds shoot and flourish in the hush," "a new moon glimpsed through tangled glass,"—and then in its recollection of simple pleasure connected with life in the country—sleeping out under the stars, fishing, observing birds—leads to the hope of restoration.

The need for restoration becomes explicit in "The Gutterial Muse," where in a witty conceit the poet compares the midnight laughter of young lovers in the parking lot below his window to the bubbles sent up by the tench, called the "doctor fish," whose slime when touched heals the wounds of other fish.

> A girl in a white dress
> Was being courted out among the cars:
> As her voice swarmed and puddled into laughs
> I felt like some old pike all badged with sores
> Wanting to swim in touch with soft-mouthed life.
>
> (FW., 28)

Heaney's fidelity to the familiar, however, does not allow him to misrepresent for the sake of an idea. While nature does provide the desired healing—"Outside a restling and twig-combing breeze/Refreshes and relents"—it also threatens, as in sonnet 8 when a storm drives the poet indoors—"Come to me quick, I am upstairs shaking./My all of you birchwood in lightning"—or in sonnet 9, when life outside the kitchen windows appears ominous, inspiring a pang of conscience, suggested in the reverberating Joycean word "inwit":

> . . . a black rat
> Sways on the briar like infected fruit:
> "It looked me through, it stared me out, I'm not
> Imagining things. Go you out to it."
> Did we come to the wilderness for this?
> We have our burnished bay tree at the gate,
> Classical, hung with the reek of silage
> From the next farm, tart-leafed as inwit.
>
> (FW., 41)

But restoration is unqualified in the poems about marriage, where Heaney reflects upon his relationship with his wife and his role as husband, lover, and companion, creating a touching epithalamium, not of the newly wed but of the very married. In "The Skunk," a startling comparison of animal and wife, he describes a mature love:

> After eleven years I was composing
> Love-letters again, broaching the word "wife"
> Like a stored cask.
>
> (FW., 48)

"An Afterwards" evokes a bittersweet moment as his wife touches upon the loss of time together:

> Why could you not have, oftener, in our years
>
> Unclenched, and come down laughing from your room
> And walked the twilight with me and your children—
> Like that one evening of elder bloom
> And hay, when the wild roses were fading?
>
> (FW., 44)

The exquisite final sonnet in the Glanmore series stresses the strength the poet draws from this enduring love:

> I dreamt we slept in a moss in Donegal
> On turf banks under blankets, with our faces
> Exposed all night in a wetting drizzle,
> Pallid as the dripping sapling birches.
> Lorenzo and Jessica in a cold climate.
> Diarmuid and Grainne waiting to be found.
> Darkly asperged and censed, we were laid out
> Like breathing effigies on a raised ground.
> And in a dream I dreamt—how like you this?—
> Our first night years ago in that hotel
> When you came with your deliberate kiss
> To raise us towards the lovely and painful
> Covenants of flesh; our separateness;
> The respite in our dewy dreaming faces.
>
> (FW., 42)

The Freudian dream within a dream, set off by the allusion to Wyatt, creates a powerful literary effect, engaging the role of the imagination to recall and arrange levels of experience.[25] Within the context of the background to *Field Work*—the notion of retreat from Belfast to Wicklow—the reference to Diarmuid and Grainne proves perfectly apt. In Irish legend these lovers flee the violent threat of Finn and his warriors, drawing strength from each other and from the natural surroundings that shelter them. Both the nature of their love and the context of their flight have taken on personal significance for Heaney, who sees his time in Glanmore as a retreat from the troubles. And while this sonnet—and the entire sequence—end with the reverberations of the word "respite," suggesting only a pause, the passion and beauty of love intensify and define the moment, hoarding it as if to transcend time.

As important as choice and commitment are, in Heaney's mind, to the success of the Glanmore Sonnets, they are more evident in "The Harvest Bow," the beautiful tribute to the poet's father. This poem draws its powerful effect from a delicate conceit, which develops throughout the piece from what it is in actuality—a woven badge of straw signifying the fruitful harvest—to what it represents symbolically, as the poet reads meaning into its golden loops and transforms it.

> I see us walk between the railway slopes
> Into an evening of long grass and midges,
> Blue smoke straight up, old beds and ploughs in hedges,
> . . . .
> You with a harvest bow in your lapel,
>
> Me with the fishing rod, already homesick
> For the big lift of these evenings.
>
> (*FW.*, 58)

As the poem moves toward its conclusion, the straw knot becomes "a drawn snare," which the spirit of corn slips, but which the poet cannot, as its burnished edges and golden loops draw him into its world, whose action cannot be relived since it "beats out of time," but whose meaning is therefore incorruptible, "that original townland/Still tongue-tied in the straw." The poet, though snared by the frail device, nevertheless works at its meaning as he must, "Gleaning the unsaid off the palpable." What aids him is the apprehension of love, also caught in the harvest bow, "a throwaway love-knot of straw," which becomes a marriage symbol, "pinned up on our dresser . . . still warm." The poem postulates a simple happiness the poet has earned through his own imaginative plaiting of the strands of moments recalled from his boyhood in rural Ireland.

"The Harvest Bow" is itself a union of elements, of the straw from the earth's harvest, of the masculine imagination shaping the bow, of the feminine stability of love and peace, of time and timelessness, and of artifice and reality. Commitment appears on many levels in the poem, implicit in marriage itself and in the "fine intent" of the weaving of the harvest bow, which extends also to the making of poetry. The description of the bow made by hands that "harked to their gift. . . . /Until your fingers moved somnambulant" echoes Heaney's own explanation of the struggle in his poetry, "a kind of somnambulist encounter between masculine will and intelligence and feminine clusters of image and emotion."[26] Here, however, the struggle is resolved in ingenious fashion. The masculine intelligence patiently shapes the frail device, braiding into it, twist by twist, the essence of rural life, and in so doing implicates a feminine sensibility in the love knot, in the simple motto "The end of art is peace," and in the poet's own marriage in the final stanza.

The delicate balance of "The Harvest Bow" informs other poems that close *Field Work*. The simple observations in "Song" reinforce what the poet sees as he spies into the straw knot: that the rhythms of nature give off a timeless and essential sound.

> There are the mud-flowers of dialect
> And the immortelles of perfect pitch
> And that moment when the bird sings very close
> To the music of what happens.
>
> (FW., 56)

That these observations became for Heaney, at this stage in his life, refreshing and also reassuring is quite apparent in his confident reverberation of Yeats in the poignant "September Song," which gives us a startling portrait of the poet at middle life: "We toe the line/between the tree in leaf and the bare tree." Here, caught between the full bloom of youth and the bare branches of old age, Heaney stresses what "The Harvest Bow" implies, a backward look, both psychologically and poetically, to find markings for the journey ahead. The conviction of the recent poetry suggests that Heaney has taken a newfound comfort, if not ease, in that backward look, a remarkable achievement when we consider how often and at what peril the modern Irish poet has searched his past.

9

The Tradition of Discontinuity: A Glance at Recent Ulster Poetry

After a century of poetic practice, questions about tradition and continuity in modern Irish poetry remain difficult and complex. In the 1880s, the most crucial problem facing the Irish writer was the lack of a distinctly Irish poetic tradition in English; one hundred years later, no longer doubting the place of tradition, the Irish writer now worries about continuity, the sense of the past in the present. This shift in the history which Irish poets have made began with Austin Clarke and continues down to the present generation. The poets of Clarke's generation worried only slightly about continuity, since they still faced the dark side of tradition, the menacing and deadly influence of a powerful precursor. The present generation, however, has learned to live with the great Yeats, as Heaney's poetry so clearly shows. Indeed, as Heaney reads him, Yeats can be a source of inspiration. What is also clear from Heaney's poetry is the sense in which other writers have become part of the fabric of Irish poetry; Kavanagh and Joyce can be important influences and can be accommodated with no great anxiety. The same holds true for Kinsella, who sees Yeats, Joyce, and Clarke as part of his poetic heritage.

The idea of tradition, then, has become more established

and less threatening as each succeeding generation has inherited a larger and more diverse poetic legacy. The problem of continuity, however, offers less comfort. Heaney's contemporary Derek Mahon, and more recent poets like Paul Muldoon and Tom Paulin have written continually about the burden of history, remarking that their chief artistic task is not to accept a poetic tradition but to connect with it. Moreover, as the Irish poetic tradition expands to include a Joycean component, the inevitable issue of the artist's dissociation from society becomes important. As Terence Brown has noted, the situation is problematic. The writer feels separate from his community, with no understanding of coherent ideology to help him bridge the gap.[1] Kinsella's own criticism confirms this, as we have seen, describing a deep sense of loss in the cultural consciousness. In a more extreme view, Seamus Deane has argued that the strain among Irish writers to uncover an unbroken continuity in Irish history has caused them to seek meaning in the contradictory notion of fragmentation.

> In reaction, we look for other sources which will be more expressive of ambiguity and complexity, which will stress the notion of discontinuity and make the themes of diversity and difference more palatable and consoling than they once were. In doing so we must recognise that our search is, to large, extent, determined by the demands of contemporary problems.[2]

Contemporary problems for writers, however, are more complex than those facing the sociologist or the political scientist who wishes to analyze the economic, political, or social issues of a community. Of course, the writer must consider these issues, and Deane's remarks suggest that Irish writers in particular cannot ignore the problems of contemporary society. But, as Deane's remarks further imply, the poet also must face creative and interpretive difficulties, which make his "contemporary problems" as much literary as they are social and political. The Irish writer must reflect the realities of his culture in his work, making, in Deane's words, "the themes of diversity and difference more palatable," but at the same time he must accept the burden of recent literary history, which, like recent Irish political and social history, shows certain patterns. The central dilemma in modern literary history, first reflected in Joyce's *Portrait,* then in Yeats's Ascendancy poetry, and finally in the work of the poets we have studied here, is the subject of discontinuity, the inevitable result of the clash of cultures. In dealing with cultural discontinuity, Irish poetry easily and naturally has evolved into a treatment of the artist himself, a probing of the psychic posture of one estranged from society. This consistent attention to the distance between poet and community has produced a legacy shared by many recent poets, a legacy that Deane believes is reinforced by contemporary social and political problems.

Dissociated Sensibility

What has emerged in post-Yeatsian Irish poetry, then, is a tradition of discontinuity which has presented its own special difficulties for recent writers. Poets can no longer simply celebrate the local and the familiar, nor can they portray their surroundings realistically without risking the charge of imitation or even of stagnation. Instead, the contemporary writer must scrutinize the condition of discontinuity, explore its consequences, and declare his own isolation; if he cannot make them new, he must attempt to push these subjects to a new plane. It is precisely on this level of poetic struggle that much of the excitement in recent Irish poetry has occurred, particularly in the poetry of Ulster writers.

The vitality in contemporary Ulster poetry grows out of the way in which each poet has accepted the curious social and cultural dilemma peculiar to a divided society. Most of the recent poetry begins with the admission of fragmentation and incoherence and works outward from that point. Tom Paulin, critical of the fictions behind national beliefs, confronts his dissociation with a skeptical view of the theory of history:

> Can you describe history I'd like to know?
> Isn't it a fiction that pretends to be fact
> like *A Journal of A Plague Year?*[3]

Paul Muldoon, one of the most critically acclaimed of the recent Ulster poets, treats his social and cultural fragmentation with staggering versatility, ranging from long narrative poems about the American West to short lyrics about life in rural Ulster. Despite the variety in subject matter, however, a consistent note of ambivalence sounds throughout Muldoon's poems, not only about contemporary values but also about the proper focus of poetry itself.

> Look, son. Just look around you.
> People are getting themselves killed
> Left, right and centre
> While you do what? Write rondeaux?
> There's more to living in this country
> Than stars and horses, pigs and trees,
> Not that you'd guess it from your poems.
> Do you never listen to the news?
> You want to get down to something true,
> Something a little nearer home.[4]

The voice of the political realist is taunting the poet, demanding that poetry be made more responsible, a demand that is keenly felt by the modern Ulster poet, as we know from Heaney's *North* and *Field Work.* Muldoon grants the political voice its due in many of his poems; at the same time, with an impressive display of poetic style, he also manages to inject vitality into those tired circus animals, the horses and pigs.

The examples of Paulin and Muldoon demonstrate the continued presence of a modernist sensibility among contemporary poets, but it is too early in either of these young poets' careers to determine the significance of that presence. It is rather in the work of Derek Mahon, a more established Ulster poet, that we understand how severely the poetic consciousness can be dissociated from its culture.[5] Mahon's questioning of history, his depiction of political instability, and his skepticism about the efficacy of poetry to provide a moral voice all confirm that the modernist tradition of discontinuity continues to haunt the Irish poetic imagination.

Recognizing Mahon's consistent productivity, commentators are now beginning to describe stages of development, balancing the latest poetry against the very early work, a sure sign that Mahon's reputation is solidifying.[6] Most of the critical commentary on him follows the main line of criticism in post-Yeatsian poetry, to place his work within the Irish poetic tradition, but to discover also his own particular sense of authenticity. One of the most intriguing versions of this perspective has come from Anthony Bradley, who has suggested that Mahon's most effective treatment of Irish themes often evolves through a contextual comparison, when the poet uses non-Irish subjects to measure what he calls "the given life," that is, life in Northern Ireland.[7]

Bradley's view is helpful in understanding the expatriated or outside perspective that Mahon employs in many of his poems. The setting for most of these pieces ranges well beyond the local shores of Ulster to include such far-flung places as Japan, Brittany, North Carolina, or the Canadian Pacific. Some, however, are set in Ulster or, more specfically, in Mahon's native Belfast, which adds a poignancy to the poet's feelings of alienation. There is a reserve in his work, a reticence to identify completely with the given life, to avoid the tendency in Kavanagh's or Heaney's work to celebrate the familiar life of the parish. The well-traveled quality of Mahon's poetry produces an uneasy cosmopolitanism, which reflects the insecurity of an individual caught between a narrow society he dislikes and the wide world beyond where he wishes to live and work.[8] The uneasiness comes through in the separation of poet from place, what Mahon calls dissociation, a final inability of the imagination to take root.[9] This dissociation is not simply an alienation from familiar home life, although that occurs often enough in

Mahon's Belfast poetry, when he writes of "the things that happen in the kitchen houses/And the echoing back-streets of this desperate city.[10] It is also present in the pervading sense of isolation in the poems, in the poet's estrangement from Catholic and Gaelic Ireland, and in his reluctance to identify with his native Protestant Ulster, which he associates with bigotry, stubbornness, and an aversion to change:

> Extraordinary people
> We were in our time,
> How we lived in our time
>
> As if blindfold
> Or not wholly serious,
> Inventing names for things
>
> To propitiate silence.
> (*Poems*, p. 61)

Nor can Mahon seem to draw any real comfort from the world at large. Often in his work foreign places serve only to underscore his loneliness or to remind him that he is far from home. Moreover, what he chooses to observe and to describe about these places are often only those surface features that a tourist might notice, further evidence of his reluctance to penetrate foreign cultures. In "A Postcard from Berlin," the details are the stuff of travel posters:

> Skies are the blue
> of postcard skies, and the leaves green
> In that quaint quarter of Berlin. . . .
> I hear the echoes of Weimar tunes
> Grosz laughter in the beer-gardens.

Not surprisingly, these surface impressions cannot hold, and the poet's mind drifts back to a friend in battle-torn Ulster.

> I can imagine your dismay
> As cornered in some zinc cafe,
> You read of another hunger-strike,
> A postman blasted off his bike.[11]

This recurring pattern of cultural dislocation has prompted Dillon Johnston to place Mahon in the tradition of Irish exiles which includes Joyce and the early Beckett, whose living abroad only reinforced the sense of home.[12] For Mahon, however, that sense of home is always bittersweet, a curious blend of impressions of the familiar and a sense of the unknown.

> And I step ashore in a fine rain
> To a city so changed
> By five years of war
> I scarcely recognize
> The places I grew up in,
> The faces that try to explain.
>
> But the hills are still the same
> Grey-blue above Belfast.
> Perhaps if I'd stayed behind
> And lived it bomb by bomb
> I might have grown up at last
> And learnt what is meant by home.
>
> (*Poems*, p. 58)

The significance of the posture of exile in Mahon's poetry is made clear in his essay on Louis MacNeice, an Ulster poet of a previous generation who explored the cultural schism of his own identity. Again, as is the case with Heaney's remarks on Hopkins's poetry, we note how self-revealing one poet is in exploring the condition of another. Mahon's commentary emphasizes MacNeice's special difficulty as an Irish writer in establishing cultural identification. As Mahon reads him, MacNeice was the true outsider, a poet without a community, whose degree of separation from his own society paradoxically qualified—if it did not make impossible—the condition of exile.

> "Exile," in the histrionic and approximate sense in which the word is used in Ireland, was an option available to Joyce and O'Casey, who "belonged" to the people from whom they wished to escape. It was not available in the same sense, to MacNeice, whose background was a mixture of Anglo-Irish and Ulster Protestant. Whatever his sympathies he didn't, by class or religious background, "belong to the people."[13]

Even a cursory reading of MacNeice's poems about Ireland confirms the general thrust of Mahon's remarks. MacNeice scrutinizes his Irishness in a number of his poems, vacillating between attraction and repulsion, but always remaining sensitive to the role of outsider: "I was the rector's son, born to the Anglican order,/Banned for ever from the candles of the Irish poor."[14] Twice-removed from Irish society, first from Catholic Gaelic Ireland by his Protestant heritage, and then from Ulster society by virtue of his English education, MacNeice nonetheless could never quite shake the attraction of the beauty of Ireland.

> Look into your heart, you will find a County Sligo,
> A Knocknarea with a navel a cairn of stones,
> You will find the shadow and sheen of a moleskin mountain
> And a litter of chronicles and bones.
>
> Look into your heart, you will find fermenting rivers,
> Intricacies of gloom and glint,
> You will find such ducats of dream and great doubloons of
>   ceremony
> As nobody today would mint.[15]

The feeling of belonging and yet not belonging echoes throughout his poetry in notes of separation:

> Born here, I should have proved a different self.
> Such vistas dare not open; . . .
> For what takes root or grows that owns no root?[16]

But even the idea of rootlessness is ambiguous. In "Western Landscape," a poem permeated with the contradictions that define MacNeice's attitude toward Ireland, the country both beckons and rebuffs, "Proves and disproves what it wants," and creates impressions that "hit and miss," that "will last and will not."

> The west of Ireland
> Is brute and ghost at once. Therefore in passing
> Among these shadows of this permanent show . . .
>   . . . let me who am neither Brandan

> Free of all roots nor yet a rooted peasant
> Here add one stone to the indifferent cairn. . . .
> With stone on the cairn, with a word on the wind, with a
>   prayer in the flesh let me honour this country.[17]

MacNeice senses he can never belong, but also that he can never completely sever himself from his origins. Thus he remains, as Mahon has noted, a tourist in his own country.

Mahon's criticism of MacNeice's poetry is interesting not only because of the sensitive reading of one poet by another but it also offers insight into Mahon's own poetic condition and reveals the extent to which the younger Ulster Protestant writer identifies with his elder. The same note of vacillation which Mahon hears in MacNeice's work—drawn by the beauty of the Irish west but cut off from the land's mythical and spiritual associations, aware of the subtle complexities of a culture yet separated from them—is the very sound of Mahon's own troubled imagination.

We recognize the resemblances between the two poets very clearly in Mahon's poetry of the Irish west. In depicting the intense beauty of the countryside, he frequently resorts to superlatives, describing hills "a deeper green/Than anywhere in the world" "the perfect northern light," or "Clear cliffs and salt water/Fields brighter than paradise." Inishere, Donegal, the Aran Islands—these places embody simple yet genuine meaning in Mahon's supreme fiction; the landscape evolves into a value, a permanent spirituality in opposition to the passing materialism of the industrial world. The people who inhabit these places live authentic, pure lives, and their daily rhythms suggest association and identification with their society and culture. This part of the fictive use of the Irish west, of course, is not original; many of the urban Revival writers, most notably Yeats and Synge, sensed in the rugged Gaelic west an authenticity and sincerity that could give shape to their work. Mahon's development of the fiction has been very different, however, since he has introduced his own reaction to these literary values. He has accepted the traditional poetic meaning of the Irish west, but ultimately has remained cut off from those values. He, too, has become a tourist in his own country, struck by the vitality of country people, but unable to share it.

> Remember the time we drove
> To Donegal and you talked
> For hours to fishermen
> You had worked with, while I,
> Out of my depth in these
> Waters, loafed on the quays?[18]

Mahon often confesses to being out of his depths "in these waters," raising the essential contradiction in his poetry. The poem "In the Aran Islands" states emphatically his attraction to a romantic Irish tradition that will bolster his poetics:

> searched with a fearful admiration
> walking over the nacreous sand
> I dream myself to that tradition
> Fifty winters off the land.
>
> (P., 34)

Yet the slightest intrusion from the real world quickly stifles desire. The poem's final image presents another form of rootlessness, the seabird pulling away from the strand: "Friend to no slant fields or the sea either,/Folds back over the forming waters." The lack of commitment implicit in this poem's final image demonstrates the paradox facing Mahon and other Ulster writers who have attempted to expand their horizons by living abroad and studying other cultures. The poet's wider perspective allows him to appreciate the beauty of his native land, but ironically prevents him from a complete and easy identification with the parish. The situation becomes more difficult in Ulster when the parochial values are tribal and sectarian and clash with the more open cosmopolitan perspective; the Ulster poet who lives abroad comes home, in Mahon's words, unable to see.

Mahon believes this diffuseness and dissociation characterizes much of recent Ulster poetry, including his own work and that of other Protestant writers such as Paulin, Michael Longley, and James Simmons.[19] It also places their work within what I have called the essentially Joycean direction of Irish poetry, that which accepts the discontinuity of Irish culture. The same struggle with the fragmentation of modern life, so troubling to the poets of Clarke's and Kinsella's generations, persists for Mahon and his fellow Ulster poets, but with an even greater sense of urgency owing to the peculiar stratification of Northern Irish society.

As an Irish poet, Mahon poses what Kinsella has called a gapped sensibility due to the death of Gaelic Ireland; but Mahon's dissociation has been compounded by his Ulster Protestant background, which remove him from the hidden Gaelic Ireland and offered very little in return. The current direction of unionist politics in Northern Ireland makes it impossible for Mahon to idealize the Protestant tradition as Yeats did; instead of great champions of liberty like Grattan and Burke, Mahon sees only the blind and narrow-minded twentieth-century Ulster variety, whom he addresses in "Ecclesiastes":

> you could
> wear black, drink water, nourish a fierce zeal
>   with locusts and wild honey, and not
> feel called upon to understand and forgive
>   but only to speak with a bleak
> afflatus . . .
>   . . . this is your
>   country, close one eye and be king.
>
> (P., 31)

Mahon's criticism of Ulster Protestantism also prevents him from identifying with the Anglo-Irish tradition as some contemporary poets have done, the most notable of whom is Richard Murphy, whom Mahon has called quite possibly the last in the tradition of which Yeats is the exemplar.[20] The same elegiac note we hear in Yeats's Ascendancy poems sounds clearly in Murphy's poem about his patrician grandmother, whose passing ended an era.

People she loved were those who worked the land
Whom the land satisfied more than wisdom:
They've gone, a tractor ploughs where horses strained,
Sometimes sheep occupy their roofless room.

Through our inheritance all things have come,
The form the means, all by our family:
The good of being alive was given through them,
We ourselves limit that legacy.

The bards in their beds once beat out ballads
Under leaky thatch listening to sea-birds,
But she in the long ascendancy of rain
Served biscuits on a tray with ginger wine.

Time can never relax like this again,
She in her phaeton looking for folk-lore,
He writing sermons in the library
Till lunch, then fishing all the afternoon.[21]

The balance of form, the controlled diction, and the overall
decorum combine to produce a distinctively Yeatsian tone which
resonates through an elegiac Ascendancy fiction of Anglo-Irish
country life: landowners who love their workers, peasant bards
attuned to nature, a leisured fisherman, all aware of custom and
ceremony. Murphy's Anglo-Irish heritage also surfaces in his
interest in building houses and shaping old ruins, a reflection
of the masculine ordering spirit of the Ascendancy families who
cultivated gardens and built great houses, transforming the dis-
order of rural Ireland into a coherent beauty. The cultivating
spirit also informs "The Reading Lesson," an interesting poem
which describes the poet's efforts to educate a fourteen-year-old
tinker boy who is reluctant to learn.

"I'll not read anymore." Should I give up?
His hands, long-fingered as a Celtic scribe's,
Will grow callous, gathering sticks or scrap;
Exploring pockets of the horny drunk
Loiterers at the fairs, giving them lice.
A neighbour chuckles. "You can never tame
The wild duck: when his wings grow, he'll fly off."

If books resembled roads, he'd quickly read:
But they're small farms to him, fenced by the page,
Ploughed into lines, with letters drilled like oats:
A field of tasks he'll always be outside.
If words were bank-notes, he would filch a wad:
If they were pheasants, they'd be in his pot
For breakfast, or if wrens he'd make them king.[22]

The central irony in these lines resides in the necessary restriction of instinctual vitality which civilization demands: the act of reading should tame the wildness in the boy. The tension produced in the struggle between civilization and natural instinct is amplified in the poet's own conflict between a well-wrought paternalism, which anticipates a life of crime for the uneducated, and a tolerant imagination, which sees the vitality and instinct of a natural spirit who can read roads and trap pheasants. The tugging between these two tendencies underlies Murphy's central preoccupation, the creation of a poetic fiction that will accommodate the two sides of his Irish identity, his Anglo-Irish Ascendancy inheritance and his attraction for the life represented by tinkers, fishermen, and the common people of Connemara. The long narrative poem "The Battle of Aughrim" explores this tension from a historical point of view, depicting both sides of the battle in 1691 between Irish and English troops. Murphy's sailing poems, "The Last Galway Hooker," "Sailing to an Island," and "The Cleggan Disaster," also grow out of this polemic, described by Seamus Heaney in his essay on Murphy as "a march between his Anglo-Irish Protestant background and his Irish Catholic surroundings . . . a parable of another journey between cultures, from the sure ground of a shared but disappearing Ascendancy world to the suspecting community of the native islanders."[23]

Derek Mahon does not share Murphy's cultural perspective and therefore can draw neither comfort nor meaning from the Ascendancy tradition. Mahon is too much a citizen of the modern world and too familiar with its filthy tide to find Yeats's and Murphy's tradition appropriate. The patrician values and the romantic conception of affinity between the noble and the begger-man will not suffice for a poet whose ladders begin in the rag-and-bone shop of contemporary Ulster. Rather, Mahon lives within the discomfort of solitude whose trope is the poet-persona isolated from his sources. A frequent version of this isolation comes in the image of a poet at his window, staring down into the night, "far from his people/and the fitful glare of his high window is as/nothing to our scattered glass." Occasionally, the solitude appears as self-doubt, particularly about the poetic act—"all this time I have my doubts/About this verse-making"—which extends into a vision of the future: "And will the year two thousand find/Me still at a window, pen in hand?" At its most extreme the isolation theme appears in the image of a physical separateness that reflects the poverty of the imagination.

> The Muse is somewhere
> Else, not here
> By this frozen lake—
> Or, if here, then I am
> Not poet enough
> To make the connection.[24]

These highly self-conscious moments of doubt do not only arise from the artist's sense of impotence to effect any change in the political world, although this anxiety has been noted by some of Mahon's readers.[25] Self-consciousness and especially self-doubt in his poems also stem from the postmodernist tendency to make poetry their subject, particularly the difficulty of the poetic imagination to thrive amid what Mahon calls the given life. The fragmentation of modern existence with its technological and material bent calls into question the very idea of permanence, a traditional value upon which poets have relied for centuries. Mahon's own poems about the Irish west reflect the recognition of and desire for this value. But the flux and transitory nature of modern life have prevented him from seeing permanence even in art, a view opposite to that which informs Yeats's "Sailing to Byzantium":

You will tell me that you have executed
A monument more lasting than bronze;
But even bronze is perishable.
Your best poem, you know the one I mean,
The very language in which the poem
Was written, and the idea of language,
All these things will pass away in time.

(Poems, 107)

The poet must settle instead for the struggle of searching and shaping, for it is only in the continual attempts to order and to question that the poet approaches meaning. In Mahon's case, however, this poetic questing has taken on a very antiromantic accent, stressing the essential discontinuity of the psyche and the dissociation of imagination. The poetic quest has become Mahon's hunt by night.

Irish Modernism

It has been the purpose of this study to trace the central preoccupations of post-Yeatsian Irish poetry in the work of major figures of the last fifty years. The chief task facing these writers has been the redirection of poetry in Ireland, away from the romantic Revivalism and the mythmaking of Yeats's Ascendancy tradition toward a Joycean acceptance of the modern world and its protean condition caused by evolving and dividing social and cultural standards. In choosing the real experiences of twentieth-century Irish life instead of a romantic version of a historical and mythical Ireland, the post-Yeatsian poet has had to surrender the security of structure for the insecurity of innovation.

Post-Yeatsian poetry, then, has moved from romanticism to modernism. The early stages of this shift were marked by what Yeats called rhetoric, the quarrel with others, chiefly with that society in which the poet lived and was writing. Clarke's satirical poetry, Kavanagh's "The Great Hunger" and "Lough Derg," and even parts of Kinsella's "Nightwalker" are examples of this early stage. Eventually, as a reaction against romanticism, writers outgrew their criticism of society, accepting their dissociation, as Irving Howe effectively has argued, as an authentic condition of the modern imagination.[26] Literature has become more subjective as writers have examined both their own psychic makeups and their relation to society and to its values. Much of this examination has considered the role of the poet and the function of art as a social force. Kinsella's inward voice in his later poetry, Montague's "The Rough Field," Heaney's self-doubt in *North* and *Field Work,* and much of Mahon's poetry demonstrate the preoccupation with the role of the poet, the making of poems, and the self-sufficiency of art. We can read the gradual but steady recognition of dissociation among these poets as they search for cultural perimeters. The deeper their sense of the loss of tradition and the greater their feeling of discontinuity with their past, the more they seem to question the difficulty of making poems. From Clarke through the most recent work of Derek Mahon, a consistent and growing tendency has appeared to make literature the subject of poetry.

With Derek Mahon's poetry, and with the brief glances at contemporary writers such as Paul Muldoon and Tom Paulin, we have recognized that discontinuity has replaced any single coherent tradition as post-Yeatsian poetry's most salient feature. These contemporary writers take their dissociation for granted and began their poetic efforts from that perspective. Their arena is the self; their task is to discover meaning and to respond authentically to the modern conditions of individual isolation and cultural fracture. Despite all of their modernist tendencies, however, these contemporary writers have, paradoxically, a genuine sense of their own identities as Irish poets. They are aware that the literary history of the past hundred years informs their poetics, just as they are aware of the achievement of Yeats and those poets who constitute that history. They have also learned that such a self-conscious poetic history cannot be ignored, since virtually all Irish poets of the twentieth century have involved themselves in its definition and development. Like Mahon's image of the stubborn growth in the desolate northwest,the Irish poetic tradition has rooted itself in native soil and has adapted to the severe climate:

> Out there you would look in vain
> For a rose bush; but find,
> Rooted in stony ground,
> A last stubborn growth
> Battered by constant rain
> And twisted by the sea-wind
>
> With nothing to recommend it
> But its harsh tenacity
> Between the blinding windows
> And the forests of the sea,
> As if its very existence
> Were a reason to continue.
>
> (*Poems*, 99)

And if it no longer resembles Yeats's right rose tree, the tradition nonetheless seems assured of some kind of continuity, its trunk apparently weathered and hardened enough to survive even its own isolation.

Notes

INTRODUCTION

1. *The Continuity of American Poetry* (Princeton: Princeton University Press, 1967), 3.

2. See T. S. Eliot's well-known description of tradition in "Tradition and the Individual Talent," *The Selected Prose of T. S. Eliot*, ed. Frank Kermode (New York: Harcourt, Brace, Jovanovich/Farrar Straus Giroux, 1975), 37–44, esp. the following: "It [Tradition] involves the historical sense . . . a perception, not only of the pastness of the past but of its presence; the historical sense compels a man to write not merely with his own generation in his bones, but with a feeling that the whole of the literature of Europe from Homer and within it the whole of the literature of his own country has a simultaneous existence and composes a simultaneous order . . . a sense of the timeless as well as of the temporal and of the timeless and the temporal together."

3. Terence Brown, *Ireland: A Social and Cultural History, 1922–1979* (Glasgow: William Collins Sons and Co., Ltd., 1981), esp. 267–304.

4. *Synge and Anglo-Irish Literature* (Cork: The Mercier Press, 1966). Corkery measures degrees of Irishness here, labeling those with a Catholic-Gaelic consciousness the most Irish. Yeats, Synge, Lady Gregory, and other Protestant Ascendancy writers who shaped the Literary Revival do not score well on Corkery's scale.

5. See esp. Austin Clarke, "Irish Poetry Today," *Dublin Magazine*, n.s., 10, 1 (January–March 1935), 26–32; Padraic Fallon, review of Yeats's *The Winding Stair and Other Poems*, *Dublin Magazine*, n.s., 9, 2 (1934), 58.

6. Quoted in Hugh A. Low, *Anglo-Irish Literature* (Dublin: Talbot Press Ltd., 1926), 277.

7. "Irish National Literature, III," *Uncollected Prose of W. B. Yeats,* vol. 1, ed. John P. Frayne (New York: Columbia University Press, 1970), 377.

8. *Later Poems* (Dublin: The Dolmen Press, 1961), 30n.

9. Maurice Harmon, *Irish Poetry After Yeats* (Boston: Little, Brown and Company, 1979), 9.

10. *English As We Speak It in Ireland*, rev. ed. (Dublin: Wolfhound Press, 1979), 7.

11. *A Colder Eye* (New York: Alfred A. Knopf, 1983), 75.

12. See Brown, *Ireland: A Social and Cultural History, 1922–1979*, 191–193; Kenner, *A Colder Eye*, 49–81.

13. James Joyce, *A Portrait of the Artist as a Young Man* (New York: Viking Press, Inc., 1968), 189.

14. "The Social Function of Poetry," *On Poetry and Poets* (New York: Farrar, Straus and Cudahy, 1957), 9–12.

15. *The Continuity of American Poetry*, 12.

16. "Irish Poetry and Irish Nationalism," *Two Decades of Irish Writing*, ed. Douglas Dunn (Chester Springs, Pa.: Dufour Editions, 1975), 8.

17. Thomas Kinsella, "The Irish Writer," *Davis, Mangan, Ferguson? Tradition and the Irish Writer* (Dublin: The Dolmen Press, 1970), 59.

18. "In the Irish Grain," introduction to *Faber Book of Irish Verse* (London: Faber and Faber, 1974).

19. "An Example of Tradition," *The Crane Bag* 3, 1 (1979), 47.

20. "The Weasel's Tooth," *Irish Times*, 7 June 1974, 7.

21. Oscar Wilde, Joyce's source for the image of the cracked mirror, confirmed the notion of export, since Wilde was the Irish wit of London's literary world in the 1880s and early 1890s.

22. "Romantic Ireland," *Yeats, Sligo and Ireland*, ed. A. Norman Jeffares (Gerrads Cross: Colin Smythe, 1980), 25.

23. See Sean O'Faolain, "Fifty Years of Irish Writing," *Studies* 51 (Spring 1962), 93–103.

24. *Selected Poems* (Winston-Salem, N.C.: Wake Forest University Press, 1982), 10.

25. See Frank Kernowski, *The Outsiders* (Fort Worth: Texas Christian University Press, 1975), for an example of this kind of criticism.

26. "The Future of Irish Literature," *Horizon* 5, 25 (January 1942), 55.

1: TRADITION AND ISOLATION

1. Quoted in *Irish Literary Portraits*, ed. W. R. Rodgers (London: British Broadcasting Corp., 1972), 19.

2. *The Poems of W. B. Yeats*, ed. Richard J. Finneran (New York: Macmillan Publishing Co., 1983), 59. Further references to Yeats's poetry will be cited parenthetically in the text as *YP*.

3. *The Selected Prose of T. S. Eliot*, 249.

4. "The Growth of a Poet, March 17, 1934," *Uncollected Prose of W. B. Yeats*, vol. 2, ed. John P. Frayne and Colton Johnson (New York: Columbia University Press, 1976), 498.

5. *Letters on Poetry from W. B. Yeats to Dorothy Wellesley* (London: Oxford University Press, 1964), 143.

6. "Under Ben Bulben" appeared as the final lyrical poem in Yeats's *Collected Poems* until Finneran's new edition in 1983.

7. Besides the well-known accounts in Yeats's *Autobiography*, Moore's *Hail and Farewell*, and Ernest Boyd's *Ireland's Literary Renaissance*, two recent studies are Phillip L. Marcus, *Yeats and the Beginning of the Irish Renaissance* (Ithaca: Cornell University Press, 1970), and Richard Fallis, *The Irish Renaissance* (Syracuse: Syracuse University Press, 1977).

8. Collected in *The Autobiography of William Butler Yeats* (New York: The Macmillan Co., Collier Books, 1967), 131.

9. *The Identity of Yeats* (New York: Oxford University Press, 1964), 12–38.

10. *The Letters of W. B. Yeats*, ed. Alan Wade (New York: The Macmillan Co., 1955).

11. Ibid., 51, 69.

12. "Irish National Literature, III: Contemporary Irish Poets," *Uncollected Prose of W. B. Yeats*, 1:382.

13. *Essays and Introductions* (New York: The Macmillan Co., 1961; First Collier Edition 1968), 187.

14. *Uncollected Prose of W. B. Yeats*, 1:348.

15. Katherine Tynan, *The Middle Years* (London, 1916), 59.

16. W. B. Yeats, *Letters to the New Island*, ed. Horace Reynolds (Cambridge, Mass.: Harvard University Press, 1934), 2 September 1888.

17. *Memoirs*, ed. Denis Donoghue (New York: The Macmillan Co., 1972), 223.

18. Thomas Parkinson, in *W. B. Yeats: Self-Critic* (Berkeley, Los

Angeles, London: University of California Press, 1971), discusses the development of Yeats's early style. The poet's own explanation of the personal significance and evolution of the use of Celtic material appears in the notes to the poetry and the introduction to the 1908 edition of *Collected Works*.

19. Richard Ellmann, *Yeats: The Man and the Masks* (New York: The Macmillan Co., 1948), 159.

20. Yeats argues for the importance of mood in an 1895 piece: "Everything that can be seen, touched, measured, explained, understood, argued over, is to the imaginative artist nothing more than a means, for he belongs to the invisible life, and delivers its new and ever ancient revelation . . . the mysterious instinct that has made him an artist, . . . teaches him to discover immortal moods in mortal desires, an undecaying hope in our trivial ambitions, a divine love in sexual passion" (*Essays and Introductions*, 195).

21. Ellman has explained that this unbalance also worried Yeats in his early use of symbolism. See *Identity of Yeats*, 78–79.

22. Ellman, *Yeats: The Man and the Masks*, 154–160.

23. Wade, 23, 434.

24. Wayne Hall, in *Shadowy Heroes* (Syracuse: Syracuse University Press, 1980), suggests that the reaction went beyond mere poetics; it centered upon the future of Irish culture. Yeats began to sense the artificiality of his poetry and the limitations of a national literary movement. Hall writes: "It was not to be his [Yeats's] own. Present culture offered the Irish Renaissance a rich and genuine literary source; for Yeats, however, grown intellectually complex and fragmented himself, the peasants of *The Celtic Twilight* could provide only a standard, and an artificially literary one at that, against which to measure his own far different world" (159).

25. J. C. Beckett, *The Anglo-Irish Tradition* (Ithaca: Cornell University Press, 1976), esp. 96–130; Brown, *Ireland: A Social and Cultural History, 1922–1979*, 124.

26. Wade, 464.

27. "Journal," January 1914, *Memoirs*, 271.

28. "Journal," March 12, 1909, *Memoirs*, 184.

29. *The Senate Speeches of W. B. Yeats*, ed. Donald R. Pearce (Bloomington: Indiana University Press, 1960), 99.

30. *W. B. Yeats and Georgian Ireland* (Evanston: Northwestern University Press, 1966), 102.

31. *Essays and Introductions*, 402.

32. Torchiana, *W. B. Yeats and Georgian Ireland*, 23–25.

33. Brown, *Ireland: A Social and Cultural History, 1922–1979*, 107.

34. "Journal," *Memoirs*, 251.

35. Torchiana, *W. B. Yeats and Georgian Ireland*, 118.

36. *Essays and Introduction*, 525.

37. "W. B. Yeats," *Dublin Magazine*, n.s. 14, 2 (1939), 10.

38. Patrick Kavanagh, *Collected Prose* (London: MacGibbon and Kee, 1967), 254.

39. "Literary Myths of the Revival: A Case for their Abandonment," *Myth and Reality in Irish Literature*, ed. Joseph Ronsley (Waterloo: Wilfred Laurien University Press, 1977), 320.

40. "The Irish Writer," *Davis, Mangan, Ferguson? Tradition and the Irish Writer*, 62.

41. Ibid., 64.

2:   REVIVALISM AND THE REVIVALISTS

1. Austin Clarke, *Poetry in Modern Ireland*, 2d ed. (Cork: The Mercier Press, n.d.), 42.

2. Wade, 795.

3. David Corkery, *Synge and Anglo-Irish Literature* (Cork: The Mercier Press, 1966), 38.

4. Ibid., 3.

5. Higgins, a Protestant, adopted the values of the school, attempting to portray Catholic life in his poetry. The portrayal of Catholic Ireland was distinctly anti-Yeats.

6. *The Dublin Magazine* 9, 2 (1934), 58.

7. *Poetry in Modern Ireland*, 49.

8. Unpublished essay on Irish poetry, National Library of Ireland, MS 10, 864.

9. Ibid.

10. Ernest Boyd, *Ireland's Literary Renaissance* (New York: Alfred A. Knopf, 1922), 255–258.

11. *New Songs* (Dublin: O'Donoghue and Co., 1904), 5.

12. Austin Clarke, *The Celtic Twilight and the Nineties* (Dublin: The Dolmen Press, 1969), 31.

13. *New Songs*, 15.

14. *Mud and Purple: Pages from the Diary of a Dublin Man* (Dublin: The Talbot Press, Ltd., 1917).

15. Ibid.

16. Ibid.

17. The high point of the Revival is usually considered to have been the period between the publication of *The Wind Among the Reeds* in 1899, the rise of the Abbey Theater, and Synge's death in 1910.

18. "Introduction," *The Poet's Circuit: Collected Poems of Ireland* (Mountrath: The Dolmen Press, 1961).

19. Richard Loftus, in *Nationalism in Modern Anglo-Irish Poetry* (Madison: University of Wisconsin Press, 1964), 176–180, discusses Colum's use of the ballad tradition and Gaelic prosody.

20. *Poetry in Modern Ireland*, 30.

21. *New Songs*, 42.

22. *The Poet's Circuit*, 110.

23. Ibid., 37.

24. Loftus, 179–180.

25. *The Poet's Circuit*, 37.

26. *Personal Remarks* (London: Peter Neville Ltd., 1953), 81–85.

27. Loftus, 15.

28. *Padraic Colum* (Carbondale: Southern Illinois University Press, 1970), 25–30.

29. Francis Stuart, "The Soft Centre of Irish Writing," *Paddy No More* (Nantucket, Mass.: Longship Press, 1977), 7.

30. *Plays, Poems and Prose* (London: J. M. Dent and Sons, 1975), 219. All references to Synge's poems are from this edition.

31. Ibid., 225.

32. *The Writings of J. M. Synge* (Indianapolis and New York: The Bobbs-Merrill Co., 1971), 163.

33. Synge, *Plays, Poems and Prose*, 221.

34. Ibid., 229.

35. Ibid., 234.

36. Synge's influence upon Yeats's later poetry is suggested but not developed in *The Writings of J. M. Synge*, 166–170. That Yeats admired Synge's treatment of Irish materials is obvious from the praise given to him in Yeats's prose and poetry.

37. "The Shell," *Collected Poems of James Stephens* (New York: Devin-Adair, 1954), 26.

38. Ibid., 176.

39. Ibid., 198.

40. *Collected Poems* (Dublin: The Dolmen Press/Oxford University

Press, 1974), 162. All subsequent references to Clarke's poetry will be from this volume and are cited parenthetically as *CCP*.

41. "Recent Irish Poetry," *Bookman* 77 (August 1934), 235–236.

42. "The Starry Mist," *Island Blood* (London: John Lane, The Bodley Head, 1925), 29.

43. Fallis, 236.

44. Devlin to McGreevy, 31 August 1934, McGreevy Papers, Trinity College Library, Dublin.

45. "The Gallivanting Poet," *Irish Writing*, 3 (November 1947), 62.

46. Loftus, 237.

47. This remark is as much autobiographical as it is theoretical, since I suspect that Higgins' knowledge of Irish was considerably less than that of his compeers Clarke and O'Flaherty.

48. Unpublished essay on Irish poetry, National Library of Ireland, MS 10, 864.

49. Loftus, 251–253.

50. *Island Blood*, 14.

51. *The Gap of Brightness* (New York: The Macmillan Co., 1940), 14.

52. Ibid., 39.

53. *Sincerity and Authenticity* (Cambridge, Mass.: Harvard University Press, 1971), 97.

54. Their collaborative popular broadsheets were published by Cuala Press in 1935.

55. *Poems* (Dublin: The Dolmen Press, 1974), 15.

56. Ibid., 147.

57. Ibid., 104.

58. Ibid., 150.

59. Ibid., 143.

60. "Austin Clarke and Padraic Fallon," *Two Decades of Irish Writing*, 55.

61. *Poems*, 143.

62. "A Poetic Legacy," *Irish Times*, 17 August 1974.

63. *Poems*, 39.

64. Ibid., 67.

65. "Austin Clarke and Padraic Fallon," *Two Decades of Irish Writing*, 57.

66. In this reading I differ from Maurice Harmon, "The Poetry of Padraic Fallon," *Studies* (Autumn 1975), 269–281, who sees Fallon successfully confronting Yeats in "Yeats' Tower at Ballylee."

67. *Poems*, 67.
68. Ibid., 55.
69. Ibid., 60.

3: "NON SERVIAM"

1. "The Irish Writer," *Davis, Mangan, Ferguson? Tradition and the Irish Writer*, 57.

2. Harold Bloom, in *The Anxiety of Influence* (New York: Oxford University Press, 1973), spells out a critical theory based on the influence of a major poet on those who follow him.

3. See W. Jackson Bate, *The Burden of the Past and the English Poet* (Cambridge, Mass.: Harvard University Press, 1970).

4. "The Influence of Yeats on Later English Poets," *Tri-Quarterly* (1965), 84–87.

5. Denis Donoghue, "Romantic Ireland," *Yeats, Sligo and Ireland*, ed. A. Norman Jeffares (Gerard Cross: Colin Smythe, 1980), 30.

6. Austin Clarke states that *A Portrait* "had long since become confused with my own memories" in *Twice Round the Black Church* (London: Routledge & Kegan Paul, 1962), 26. Clarke and Patrick Kavanagh both admired Joyce's stance in dramatizing the artist's ability to speak out.

7. "The Holy Office," *The Critical Writings of James Joyce*, eds. Ellsworth Mason and Richard Ellmann (New York: The Viking Press, 1959), 151.

8. Ibid., 45.

9. Ibid., 152.

10. "An Irish Poet," in ibid., 84–87.

11. "The Day of the Rabblement," *The Critical Writings of James Joyce*, 71.

12. "The Soul of Ireland," *The Critical Writings of James Joyce*, 104.

13. *The Critical Writings of James Joyce*, 91.

14. Herbert Howarth, in *The Irish Writers* (New York: Hill and Wang, 1958), 253–254, suggests that Joyce debunks Yeats's popular ideal in the play *Cathleen ni Houlihan* by splitting Kathleen from Holohan and having them argue over money.

15. Frank O'Connor, *A Backward Look* (New York: Capricorn Books, 1968), 194–196.

16. "The Day of the Rabblement," *The Critical Writings of James Joyce*, 71.

17. "The Irish Writer," *Davis, Mangan, Ferguson? Tradition and the Irish Writer*, 65.

18. Kavanagh's acceptance of parochialism—"a mentality which is never in any doubt about the social and artistic validity of his parish"—and his reference to Joyce as one of the two great Irish parishioners (the other was George Moore) were important to his overall aesthetic thinking. See *Kavanagh's Weekly*, 24 May 1952, 2, in facsimile ed. (The Curragh: Goldsmith Press, 1981).

19. "The Irish Writer," *Davis, Mangan, Ferguson? Tradition and the Irish Writer*, 64.

20. *Chamber Music* (London: Jonathan Cape Ltd., 1971), 10.

21. Ibid., 36.

22. Ibid., 13.

23. Harry Levin, *James Joyce: An Introduction* (New York: New Directions Publishing Co., 1960), 27.

24. *Poems Penyeach* (London: Faber and Faber, 1966), 18.

25. Ibid., 16.

26. Ibid., 45.

27. Ibid., 13.

28. "James Joyce, Irish Poet," *James Joyce Quarterly* 2 (1965), 264.

29. *Letters of James Joyce*, vol. 1, ed. Stuart Gilbert (New York: The Viking Press, 1952), 62–64.

30. *James Joyce: The Critical Heritage*, 527.

31. *Twice Round the Black Church*, 25–26.

32. "Kafka and his Precursors," *Other Inquisitions, 1937–1952*, trans. Ruth L. Simms (Austin: University of Texas Press, 1964), 108. In addition to discussing the obvious case of literary influence, in which one writer is shaped by another, Borges hints at a more subtle case, in which a younger writer "influences" the reading of an older text: "The poem 'Fears and Scruples' by Robert Browning is like a prophecy of Kafka's stories, but our reading of Kafka refines and changes our reading of the poem perceptibly." While this is overstating the case with Joyce, it nevertheless shows how in viewing Clarke's poetry about religious doubt, we see *A Portrait* in the background just as Clarke himself surely did.

33. *A Portrait*, 144–145.

34. Ibid., 247.

35. John Haffenden, *Viewpoints: Poets in Conversation* (London: Faber and Faber, 1981), 100.

36. *Letters of James Joyce,* vol. 2, ed. Richard Ellmann (New York: The Viking Press, 1966), 134.

37. "The Irish Writer," *Davis, Mangan, Ferguson? Tradition and the Irish Writer,* 65. Kinsella seems reluctant to name this group, but he means the Catholic bourgoisie.

38. Joyce's example lent considerable authority and support to those writers who were fighting severe government censorship in the 1940s. See O'Connor, *A Backward Look,* 214–216.

39. "Recent Irish Poetry," 236.

40. Ibid.

41. Letter to Thomas McGreevy, 18 July 1965, McGreevy Papers, Trinity College Library, Dublin.

42. Coffey edited and wrote an introduction to Devlin's *Collected Poems;* Beckett wrote an introduction to McGreevy's *Collected Poems.*

43. 25 October 1962, McGreevy Papers, Trinity College Library, Dublin.

44. Dierdre Bair, *Samuel Beckett* (New York: Harcourt Brace Jovanovich, 1978), 71.

45. *Collected Poems* (Dublin: New Writers' Press, 1971), 24.

46. Ibid., 72.

47. Bair, *Samuel Beckett,* 141.

48. *Poems in English* (New York: Grove Press, Inc., 1961), 24–25.

49. "Devlin's Poetry: Love in Abeyance," *Concerning Poetry* 14, 2 (Fall 1981), 30.

50. *Collected Poems,* ed. Brian Coffey (Dublin: The Dolmen Press Ltd., 1964), 31.

51. "Dead Season," *Three Poems* (Paris: F. Paillait, 1933).

52. "Come Out," *Three Poems.*

53. Austin Clarke confessed that Joyce had no interest in reading his poetry and asked him only about places and persons in Dublin; see *Twice Round the Black Church,* 24–27. Bair reports that Joyce gave Beckett's work only cursory recognition; see *Samuel Beckett,* 67–113.

54. *A Portrait,* 252.

4: TRADITION AND CONTINUITY I: AUSTIN CLARKE

1. Those who have pointed to the insularity and limitations of Clarke's poetry because of its self-consciously Irish quality are Samuel Beckett, "Recent Irish Poetry"; Patrick Kavanagh, "Poetry in Ireland Today," *The Bell* 16 (April 1948), 39–42; Donald Torchiana, "Some Dublin Afterthoughts," *Tri-Quarterly* 4 (Autumn 1965), 140–145. Those who have praised the use of Irish material and technique are Robert Farren, *The Course of Irish Verse* (London: Sheed and Ward, 1948), 140–155; Susan Halpern, *Austin Clarke, his Life and Works* (Dublin: The Dolmen Press, 1974), 61–91, 146–147; John Montague, "Global Regionalism, An Interview with John Montague," *Literary Review* 22, 2 (Winter 1979); Craig Tapping, *Austin Clarke, A Study of His Writings* (Totowa, N.J.: Barnes and Noble, 1981); Gregory A. Schirmer, *The Poetry of Austin Clarke* (Notre Dame: University of Notre Dame Press, 1983), esp. 5–11, 49–65.

2. Clarke, *A Penny in the Clouds* (London: Routledge & Kegan Paul, 1968), 2–3, 10–11.

3. *Twice Round the Black Church,* 169.

4. "Recent Irish Poetry," 134.

5. Seamus O'Sullivan Collection, Huntington Library MS.

6. "Irish Poetry Today," *Dublin Magazine* 10, 1 (January–March 1935), 28.

7. The wandering clerk gave Clarke a chance to pun on his own name; it also testifies to the autobiographical significance of the scholar in Clarke's medieval works.

8. Roger McHugh, "The Plays of Austin Clarke," *Irish University Review* 9, 1 (Spring 1974), 52–64.

9. *CCP.,* 545.

10. My reading of *Pilgrimage* as a revivalist text, or at least one prompted by the aims of the Revival, generally meshes with Gregory Schirmer's reading in his *The Poetry of Austin Clarke,* 23–43.

11. *Twice Round the Black Church,* 169; *A Penny in the Clouds,* 22–24.

12. "Austin Clarke and the Gaelic Poetic Tradition," *Irish University Review* 4, 1 (Spring 1974), 41–45.

13. *CCP.,* 547.

14. *The Literary Review* 22, 2 (Winter 1979), 161.

15. "The Poetic Career of Austin Clarke," *Irish University Review* 4, 1 (Spring 1974), 133.

16. Ibid., 131.

17. "Austin Clarke and Padraic Fallon," *Two Decades of Irish Writing*, 46.

18. Vivian Mercier, "Mortal Anguish, Mortal Pride: Austin Clarke's Religious Lyrics," *Irish University Review* 4, 1 (Spring 1974), 95.

19. *A Portrait*, 172.

20. Maurice Harmon, "The Later Poetry of Austin Clarke," *The Celtic Cross*, eds. Ray B. Browne, William John Roscelli, and Richard J. Loftus (West Lafayette: Purdue University Press, 1964), 39–55; Charles Tomlinson, "Poets and Mushrooms," *Poetry* (1962), 113; Augustin Martin, "The Rediscovery of Austin Clarke, *Studies* 54 (1965), 420–436.

21. I have elaborated on this point in "Austin Clarke in Transition," *Irish University Review* 4, 1 (Spring 1974), 106–110. See also Terence Brown, "Dublin in Modern Irish Poetry," *Irish University Review* 6, 1 (Spring 1976), 4–16.

22. "Miss Rosanna Ford," *CCP.*, 436; "Miss Marnell," *CCP.*, 210; "The Knock," *CCP.*, 272.

23. *Dublin's Joyce* (Boston: Beacon Press, 1956), 214–224.

24. "A Jocular Retort," *CCP.*, 475; "Ex Trivio," *CCP.*, 471: "The Dead Sea Scrolls," 228.

25. "The Later Poetry of Austin Clarke," 50; "Celebrations," *CCP.*, 195.

26. "The Irish Writer," *Davis, Mangan, Ferguson? Tradition and the Irish Writer*, 64–66; see also *An Duanaire, Poems of the Dispossessed*, xix–xxxix.

27. Corelli's *The Sorrows of Satan* (London, 1895) is referred to in *Ulysses*, 184. Joyce also read *Ziska, The Problems of a Wicked Soul* (London, 1897). See letter to Stanilaus Joyce, 28 February 1905, *Letters of James Joyce*, 2:82–23. Malloy's "Love's Old Sweet Song" reverberates throughout *Ulysses*.

28. Clarke's play *Liberty Land* (Dublin: The Dolmen Press, 1978) features the street culture of nineteenth-century Dublin.

29. He identifies the following initials: W. B. Y. (Yeats), A. G. (Lady Gregory), A. J. (Augustus John), AE (George Russell), and S. O'C (Sean O'Casey).

30. Clarke's sermon, or lecture, on Swift, "The Poetry of Swift,"

appears in *Jonathan Swift, 1667–1967: A Dublin Tercentenary Tribute*, eds. Roger McHugh and Philip Edwards (Dublin: The Dolmen Press, 1967), 94–115.

31. Vivian Mercier, *The Irish Comic Tradition* (New York: Oxford University Press, 1962), 201–205; Richard Weber, "Austin Clarke: The Arch-Poet of Dublin," *Massachusetts Review* 11, 2 (1970), 298–301; Robert F. Garratt, "Aware of my Ancestor: Austin Clarke and the Legacy of Swift," *E-I* 11, 3 (Summer 1976), 92–103.

32. "W. B. Yeats," *Dublin Magazine*, n.s., 14 (April–June 1939), 10.

33. "Introduction," *Selected Poems of Austin Clarke* (Dublin: The Dolmen Press/Winston-Salem: Wake Forest University Press, 1976), ix.

34. See Gerard Lyne, "Austin Clarke, A Bibliography," *Irish University Review* 4, 1 (Spring 1974), 137–155.

5: Tradition and Continuity II: Patrick Kavanagh

1. "The Intangible," *Irish Statesman*, 19 October 1929; "Ploughman," *Irish Statesman*, 15 February 1930; and "Beech Tree," *Dublin Magazine* (October 1931).

2. *The Complete Poems of Patrick Kavanagh*, ed. Peter Kavanagh (New York: The Peter Kavanagh Hand Press, 1972), 1. All subsequent references to Kavanagh's poems are from this edition and will be cited parenthetically as *KCP*.

3. *The Green Fool* (Harmondsworth: Penguin Books, 1975), 222–231.

4. "Austin Clarke and Padraic Fallon," *Two Decades of Irish Writing*, 42.

5. Typical of the humor at Kavanagh's expense is the following remark of Seamus O'Sullivan, quoted in Clarke's *A Penny in the Clouds*, 71: "One evening, looking from the drawing-room of his house in Morehampton Road, he [S.O'S] saw a man pushing a handcart with a small load of manure. 'I see that Paddy Kavanagh is moving. There go his furniture and effects.'" See also Anthony Cronin, *Dead as Doornails* (Dublin: Poolbeg Press, 1975), esp. 63–92, which, while more affectionate, also describes Kavanagh's uncouth appearance and his clumsiness.

6. Letter to Peter Kavanagh, August Bank Holiday, 1947, *Lapped Furrows*, ed. Peter Kavanagh (New York: The Peter Kavanagh Hand Press, 1969).

7. Quoted in Peter Kavanagh, *Sacred Keeper: A Biography of Patrick Kavanagh* (Atlantic Highlands, N.J.: Humanities Press, 1980), 173.

8. "St. Stephens's, Trinity Term, 1962," quoted in *The Journal of Irish Literature* 6, 1 (January 1977), 28.

9. *Irish Times*, 15 August 1942.

10. "William Butler Yeats," *Collected Pruse* (London: MacGibbon and Kee, 1967), 254.

11. "On a Liberal Education," *November Haggard*, ed. Peter Kavanagh (New York: The Peter Kavanagh Hand Press, 1971), 80.

12. *Kavanagh's Weekly*, 17 May 1952, 7.

13. "Auden and the Creative Mind, *Collected Pruse*, 251.

14. "Poetry in Ireland Today," *The Bell* (April 1948), 40.

15. *Kavanagh's Weekly*, 24 May 1952, 2.

16. Ibid., 31 May 1952, 3.

17. *Self-Portrait* (Dublin: The Dolmen Press, 1964), 20.

18. Letter to Peter Kavanagh, December 1950, *Lapped Furrows*.

19. "The Literary Movement in Ireland," 27 April 1899, *Uncollected Prose of W. B. Yeats*, 2:184–186.

20. *YP.*, 321.

21. Darcy O'Brien, *Patrick Kavanagh* (Lewisburg: Bucknell University Press, 1975), 19–26, in an interesting reading of "The Great Hunger," Kavanagh's poetry alludes to but does not develop the Joycean twist.

22. Kavanagh had the following passage in mind: "when the soul of a man is born in this country. . . . "

23. Weldon Thornton, "Virgin or Hungry Fiend? The Failure of the Imagination in Patrick Kavanagh's 'The Great Hunger,'" *Mosaic* 12, 3 (Spring 1979), 157.

24. For discussions of this poem, see Seamus Heaney, "From Monaghan to the Grand Canal," *Pre-occupations* (London: Faber and Faber, 1980), 117–118; Adrian Frazer, "The Sincerity of Patrick Kavanagh," *The Malahat Review*, no. 53 (January 1980), 114–116.

25. The phrasing and rhythm in "Candida" owe much to Swift's birthday poems to Stella.

26. John Nemo divides the final phase of Kavanagh's career into four phases: artistic disorientation, spiritual rebirth, carelessness, and creative loss; see *Patrick Kavanagh* (Boston: Twayne Publishers, 1979), 115–116.

6:   POETRY AT MID-CENTURY I: THOMAS KINSELLA

1. "The Impact of International Modern Poetry on Irish Writing," *Irish Poets in English*, ed. Sean Lucy (Cork: The Mercier Press, 1973), 155.

2. "The Irish Writer," *Davis, Mangan, Ferguson? Tradition and the Irish Writer*, 66.

3. The case for internationalism as a major feature of modernism has been made by, among others, Harold Rosenberg, in "The Fall of Paris," *The Tradition of the New* (New York: McGraw-Hill, 1965), 209–220, and Delmore Schwartz, in "T.S. Eliot as the International Hero," *The Idea of the Modern*, ed. Irving Howe (New York: Horizon Press, 1967), 277–287. Irish modernist poetry recognizes international influences yet retains a distinct Irish accent.

4. Each generation of modern Irish poets, beginning with Yeats's continuing through Higgins's and Clarke's, and now including Kinsella's and Montague's, has felt compelled to explain itself.

5. Thomas Kinsella and John Montague, eds., *Dolmen Miscellany of Irish Writing* (Dublin, The Dolmen Press, 1962).

6. "The Irish Writer," *Davis, Mangan, Ferguson? Tradition and the Irish Writer*, 66.

7. Haffenden, *Viewpoints*, 112.

8. "The Irish Writer," *Davis, Mangan, Ferguson? Tradition and the Irish Writer*, 59.

9. Kinsella delivered the paper "The Irish Writer" at the annual meeting of the Modern Language Association in New York in 1966. The paper was revised and published in *Davis, Mangan, Ferguson? Tradition and the Irish Writer* in 1970. A further revision with additions appeared as "The Divided Mind" in *Irish Poets in English*, ed. Sean Lucy (Cork: The Mercier Press, 1973), 208–218. Carolyn Rosenberg lists another version, "The Irish Writer," *E-I* 1, no. 2 (1967), 8–15, in her unpublished dissertation, *Let Our Gaze Blaze: The Recent Poetry of Thomas Kinsella*, Kent State University, 1980, 653.

10. *Poems, 1956–1973* (Winston-Salem, N.C.: Wake Forest University Press, 1979), 31. All subsequent references to this volume will be cited parenthetically as *P*.

11. *Another September* (Dublin: The Dolmen Press, 1958), 1.

12. "Searching the Darkness: The Poetry of Richard Murphy,

Thomas Kinsella, John Montague and James Simmons," *Two Decades of Irish Writing*, 133.

13. *Eight Contemporary Poets* (London: Oxford University Press, 1974), 120.

14. *The Poetry of Thomas Kinsella* (Atlantic Highlands, N.C.: Humanities Press, 1975), 24.

15. *National Student* (University College, Dublin) 114 (Mar 1952), 5–7.

16. "The Irish Writer," *Davis, Mangan, Ferguson? Tradition and the Irish Writer*, 65.

17. Harmon, 14–15; Brown, "Dublin in Modern Irish Poetry," 8–10; John Reese Moore, "Thomas Kinsella's *Nightwalker:* A Phoenix in the Dark," *The Hollins Critic* 5, 4 (October 1968), 3–6.

18. Hugh Kenner, "Thomas Kinsella: An Anecdote and Some Reflections," *Genres of the Literary Revival*, ed. Ronald Schleifer (Pilgrim Books, 1980), 186.

19. "Introduction," *An Duanaire, 1600–1900: Poems of the Dispossessed*, xxv–xxvii.

20. "The Influence of Yeats on Later English Poets," 85.

21. Commentary has generally stressed Eliot's "The Waste Land" as the major presence behind "Nightwalker." This observation would seem to demand the quibble about Eliot's debt to *Ulysses;* most critics do not discuss Joycean technique in "Nightwalker." See Longley, 134; Bedient, 127–128; Harmon, 60.

22. *The Poetry of Thomas Kinsella*, 64–65.

23. Kenner identifies "Father of Authors! It is himself," "son-husband," and "big white harse" as being from *Finnegans Wake* in "Thomas Kinsella: An Anecdote and Some Reflections," 183n. There is also an echo of the "Proteus" chapter in *Ulysses* in "the smell of seaweed, a spectral stink of horse/And rider's sweat" as the tide at Sandymount strand draws back.

24. Harmon, 67, identifies the bird as Amhairgin, the spirit of the Irish language and nationality.

25. Kinsella published *Nightwalker* with Dolmen Press in 1967. An American version, slightly changed, appeared with Alfred A. Knopf in 1968 and was reprinted in 1969. None of these contains the new punctuation in *Notes*. For commentary, see Harmon, 80; Peggy F. Broder, "Breaking the Shell of Solitude: Some Poems of Thomas Kinsella," *Eire-Ireland* 14, 2 (Summer 1979), 80; Arthur E. McGuinness, "Bright Quincunx Newly Risen: Thomas Kinsella's Inward 'I,'" *Eire-Ireland* 15,

4 (Winter 1980), 118. The connection with *Finnegans Wake,* whose beginning Kinsella may have had in mind when planning the changes in *Notes* is not mentioned in the criticism.

26. *Peppercanister Poems, 1972–1978* (Winston-Salem: N.C.: Wake Forest University Press, 1979), 69. Further references to this volume will be cited parenthetically as *PP.*

27. Moore, 4.

28. "The Irish Writer," *Davis, Mangan, Ferguson? Tradition and the Irish Writer,* 59.

29. *The Tain* (London: Oxford University Press, 1970); *An Duanaire, 1600–1900: Poetry of the Dispossessed.*

30. Kinsella outlines the route in his introduction to *The Tain.*

31. "Art of Austin Clarke," *Irish Press,* 16 June 1956.

32. "Introduction," *Selected Poems of Austin Clarke,* x–xi.

33. "The Irish Writer," *Davis, Mangan, Ferguson? Tradition of the Irish Writer,* 62–64.

34. See McGuiness, "Bright Quincunx Newly Risen: Thomas Kinsella's "Inward 'I,'" which argues for Yeats's presence in Kinsella's later poems.

35. Carol Rosenberg develops these comparisons thoroughly in *Let Our Gaze Blaze: The Recent Poetry of Thomas Kinsella,* 417–438.

7:   POETRY AT MID-CENTURY II: JOHN MONTAGUE

1. "The Irish Writer," *The Bell,* 17, 7 (October 1951), 8.

2. Ibid., 10.

3. *Poisoned Lands,* new ed. (Dublin: The Dolmen Press, 1977), 9.

4. Mary Leland, "John Montague in Cork," *Irish Times,* 23 November 1976.

5. Adrian Frazer, "Interview with John Montague," *The Literary Review* 22, 2 (Winter 1979), 153–154.

6. Ibid., 156.

7. *A Portrait,* 252.

8. *Selected Poems* (Winston-Salem, N.C.: Wake Forest University Press, 1982), 18. All subsequent references to Montague's *Selected Poems* will be cited parenthetically as *SP.*

9. A. K. Weatherhead, "John Montague: Exiled from Order," *Concerning Poetry* 14, 2 (Fall 1981), 97–101.

10. Edna Longley, "Searching the Darkness: The Poetry of Richard Murphy, Thomas Kinsella, John Montague and James Simmons," *Two Decades of Irish Writing*, 138–145; Thimothy Kearney, "The Poetry of the North: A Post-modernist Perspective," *The Crane Bag* 3, 2 (1979), 48; Terence Brown, *Northern Voices* (Dublin: Gill and Macmillan, 1975), 147–156.

11. Heaney, "The Poetry of Patrick Kavanagh: From Monaghan to the Grand Canal"; Deane, "Irish Poetry and Irish Nationalism: A Survey," esp. 10–20; Michael Allen, "Provincialism and Recent Irish Poetry," 23–36; all in *Two Decades of Irish Writing*.

12. *The Rough Field*, 3d ed. (Winston-Salem: Wake Forest University Press, 1979), 7. All subsequent references to this volume will be cited parenthetically as *RF*.

13. *A Chosen Light* (London: MacGibbon and Kee, 1967).

14. "Boats," *Tides* (Dublin: The Dolmen Press, 1970), 59.

15. Brown, *Northern Voices*, 157.

16. "Seamless Garment and the Muse," *Agenda* 5, 4; 6, 1 (Autumn–Winter 1967), 27.

17. Deane, "Irish Poetry and Irish Nationalism: A Survey," 15–16; Sean Lucey, "Three Poets from Ulster," *Irish University Review* 3, 2 (Autumn 1973), 191–192; D. E. S. Maxwell, "The Poetry of John Montague," *Critical Quarterly* 15 (Summer 1973), 180–185, all see Montague as largely successful. Brown, *Northern Voices*, 167–168; Longley, 144–145; Kearney, 47–48, do not.

18. *Northern Voices*, 157. Brown sees this problem as central to all of Montague's poetry.

19. "The Speckled Hill, the Plower's Share: Northern Irish Poetry Today," *Encounter* 41 (December 1973), 72. See also *Two Decades of Irish Writing*, 146n.

20. *Northern Voices*, 167–168.

21. Longley, "Searching the Darkness," 143–146.

22. Frazer, "Interview with John Montague," 157.

23. Ibid., 173.

24. "A Note on Rhythm," *Agenda* 10, no. 4–11, 1 (Autumn–Winter 1972), 41.

25. Weatherhead, 104.

26. *Faber Book of Irish Verse* (London: Faber and Faber, 1974), 37–38.

27. *A Slow Dance* (Dublin: The Dolmen Press, 1975), Further references to *A Slow Dance* will be cited parethetically as *SD*.

8: The Poetry of Commitment: Seamus Heaney

1. "Poetry in Northern Ireland," *Twentieth Century Studies* 4 (November 1970), 89–93.

2. Those who argue that Heaney has transcended terror include Richard Murphy, "Poetry and Terror," *New York Review of Books*, 30 September 1976, 38–40; Arthur McGuinness, "'Hoarder of Common Ground': Tradition and Ritual in Seamus Heaney's Poetry," *Eire-Ireland* 13, 2 (Summer 1978), 71–92. Those who sense in varying degrees hints of reluctance to confront issues are, among others, Kearney, "The Poetry of the North," 45–53; Shaun O'Connell, "Seamus Heaney: Poetry and Power," *New Boston Review* 5, 5/6 (August–September 1980), 3–5; Mark Patrick Hederman, "Seamus Heaney, the Reluctant Poet," *The Crane Bag* 3, 2 (1979), 61–70; Wlliam Bedford, "To Set the Darkness Echoing," *Delta*, no. 56 (1977), 2–7.

3. Politics and literature have been inseparable in modern Ireland. See Malcolm Brown, *Politics of Irish Literature* (Seattle: University of Washington Press, 1972), for background. For more recent commentary, see Seamus Deane, "The Writer and the Troubles," *Threshold*, no. 25 (Summer 1974), 13–17.

4. See esp. interview with Seamus Deane, *The Crane Bag*, 1, 1 (1977), 66–72; Haffenden, *Viewpoints*, 57–75.

5. *Pre-occupations, Selected Prose 1968–1978* (London: Faber and Faber, Ltd., 1980), 41.

6. Ibid., 34–35.

7. *Door into the Dark* (London: Faber and Faber, Ltd., 1969), 56.

8. *Death of a Naturalist* (London: Faber and Faber, Ltd., 1966), 14.

9. See McGuiness, "'Hoarder of Common Ground': Tradition and Ritual in Seamus Heaney's Poetry"; Seamus Deane, "The Appetites of Gravity: Contemporary Irish Poetry," *Sewanee Review* 84, 1/2 (1976) 202–205; Bernard Sharratt, "Memories of Dying: The Poetry of Seamus Heaney II," *New Blackfriars* 57 (August 1976), 371–377.

10. *North* (New York: Oxford University Press, 1975), 41–43. Subsequent references to *North* will be cited parenthetically as *N*.

11. Seamus Deane, "Interview with Seamus Heaney," *The Crane Bag* 1, 1 (Spring 1977), 63.

12. Hederman, in "Seamus Heaney, the Reluctant Poet," identifies this struggle in Heaney's poetry, but, I believe, misinterprets its effect and direction.

13. *Pre-occupations*, 56–57.

14. Dean, "Interview with Seamus Heaney," 65.

15. *Pre-occupations*, 88.

16. *A Hopkins Reader*, ed. John Pick (New York: Oxford University Press, 1953).

17. Ibid., 31.

18. Haffenden, *Viewpoints*, 69.

19. *Pre-occupations*, 120.

20. Ibid., 110.

21. Heaney's version of this polemic shapes his view of authenticity: "You have to be true to your own sensibility, for the faking of feelings is a sin against the imagination. Poetry is out of the quarrel with ourselves and the quarrel with others is rhetoric" (*Pre-occupations*, 34).

22. For Heaney's own hints about the design of *North*, see Haffenden, *Viewpoints*, 69–70; Deane, "An Interview with Seamus Heaney," 63–65.

23. *Field Work* (New York: Farrar, Straus, Giroux, 1979), 13. Subsequent references to *Field Work* will be cited parenthetically as *FW*.

24. "A Familiar Ghost," *Irish Times*, Special Supplement, 2 February 1982. A revision of this poem appears in Heaney's new book *Station Island* (New York: Farrar, Straus and Giroux, 1985), which arrived too late for me to include in my remarks here.

25. Sigmund Freud, *The Interpretation of Dreams*, trans. James Strackey (New York: Science Editions, Inc., 1961), 338. Freud contended that the "dream within a dream" constitutes a true recollection of reality, as opposed to the mere wishes of a single dream.

26. *Pre-occupations*, 34.

9:   TRADITION OF DISCONTINUITY

1. Brown, *Ireland: A Social and Cultural History, 1922–1979*, 317.

2. "Postscript," *The Crane Bag* 3, 2 (1979), 512.

3. "Martello," *Liberty Tree* (London: Faber and Faber, 1983), 55.

4. "Lunch with Pancho Villa," *Mules* (Winston-Salem: Wake Forest University Press, 1977), 11.

5. Mahon's poetry ranges over twenty years and appears in five books, allowing readers to observe his poetic development: *Night-Crossing* (London: Oxford University Press, 1968); *Lives* (London: Oxford

University Press, 1972); *The Snow Party* (London: Oxford University Press, 1975); *Poems: 1962–1978* (London: Oxford University Press, 1979); *The Hunt by Night* (Winston-Salem: Wake Forest University Press, 1983).

6. See, for example, reviews by Arthur E. McGuinness, *Eire-Ireland* 16, 1 (Spring 1981), and Adrian Frazer, in *Eire-Ireland* 19, 1 (Spring 1984).

7. Bradley, *Contemporary Irish Poetry* (Berkeley, Los Angeles, London: University of California Press, 1980), 10.

8. Brown, *Northern Voices*, 196.

9. "Poetry in Northern Ireland," *Twentieth Century Studies*, 4 (November 1970).

10. "The Spring Vacation," *Poems: 1962–1978*, 4. Subsequent references to this volume will be cited parenthetically as *Poems*.

11. *The Hunt by Night*, 49.

12. "Unaccommodated Mahon: An Ulster Poet," *The Hollins Critic* 17, 5 (December 1980), 2.

13. "MacNeice in England and Ireland," *Time Was Away*, eds. Terence Brown and Alec Reid (Dublin: The Dolmen Press, 1974), 117.

14. "Carrickfergus," *Selected Poms of Louis MacNeive*, ed. W. H. Auden (London: Faber and Faber, 1964), 29.

15. "Neutrality," *Selected Poems of Louis MacNeice*, 77.

16. "The Once in Passing," *Selected Poems of Louis MacNeice*, 106.

17. Ibid., 96.

18. *The Hunt by Night*, 34.

19. "Poetry in Northern Ireland," *Twentieth Century Studies* (1970).

20. Ibid., 92.

21. *Selected Poems* (London: Faber and Faber, 1979), 20.

22. *High Island* (New York: Harper and Row, 1974), 107.

23. "The Poetry of Richard Murphy," *Irish University Review* 7, 1 (Spring 1977), 19.

24. *The Hunt by Night*, 41.

25. See D. E. S. Maxell, "Contemporary Poetry in the North of Ireland," *Two Decades of Irish Writing*, 179–183; Dillon Johnston, "Unaccommodated Mahon: An Ulster Poet," 2–6; and Adrian Frazer, "Proper Portion: Derek Mahon's *The Hunt by Night*," *Eire-Ireland* 18, 4 (Winter 1983), 136–143.

26. "The Idea of the Modern," *The Idea of the Modern*, 11–40.

Selected Bibliography

Primary Sources

Beckett, Samuel. *Poems in English*. New York: Grove Press Inc., 1961.

Clarke, Austin. *The Celtic Twilight and the Nineties*. Dublin: The Dolmen Press, 1969.

————. *Collected Poems*. Dublin: The Dolmen Press in association with Oxford University Press, 1974.

————. *A Penny in the Clouds*. London: Routledge & Kegan Paul, 1968.

————. *Poetry in Modern Ireland*. Cork: Mercier Press, 1966.

————. *Twice Round the Black Church*. London: Routledge & Kegan Paul, 1962.

Coffey, Brian. *Three Poems*. Paris: F. Paillait, 1933.

Colum, Padraic. *The Poet's Circuit: Collected Poems of Ireland*. Mountrath and Portlaoise: The Dolmen Press, 1961.

Devlin, Denis. *Collected Poems*. Ed. Brian Coffey. Dublin: The Dolmen Press, 1964.

Fallon, Padraic. *Poems*. Dublin: The Dolman Press, 1974.

Heaney, Seamus. *Death of a Naturalist*. London: Faber and Faber Ltd., 1966.

————. *Door into the Dark*. London: Faber and Faber Ltd., 1969.

————. *Field Work*. New York: Farrar, Straus, Giroux, 1979.

————. *North*. New York: Oxford University Press, 1975.

————. *Pre-occupation: Selected Prose, 1968–1978*. London: Faber and Faber Ltd., 1980.

Higgins, F. R. *The Gap of Brightness*. New York: Macmillan Co., 1940.

————. *Island Blood*. London: John Lane, The Bodley Head Ltd., 1925.

Joyce, James. *Chamber Music*. London: Jonathan Cape Ltd., 1971.

————. *The Critical Writings*. Ed. Ellsworth Mason and Richard Ellmann. New York: The Viking Press, 1959.

————. *Letters*. Vol. I. Ed. Stuart Gilbert; Vol. II. Ed. Richard Ellman. New York: The Viking Press, 1957 and 1966.

————. *Poems Penyeach*. London: Faber and Faber Ltd., 1966.

————. *A Portrait of the Artist as a Young Man*. New York: The Viking Press, 1968.

Kavanagh, Patrick. *Collected Prose*. London: MacGibbon and Kee, 1967.

————. *The Complete Poems*. Ed. Peter Kavanagh. New York: The Peter Kavanagh Hand Press, 1972.

————. *The Green Fool*. Harmondsworth: Penguin Books, Ltd., 1975.

————. *Lapped Furrows*. Ed. Peter Kavanagh. New York: The Peter Kavanagh Hand Press, 1969.

————. *Kavanagh's Weekly*, fascimile edition. The Curragh Co. Kildare, Ireland: Goldsmith Press, 1981.

————. *November Haggard*. Ed. Peter Kavanagh. New York: The Peter Kavanagh Hand Press, 1971.

————. *Self-Portrait*. Dublin: The Dolmen Press, 1964.

Kinsella, Thomas, trans. *An Duanaire: 1600–1900: Poetry of the Dispossessed*. Selected by Sean O'Tuama. Dublin: The Dolmen Press, 1981.

————. *Another September*. Dublin: The Dolmen Press, 1958.

————. "The Irish Writer," *Davis, Mangan, Ferguson? Tradition and the Irish Writer*. Dublin: The Dolmen Press, 1970. Pp. 57–66.

————. *Peppercanister Poems, 1972–1978*. Winston-Salem: Wake Forest University Press, 1979.

————. *Poems, 1956–1973*. Winston-Salem: Wake Forest University Press, 1979.

————, trans. *The Tain*. London: Oxford University Press, 1970.

MacGreevey, Thomas. *Collected Poems*. Dublin: New Writer's Press, 1971.

MacNeice, Louis. *Selected Poems of Louis MacNeice*. Ed. W. H. Auden. London: Faber and Faber Ltd., 1964.

Mahon, Derek. *The Hunt by Night*. Winston-Salem: Wake Forest University Press, 1983.

————. *Lives*. London: Oxford University Press, 1972.

————. *Night-Crossing*. London: Oxford University Press, 1968.

————. *Poems: 1962–1978*. London: Oxford University Press, 1979.

————. *The Snow Party*. London: Oxford University Press, 1975.

Montague, John A. *A Chosen Light*. London: MacGibbon and Kee, 1967.

————, ed. *Faber Book of Irish Verse*. London: Faber and Faber Ltd., 1974.

————. *Poisoned Lands*. Dublin: The Dolmen Press, 1977.

————. *The Rough Field*. Winston-Salem: Wake Forest University Press, 1979.

————. *Selected Poems*. Winston-Salem: Wake Forest University Press, 1982.

————. *Tides*. Dublin: The Dolmen Press, 1970.

Muldoon, Paul. *Mules*. Winston-Salm: Wake Forest University Press, 1977.

Murphy, Richard. *High Island*. New York: Harper and Row, 1974.

————. *Selected Poems*. London: Faber and Faber Ltd., 1979.

O'Sullivan, Seamus. *Mud and Purple: Pages from the Diary of a Dublin Man*. Dublin: The Talbot Press Ltd., 1917.

Paulin, Tom. *Liberty Tree*. London: Faber and Faber Ltd., 1983.

Russell, George. pseud. [Æ] *New Songs*. Dublin: O'Donoghue and Co., 1904.

Stephens, James. *Collected Poems*. New York: Deven-Adair, 1954.

Synge, J. M. *Plays, Poems, and Prose*. London: J. M. Dent and Sons, 1975.

Yeats, W. B. *The Autobiography of William Butler Yeats*. New York: The Macmillan Co., 1967.

————. *Essays and Introductions*. New York: The Macmillan Co., 1961.

————. *Later Poems*. Dublin: The Dolmen Press, 1961.

————. *Letters on Poetry from W. B. Yeats to Dorothy Wellesley*. London: Oxford University, 1964.

————. *Letters to the New Island*. Ed. with introd. Horace Reynolds. Cambridge, Mass.: Harvard University Press, 1934.

————. *Memoirs*. Ed. Denis Donoghue. New York: The Macmillan Co., 1972.

————. *The Poems of W. B. Yeats*. 3d ed. Richard J. Finneran. New York: Macmillan Co., 1983.

————. *Senate Speeches of W. B. Yeats*. Ed. Donald R. Pearce. Bloomington: Indiana University Press, 1960.

————. *Uncollected Prose of W. B. Yeats*. Vol. I. Ed. John Frayne. New York: Columbia University Press, 1970.

————. *Uncollected Prose of W. B. Yeats*. Vol. II. Eds. John Frayne and Colton Johnson. New York: Columbia University Press, 1976.

Secondary Material

Bair, Dierdre. *Samuel Beckett*. New York: Harcourt Brace Jovanovich, 1978.

Bate, W. Jackson. *The Burden of the Past and the English Poet*. Cambridge: Harvard University Press, 1970.

Beckett, J. C. *The Anglo-Irish Tradition*. Ithaca: Cornell University Press, 1976.

Beckett, Samuel. "Recent Irish Poetry," *Bookman*, LXXVII (August 1934).

Bedford, William. "To Set the Darkness Echoing," *Delta*, no. 36 (1977), pp. 2–7.

Bedient, Calvin. *Eight Contemporary Poets*. London: Oxford University Press, 1974.

Bloom, Harold. *The Anxiety of Influence*. New York: Oxford University Press, 1973.

Boland, Eaven. "The Weasel's Tooth," *Irish Times*, 7 June 1974, p. 7.

Borges, Jorge Luis. *Other Inquisitions, 1937–1952*. Austin: University of Texas Press, 1964.

Bowen, Zack. *Padraic Colum*. Carbondale: Southern Illinois University Press, 1970.

Boyd, Ernest. *Ireland's Literary Renaissance*. New York: Alfred A. Knopf, 1922.

Bradley, Anthony, ed. *Contemporary Irish Poetry: An Anthology*. Berkeley, Los Angeles, London: University of California Press, 1980.

Broder, Peggy F. "Breaking the Shell of Solitude: Some Poems of Thomas Kinsella," *Eire-Ireland*, XIV, 2 (Summer 1979), 80–92.

Brown, Malcolm. *The Politics of Irish Literature*. Seattle: University of Washington Press, 1972.

Brown, Terence. "Dublin in Modern Irish Poetry," *Irish University Review*, 6, 1 (Spring 1976), 4–16.

———. *Northern Voices: Poets from Ulster*. Dublin: Gill and Macmillan, 1975.

———. *Ireland: A Social and Cultural History, 1922–1979*. Glasgow: William Collins Sons and Co. Ltd., Fontana Paperbacks, 1981.

———, and Alec Reid, eds. *Time Was Away*. Dublin: The Dolmen Press, 1974.

Clarke, Austin. "Irish Poetry Today," *Dublin Magazine*, X, 1 (January–March 1935), 26–32.

———. "W. B. Yeats," *The Dublin Magazine*, 14 (April–June 1939), 6–10.

Corkery, Daniel. *Synge and Anglo-Irish Literature*. Cook: The Mercier Press, 1966.

Cronin, Anthony. *Dead as Doornails*. Dublin: Poolbeg Press, 1975.

Davie, Donald. "Austin Clarke and Padraic Fallon": *Two Decades of Irish*

Writing. Ed. Douglas Dunn. Chester Springs, Pa.: Dufour Editions, Inc., 1975.

Deane, Seamus. "The Appetites of Gravity: Contemporary Irish Poetry," *Sewanee Review,* 84, 1/2 (1976), 202–205.

———. "An Example of Tradition," *The Crane Bag,* 3, 1 (1979), 41–47.

———. "Irish Poetry and Irish Nationalism: A Survey," *Two Decades of Irish Writing.* Ed. Douglas Dunn. Chester Springs, Pa.: Dufour Editions, Inc., 1975.

———. "Literary Myths and the Revival: A Case for Their Abandonment," *Myth and Reality in Irish Literature.* Ed. Joseph Ronsley, Waterloo: Wilfred Laicrien University Press, 1977. P. 320.

———. "Postscript," *The Crane Bag,* 3, 2 (1979), 512.

———. "The Writer and the Troubles," *Threshold,* no. 25 (Summer 1974), pp. 13–17.

Donoghue, Denis. "Romantic Ireland," *Yeats, Sligo, and Ireland.* Ed. A. Norman Jeffares. Gerrads Cross, Buckinghamshire, England: Colin Smythe, 1980. Pp. 17–30.

Dunn, Douglas, ed. *Two Decades of Irish Writing.* Chester Springs, Pa.: Dufour Editions, Inc., 1975.

Eliot, T. S. *The Selected Prose of T. S. Eliot.* Ed. Frank Kermode. New York: Harcourt, Brace, Jovanovich and Farrar, Straus, Giroux, 1975.

———. "The Social Function of Poetry," *On Poetry and Poets.* New York: Farrar, Straus, and Cudahy, 1957. Pp. 9–12.

Ellmann, Richard. *The Identity of Yeats.* New York: Oxford University Press, 1964.

———. *Yeats: The Man and the Masks.* New York: The Macmillan Co., 1948.

Fallis, Richard. *The Irish Renaissance.* Syracuse: Syracuse University Press, 1977.

Fallon, Padraic. "The Winding Stair and Other Poems by W. B. Yeats," *The Dublin Magazine,* 9, 2 (1934), 58.

Farren, Robert. *The Course of Irish Verse.* London: Sheed and Ward, Ltd., 1948.

Frazer, Adrian. "Interview with John Montague," *The Literary Review,* XXII, 2 (Winter 1979), 153–154.

———. "Proper Portion: Derek Mahon's The Hunt by Night," *Eire-Ireland,* XVIII, 4 (Winter 1983), 136–143.

———. "The Sincerity of Patrick Kavanagh," *Malahat Review* 53 (January 1980), 110–131.

Garratt, Robert F. "Austin Clarke in Transition," *Irish University Review* 53 (Spring 1974), 100–116.

——. "Aware of My Ancestor: Austin Clarke and the Legacy of Swift," *Eire-Ireland*, XI, 3 (Summer 1976), 92–103.

Haffenden, John. *Viewpoints: Poet in Conversation*. London: Faber and Faber, 1981.

Hall, Wayne E. *Shadowy Heroes: Irish Literature of the 1890s*. Syracuse: Syracuse University Press, 1980.

Harmon, Maurice. *Irish Poetry After Yeats*. Boston: Little, Brown, and Company, 1979.

——. "The Later Poetry of Austin Clarke," *The Celtic Cross*. Ed. Ray B. Browne, William John Roscelli, and Richard J. Loftus. West Lafayette, Ind.: Purdue University Press, 1964. Pp. 39–55.

——. "The Poetry of Padraic Fallon," *Studies* (Autumn 1975). Pp. 269–281.

——. *The Poetry of Thomas Kinsella*. Atlantic Highlands, N.J.: Humanities Press, 1975.

Hederman, Mark Patrick. "Seamus Heaney: The Reluctant Poet," *The Crane Bag*, 3, 2 (1979), 61–70.

Howarth, Herbert. *The Irish Writers, 1880–1940*. New York: Hill and Wang, 1958.

Howe, Irving, ed. *The Idea of the Modern*. New York: Horizon Press, 1967.

Johnston, Dillon. "Devlin's Poetry: Love in Abeyance," *Concerning Poetry*, 14 (Fall 1981), 27–43.

——. "Unaccommodated Mahon: An Ulster Poet," *The Hollins Critic*, 17, 5 (December 1980).

Joyce, P. W. *English As We Speak it in Ireland*. Rev. ed. Dublin: Wolfhound Press, 1979.

Kavanagh, Patrick. "The Gallivanting Poet," *Irish Writing*, no. 3 (November 1947), pp. 63–70.

——. "Poetry in Ireland Today," *The Bell*, XVI (April 1948), 36–43.

Kearney, Timothy. "The Poetry of the North: A Post-Modernist Perspective," *The Crane Bag*, 3, 2 (1979), 43–53.

Kenner, Hugh. *A Colder Eye: The Modern Irish Writers*. New York: Alfred A. Knopf, 1983.

——. *Dublin's Joyce*. Boston: Beacon Press, 1956.

——. "Thomas Kinsella: An Anecdote and some Reflections," in *Genres of the Irish Literary Revival*. Ed. Ronald Schleifer. Pilgrim Books, 1980. Pp. 179–187.

Levin, Harry. *James Joyce: An Introduction*. New York: New Directions Publishing Company, 1960.

Loftus, Richard J. *Nationalism in Modern Anglo-Irish Poetry*. Madison: University of Wisconsin Press, 1964.

Longley, Edna. "Searching the Darkness: The Poetry of Richard Murphy, Thomas Kinsella, John Montague, and James Simmons," *Two Decades of Irish Writing*. Ed. Douglas Dunn. Chester Springs: Dufour Editions, Inc., 1975. Pp. 138–145.

Low, Hugh. *Anglo-Irish Literature*. Dublin: Talbot Press Ltd., 1926.

Lucy, Sean. "Three Poets from Ulster," *Irish University Review*, 3, 2 (Autumn 1973), 179–193.

McGuinness, Arthur. "Hoarder of Common Ground: Tradition and Ritual in Seamus Heaney's Poetry." *Eire-Ireland*, XIII, 2 (Summer 1978), 71–92.

———. "Bright Quincunx Newly Risen: Thomas Kinsella's Inward 'I,' " *Eire-Ireland*, XV, 4 (Winter 1980), 106–125.

Mahon, Derek. "Poetry in Northern Ireland," *Twentieth Century Studies*. 4 (November 1970), 89–93.

Marcus, Philip. *Yeats and the Beginning of the Irish Renaissance*. Ithaca: Cornell University Press, 1970.

Martin, Augustine. "The Rediscovery of Austin Clarke," *Studies*, LIV, 216 (Summer 1965), 420–436.

Maxwell, D. E. S. "Contemporary Poetry in the North of Ireland," *Two Decades of Irish Writing*. Ed. Douglas Dunn. Chester Springs: Dufour Editions, Inc., 1975.

———. "The Poetry of John Montague," *Critical Quarterly*, XV (Summer 1973), 180–185.

Mercier, Vivian. *The Irish Comic Tradition*. New York: Oxford University Press, 1962.

———. "Mortal Anguish, Mortal Pride: Austin Clarke's Religious Lyrics," *Irish University Review*, 4, 1 (Spring 1974), 91–99.

Montague, John. "The Impact of International Poetry on Irish Writing," *Irish Poets in English*. Ed. Sean Lucy. Cork: The Mercier Press, 1973. Pp. 144–158.

———. "The Irish Writer," *The Bell*, XVII (October 1951), 5–12.

———. "Seamless Garment and the Muse," *Agenda*, 5, 4 (Autumn–Winter 1966–1967), 27–34.

Moore, John Reese. "Thomas Kinsella's *Nightwalker*: A Phoenix in the Dark," *The Hollins Critic*, V, 4 (October 1968), 3–6.

Nemo, John. *Patrick Kavanagh*. Boston: Twayne Publishers, 1979.

O'Brien, Darcy. *Patrick Kavanagh*. Lewisburg, Pa.: Bucknell University Press, 1975.

O'Connor, Frank. *A Backward Look*. New York: Capricorn Books, 1968.

————. "The Future of Irish Literature," *Horizon*, V, 25 (January 1942), 55–63.

O'Faolain, Sean. "Fifty Years of Irish Writing," *Studies*, 51 (Spring 1962), 93–103.

Parkinson, Thomas. *W. B. Yeats: Self-Critic*. Berkeley, Los Angeles, London: University of California Press, 1971.

Pearce, Roy Harvey. *The Continuity of American Poetry*. Princeton: Princeton University Press, 1961.

Rodgers, W. R., ed. *Irish Literary Portraits*. London: British Broadcasting Corporation, 1972.

Rosenberg, Harold. *The Tradition of the New*. New York: McGraw-Hill, 1965.

Schirmen, Gregory A. *The Poetry of Austin Clarke*. Notre Dame: University of Notre Dame Press, 1983.

Scholes, Robert. "James Joyce, Irish Poet," *James Joyce Quarterly*, 2 (1965), 255–270.

Schwartz, Delmore. "T. S. Eliot as the International Hero," *The Idea of the Modern*. Ed. Irving Howe. New York: Horizon Press, 1967. Pp. 277–285.

Skelton, Robin. *The Writings of J. M. Synge*. Indianapolis-New York: The Bobbs-Merrill Co., 1971.

Spender, Stephen. "The Influence of Yeats on Later English Poets," *Tri-Quarterly* 4 (1965), 82–89.

Strong, L. A. G. *Personal Remarks*. London: Peter Neville Ltd., 1953.

Stuart, Francis. "The Soft Centre of Irish Writing," *Paddy No More*. Nantucket: Longship Press, 1977. P. 7.

Tapping, Craig. *Austin Clarke, A Study of His Writings*. Totowa, N.J.: Barnes and Noble, 1981.

Thorton, Weldon. "Virgin or Hungry Fiend? The Failures of the Imagination in Patrick Kavanagh's 'The Great Hunger,'" *Mosaic*, XII, 3 (Spring 1979), 152–162.

Torchiana, Donald. "Some Dublin Afterthoughts," *Tri-Quarterly Review*, IV (Autumn 1965), 140–145.

————. *W. B. Yeats and Georgian Ireland*. Evanston: Northwestern University Press, 1966.

Trilling, Lionel. *Sincerity and Authenticity*. Cambridge: Harvard University Press, 1971.

Wade, Allan, ed. *The Letters of W. B. Yeats*. New York: The Macmillan Co., 1955.

Weatherhead, A. K. "John Montague: Exiled from Order," *Concerning Poetry*, 14, 2 (Fall 1981), 97–101.

Weber, Richard. "Austin Clarke, The Arch-poet of Dublin," *Massachusetts: Review*, XI, 2 (1970), 289–301.

Welch, Robert. "Austin Clarke and the Gaelic Poetic Tradition," *Irish University Review*, 4, 1 (Spring 1974), 41–51.

Acknowledgments

Selections by Austin Clarke reprinted by permission of the estate of Austin Clarke and Wake Forest University Press.

Excerpts by Seamus Heaney reprinted by permission of Farrar, Straus and Giroux, Inc., from *Poems 1965–1975*, copyright 1966, 1969, 1972, 1975, 1980 by Seamus Heaney; *Field Work*, copyright 1976, 1979 by Seamus Heaney. *Preoccupations: Selected Prose 1968–1978*. Copyright 1980 by Seamus Heaney; and by permission of Faber and Faber, Ltd., from *North, Field Work*, and extracts from *Death of A Naturalist* and *Door Into the Dark* by Seamus Heaney.

Selected by Patrick Kavanagh quoted with permission by The Peter Kavanagh Hand Press, New York, and The Goldsmith Press, Newbridge, Ireland.

Selections by Thomas Kinsella reprinted by permission of Thomas Kinsella and Wake Forest University Press.

Selections by Louis MacNeice reprinted by permission of Faber and Faber, Ltd., from *The Collected Poems of Louis MacNeice*.

Extracts by Derek Mahon reprinted by permission of Oxford University Press, from *Poems 1962–1978*, copyright 1979, and *The Hunt by Night*, copyright 1982 by Derek Mahon.

Selections by John Montague reprinted by permission of John Montague and Wake Forest University Press.

Selections by Paul Muldoon reprinted by permission of Paul Muldoon and Wake Forest University Press, and by permission of Faber and Faber, Ltd.

Selections by Richard Murphy reprinted by permission of Richard Murphy and Faber and Faber, Ltd.

Selections by W. B. Yeats are reprinted with permission of Macmillan Publishing Company, from *The Poems*, W. B. Yeats, ed. Richard J. Finneran, copyright 1912, 1933 by Macmillan Publishing Company, renewed 1940, 1961 by Bertha Georgie Yeats, copyright 1940 by Georgie Yeats, renewed 1968 by Bertha Georgie Yeats, Michael Butler Yeats, and Anne Yeats; from *The Trembling of the Veil*, W. B. Yeats, copyright 1924 by Macmillan Publishing Company, renewed 1952 by Bertha Georgie Yeats; and with permission of Michael Butler Yeats and Macmillan Ltd., London.

Index

230; "Elegy," 247; "Exposure," 234, 244–247; *Field Work,* 231, 246–257; Glanmore Sonnets, 251–256; "The Gutteral Muse," 254; "The Harvest Bow," 256–257; "Hercules and Antaeus," 238–245; "Kinship," 235; *North,* 230; "Punishment," 234; "September Song," 258; "Song," 257; "The Skunk," 255; "Triptych," 246; "Viking Dublin: Trial Pieces," 234

"Heavenly Foreigner, The" (Devlin), 98

"He Wishes for the Cloths of Heaven" (Yeats), 31

Higgins, F. R., 4, 5, 16, 46, 48, 66, 106; influenced by Yeats, 68–69; and Irish Literary Revival, 50; Irish School of Poetry, 63; as a revivalist, 66–70; Works: "The Dark Breed," 66; "The Gap of Brightness," 66; "Island Blood," 66

"Holy Office, The" (Joyce), 79, 86, 87

"Home Again" (Montague), 212

Homeward: Songs by the Way (AE), 27

Hopkins, Gerard Manley, Works: "To R. B.," 242; "The Wreck of the Deutschland," 241

Howe, Irving, 274

Hyde, Douglas, 26, 27, 118; Works: *Love Songs of Connacht,* 54, 61, 105

"Inniskeen Road: July Evening" (Kavanagh), 155

Insurrections (Stephens), 61

"Intimate Parnassus" (Kavanagh), 162

Ireland, cultural history, 5, 8–9, 10, 11, 21, 81–82, 188–190, 232–233, 259–261; and Catholicism, 5, 33–34; Georgian period, 34, 35; literary nationalism, 2, 21–23, 44–51; politics and literature, 2, 34–35, 238–239; and Protestantism, 35–37, 47–48, 268–269; romantic literary portrayal of, 47–48, 50–73 passim, 148–149

Irish Academy of Letters, 46, 100

"Irish-American Dignitary" (Clarke), 123

Irish Folk Tradition, 24; in poetry of Padraic Colum, 54

Irish Free State, 12, 35, 45

Irish Language, 7–9, 45, 104–105, 110, 170, 190, 214, 218–220; dialect in English, 7

Irish Literary Revival, 2, 3, 4, 6, 8, 12–13, 44; Clarke's break with, 113–124; and continuity, 9–11, 106, 169–171, 239–262; and first generation of writers, 15, 44–63; Joyce's critique of, 79–83; Kavanagh's attack upon, 141–148; Post-Yeatsian Practitioners of, 3, 15, 26–28, 44–77; and second generation of writers, 6, 63–77; Yeats and founding of, 17–29

Irish Statesman (AE), 139

"Irish Street Scene, with Lovers" (Montague), 202

"Irish Writer, The" (Kinsella), 196

"Irish Writer, The" (Montague), 198

Island Blood (Higgins), 66

Johnson, Lionel, 26

Johnston, Dillon, 98, 265

"Johnstown Castle" (Fallon), 74

Joyce, James, 11, 12, 78–102; and Clarke, 88–89, 114, 125; and connection with Gaelic poetry,

Designer: U.C. Press Staff
Compositor: Janet Sheila Brown
Printer: Malloy Lithographing, Inc.
Binder: John H. Dekker & Sons
Text: 10/13 Palatino
Display: Palatino